# CAPITAL IDEAS

# CAPITAL IDEAS

## The Improbable Origins of Modern Wall Street

*Peter L. Bernstein*

**THE FREE PRESS**

New York   London   Toronto   Sydney   Tokyo   Singapore

The Free Press
A Division of Simon & Schuster Inc.
1230 Avenue of the Americas
New York, N.Y. 10020

First Free Press Paperback Edition 1993

Printed in the United States of America

printing number
    4  5  6  7  8  9  10

Library of Congress Cataloging-in-Publication Data

Bernstein, Peter L.
    Capital ideas: the improbable origins of modern Wall Street/
Peter L. Bernstein.
        p.      cm.
    Includes bibliographical references (p.      ) and index.
    ISBN 0-02-903012-9
    1. Finance     2. Wall Street.     I. Title.
    HG173.B47      1992
332.63'2—dc20                                          91-23269
                                                          CIP

For Barbara

*What is history all about if not the exquisite delight of knowing the details and not only the abstract patterns?*

—Stephen Jay Gould

# Contents

# Contents

# Acknowledgments

A ll authors who undertake projects like this need help from others. I have been unusually fortunate in having had such generous and essential assistance from the people named below.

The book could never have taken shape without the participation of the people whose work it describes: Fischer Black, Eugene Fama, William Fouse, Hayne Leland, Harry Markowitz, John Mc-Quown, Robert C. Merton, Merton Miller, Franco Modigliani, Barr Rosenberg, Mark Rubinstein, Paul Samuelson, Myron Scholes, William Sharpe, James Tobin, Jack Treynor, and James Vertin. Each of them spent long periods of time with me in interviews, and most of them engaged in voluminous correspondence and telephone conversations as well. All of them read drafts of the chapters in which their work is discussed and gave me important criticisms and suggestions that enrich virtually every page of the book. Most of them also provided their photographs.

Each in his own way contributed to my understanding of the subject matter well beyond the chapters that were their immediate concern. In this regard, I hope I may be forgiven if I single out Paul Samuelson, my friend of more than fifty years. He served uncomplainingly as my mentor, inspiration, and inexhaustible research associate from the very beginning; the accumulation of handwritten wisdom that passed from his fax to my fax is a treasure in itself. And my thanks as well to Janice Murray, who made our communication so easy and rewarding.

I have also benefited from those who were kind enough to undertake the onerous task of reading the complete manuscript. Michael Granito, Bernard Obletz, Roger Kennedy, Patricia Carry Stewart, and Byron Wien were especially helpful in providing me with many suggestions, which I have made every effort to put to good use. Richard Brealey's bounteous contribution to both the theoretical and the historical aspects of the story was invaluable. Robert Heilbroner, my oldest friend and sometime co-author, combined painstaking editorial advice with broad critical observations whose influence is apparent throughout.

I am deeply indebted to Peter Brodsky, Michael Keran, William Lee, and Lawrence Seltzer, whose encouragement after their careful reading of early drafts gave me the impetus to carry on when the going was hardest.

Many other people helped in supplying or guiding me to research material without which the project would have run into sand early in the game. I am especially grateful to John Brush, Richard Cowles, Charles D'Ambrosio, David Durand, Charles Ellis, Martin Fridson, Charles Henry, Judith Kimball, the staff of the Marlboro College Library in Marlboro, VT, Donald McCloskey, Joseph Murphy, M. F. M. Osborne, Earle Partridge, Edward Renshaw, Andrew Roy, Richard Russell, Hugh Weed, and Richard West.

I owe a special debt to Martin Leibowitz. The orginal plan of the book included a long section on the bond market, where Leibowitz has been the acknowledged leader as both theoretician and practitioner. When considerations of space and format led me to restrict the subject matter to the equity markets, I was unable to use the help that he had so generously provided. I hope to make up for that omission on an early occasion.

I have had enough experience as both writer and editor to know an editors' editor when I meet one. Peter Dougherty is it. His participation in this endeavor was my great good fortune. He enlarged the scope of the book beyond my own more limited concepts. He sharpened its literary quality even as he deepened the quality of the content. Without his understanding of the subject and knowledge of the personalities, I would all too frequently have ended up in the wilderness. I have never known a more merciless taskmaster who could at the same time make the job great fun.

The convention on these occasions is for the author to describe his or her spouse as a nonentity whose main contribution is to keep the author isolated from the clutter of daily life. The good spouse arranges matters so that the author's wondrous flights of creativity can soar to heights reserved only to those human beings blessed by such a self-effacing life's companion.

When I acknowledge that my Barbara performed to perfection the dreary job of isolating me from the clutter of daily life, I only hint at her contribution. She provided light when there was dark and brought me back to reality when I succumbed to euphoria. But even that was not all. Her most valuable gift was to be in the foreground rather than the background. She has been a close collaborator in every phase of the project, from the interviews to the planning and writing of each chapter. Every part of the book has been improved by her participation.

Even with all this help and support, I am certain that flaws remain. They comprise the only part of the book that is my responsibility alone.

# Introduction:
# The Revolution
# in the Wealth of Nations

*. . . the machine-gun clatter of fingers on a keyboard.*

Americans have always welcomed change. Revolution is our birthright. We take it as a sign of our youth that we prefer the new to the old. We are fascinated by innovation and lionize the innovators. We are partial to tinkerers and make folk-heroes out of people like Thomas Edison, Henry Ford, and Benjamin Franklin.

But sometimes change seems to run amuck and things appear to be out of control. Then fear takes over and spoils our appetite for novelty. That is what has happened in Wall Street over the past fifteen or twenty years.

The complexity and speed of financial innovation have reached a point where it is hard to grasp what is happening from moment to moment. Amateur investors and many professionals are wary of space-age trading strategies and kinky financial instruments that seem beyond their understanding. Individual investors grumble that they are the last to receive information about the stocks they own and the last to find buyers when security prices are dropping. Giant financial institutions complain that security prices are dangerously volatile. There is a widely held perception that overpaid MBAs, corporate raiders, and investment managers who talk like astrophysicists are living in a world of their own, detached from the realities of people who really work for a living.

But that is only part of the story. The untold part, which is what this book is about, reveals that much of this fear and resentment is misplaced. Baffling as it may be to some, Wall Street is vital and productive, a model for the rest of the world, including former socialist countries seeking the path to prosperity and freedom.

The gap in understanding between insiders and outsiders in Wall Street has developed because today's financial markets are the result of a recent but obscure revolution that took root in the groves of ivy rather than in the canyons of lower Manhattan. Its heroes were a tiny contingent of scholars, most at the very beginning of their careers, who had no direct interest in the stock market and whose analysis of the economics of finance began at high levels of abstraction.

Yet the message they brought to Wall Street was simplicity itself, based on two of the most basic laws of economics. There can be no reward without risk. And gaining an advantage over skilled and knowledgeable competitors in a free market is extraordinarily difficult. By combining the linkage between risk and reward with the combative nature of the free market, these academics brought new insights into what Wall Street is all about and devised new methods for investors to manage their capital.

Much of what these scholars had to say often seemed strange and uninviting to hungry investors and to the aggressive salesmen who inhabit Wall Street. But in their quiet way the academics eventually overcame the old guard and liberated the city of capital. Before they were done, they had transformed today's wealth of nations and the lives of all of us, as citizens, savers, and breadwinners.

Today investors are more keenly aware of risk, and better able to deal with it, than at any time in the past. They have a more sophisticated understanding of how financial markets behave and are capable of using to advantage the vast array of new vehicles and new trading strategies specifically tailored to their needs. Innovative techniques of corporate finance have led to more careful evaluation of corporate wealth and more effective allocation of capital. The financial restructuring of the 1980s created novel solutions to the problems arising from the separation of ownership and control and made corporate managers more responsive to the interests of shareholders.

The first signs of the revolution in finance and investing appeared in October 1974, with the culmination of the worst bear market in common stocks since the Great Crash of 1929. By the time

*2*

prices finally touched bottom, market values had fallen more than 40 percent from what they had been two years earlier.

That was not all. An overheated domestic economy and the rapacity of the OPEC countries had sent inflation soaring. In just a year and a half, the cost of living jumped 20 percent, more than 1 percent a month. After adjustment for inflation, the entire rise in stock prices since 1954 had been erased. At the same time, the bond market, the traditional haven for the risk-averse, suffered a 35 percent loss of purchasing power.

No one emerged unscathed. Employees found that the decline in the value of their pension funds threatened the security of their retirement. Distress brought pressure for change throughout the world of finance: the way professionals managed their clients' capital, the structure of the financial system itself, the functioning of the markets, the range of investment choices available to savers, and the role of finance in the profitability and competitiveness of American companies. Many of the star portfolio managers of the go-go years of the 1960s disappeared in the rubble, along with Richard Nixon's price controls and Gerald Ford's W.I.N. buttons. Respected banks, major industrial corporations, and even the City of New York stood at the brink of bankruptcy.

Had it not been for the crisis of 1974, few financial practitioners would have paid attention to the ideas that had been stirring in the ivory towers for some twenty years. But when it turned out that improvised strategies to beat the market served only to jeopardize their clients' interests, practitioners realized that they had to change their ways. Reluctantly, they began to show interest in converting the abstract ideas of the academics into methods to control risk and to staunch the losses their clients were suffering. This was the motivating force of the revolution that shaped the new Wall Street.

Even an incomplete list of the innovations that have emerged since the mid-1970s reminds us of how profoundly the present differs from the past. The unfamiliarity of some of the new terminology suggests the magnitude of that break with tradition.

Today there are money market funds, bank CDs for small savers, unregulated brokerage commissions, and discount brokers. There are hundreds of mutual funds specializing in big stocks, small stocks, emerging growth stocks, Treasury bonds, junk bonds, index funds, government-guaranteed mortgages, and international stocks and bonds from all around the world. There is ERISA to regulate corporate pension funds, and there are employee savings plans that enable employees to manage their own pension funds. There are markets for options (puts and calls) and markets for futures, and markets for options on futures. There is program trading, index arbitrage, and risk arbitrage. There are managers who provide portfolio insurance and managers who offer something called tactical asset allocation. There are butterfly swaps and synthetic equity. Corporations finance themselves with convertible bonds, zero-coupon bonds, bonds that pay interest by promising to pay more interest later on, and bonds that give their owners the unconditional right to receive their money back before the bonds come due.

The world's total capital market of stocks, bonds, and cash had ballooned from only $2 trillion in 1969 to more than $22 trillion by the end of 1990; the market for stocks alone had soared from $300 billion to $5.5 trillion. Today, more than half of the global market, nearly $12 trillion, trades outside the United States, compared to only one-third of the market in 1969. Hence, the wealth of nations.

Over $2 trillion, more than 50 percent of the common stock outstanding in the United States, is now owned by pension funds, mutual funds, educational endowments, and charitable foundations, compared with 40 percent in 1980 and less than 15 percent in 1950. These institutions account for 80 percent of all trading activity in the stock market, and none of them pays income taxes or taxes on capital gains. More than 70 percent of all outstanding shares changes hands in the course of a year, up from only 20 percent or so in the 1970s. The average transaction of the New York Stock Exchange now exceeds 2,000 shares, nearly six times what it was in 1974; half of the daily volume of trading takes place in blocks of 10,000 shares or more. Meanwhile, individual investors who buy and sell for their own accounts are a disappearing breed. Their direct holdings of common stocks now represent only 16 percent of their financial assets, down from 44 percent in the late 1960s.* Odd-lots (transactions of less than 100 shares) have fallen from 5 percent of total volume to less than 2 percent.

*Some, but by no means all, of this money has come back into the stock market through individual purchases of mutual funds. Distaste for the difficulties individual investors encounter when they try to manage direct holdings of common stocks explains the dramatic growth of the mutual fund business over the past fifteen years.

Financial assets now change hands with dizzying speed. Daily trading on the New York Stock Exchange averages over 150 million shares, more than ten times the daily average of 1974, five times the average in the highest year of the 1970s, and 100 times the average in the early 1950s. On Black Monday of October 1987, 604 million shares were traded. Millions of additional shares are traded directly across computers, bypassing the organized exchanges altogether. The volume of shares traded in the markets for futures and options often exceeds the volume traded on the organized exchanges. Trading in Tokyo is ten times what it was in 1982, in Frankfurt twelve times, and in London thirty times.

The pace is even swifter in the once-sedate bond market. Daily trading in U.S. government bonds runs about $100 billion. That means that the ownership of the entire national debt is turning over ten times a year. Trading is swifter still in the foreign-exchange markets: Transactions in the United States exceed $100 billion a day, while Tokyo does some $30 billion and other world markets do another $100 billion.

Such volume would be impossible without the computer. Many complex securities could not even be priced without the computer's speed and mathematical capabilities. So-called DOT transactions automate small trades on the New York Stock Exchange and transmit them instantaneously from the customer's broker to the post where the order is executed. The whole world, it seems, is becoming computerized. Even Latin America and Spain rely on computers to carry out trades, check customer credits, and post the transaction results for records and statements.* In an article titled "The Wild, Wired World of Electronic Exchanges," *Institutional Investor* magazine for September 1989 paints the scene: "Say good-bye to the heady roar of the exchange floor. Forget the terse shouting of two traders on the phone. The new sound of finance is the machine-gun clatter of fingers on a keyboard. And it can already be heard on thousands of trading desks in dozens of markets around the world."[1]

Financial markets are among the most dazzling creations of the

---

*Institutions yield sluggishly to technology. The Hong Kong exchange has a new trading floor filled with rows of people sitting at computing desks. With everything being done by the computer, a "trading floor" is no longer needed. But there always has been a trading floor, so there still is.

modern world. Popular histories of financial markets from the City of London to Wall Street tell the story of panics, robber barons, crooks, and rags-to-riches tycoons. But such colorful tales give little hint of the seriousness of the business that goes on in those markets. John Maynard Keynes once remarked that the stock market is little more than a beauty contest and a curse to capitalism. And yet no nation that has abandoned socialism for capitalism considers the job complete until it has a functioning financial market.

Simply put, Wall Street shapes Main Street. It transforms factories, department stores, banking assets, film producers, machinery, soft-drink bottlers, and power lines into something that can be easily convertible into money and into vehicles for diversifying risks. It converts such entities into assets that you can trade with anonymous buyers or sellers. It makes hard assets liquid, and it puts a price on those assets that promises that they will be put to their most productive uses.

Wall Street also changes the character of the assets themselves. It has never been a place where people merely exchange money for stocks, bonds, and mortgages. Wall Street is a focal point where individuals, businesses, and even entire economies anticipate the future. The daily movements of security prices reveal how confident people are in their expectations, what time horizons they envisage, and what hopes and fears they are communicating to one another.

The ancients left prediction to the Sphinx, to the Delphic oracle, or to those who could read the entrails of animals. Ecclesiastes tells us that "there is no remembrance of things past, neither shall there be remembrance of things to come." Dante reserved a seat in hell for anyone "whose glance too far before him ranged," and twisted their heads back-to-front.[2]

Today anticipating the future is a necessity, not an arcane game. Yet how do we make decisions when our crystal ball turns cloudy? How much risk can we afford to take? How can we tell how big the risk actually is? How long can we afford to wait to discover whether our bets are going to pay off?

The innovations triggered by the revolution in finance and investing provide answers to such questions. They help investors deal with uncertainty. They provide benchmarks for determining whether expectations are realistic or fanciful and whether risks make sense or are foolish. They establish norms for determining

*6*

how well a market is accommodating the needs of its participants. They have reformulated such familiar concepts as risk, return, diversification, insurance, and debt. Moreover, they have quantified those concepts and have suggested new ways of employing them and combining them for optimal results. Finally, they have added a measure of science to the art of corporate finance.

Many of these innovations lay hidden in academic journals for years, unnoticed by Wall Street until the financial turbulence of the early 1970s forced practitioners to accept the harsh truth that investment is a risky business. This was the key insight that the academics brought to Wall Street. Waiting for one's ship to come in is inevitably uncomfortable and uncertain, they declared, but there is no way to avoid the discomfort or to foretell just what the future holds in store.

Wall Street responded to this urgent message by expanding the variety of mutual funds, by showing heightened interest in international investing, and by devising new instruments of corporate finance. Moreover, it discovered new sources of return in such risk-controlling techniques as options, futures, swaps, portfolio insurance, and other exotic measures.

Some of these innovations produced unforeseen and undesirable outcomes. Financial markets, like many other creations of the human imagination, mix dangerous tendencies with wholesome impulses.

Most economic crises, in one way or another, have originated from abuses in the financial system, which may explain why orthodox economists have traditionally shunned their brethren in the finance departments. Stocks and bonds, for example, by their very nature, invite speculation and even corruption: No one buys them with the lofty purpose of making the allocation of the nation's capital more efficient. People buy them only in the hope of catching a ride on the road to riches.

Because stocks and bonds are liquid, decisions to buy or sell them can be easily reversed. They change hands anonymously as their prices march across the computer screen. Because they move in response to information of all types, the player who gets the information first has an enormous advantage.

They fluctuate in sympathy with one another, so that trouble in one place often spreads across the markets: chaos theory reminds us that the flutter of a butterfly's wings in Mexico can turn out to be the cause of a tidal wave in Hawaii. Most important, the prices of stocks and bonds reflect people's hopes and fears about the future, which means they can easily wander away from the realities of the present.

There is no way to purge financial markets of these attributes. Efforts to do so—and regulation has come in many different forms—impair the efficiency with which financial assets perform the broad social function of serving as a store of value. Liquidity, low transaction costs, and the freedom of investors to act on information are essential to that function.

If individual investors had dominated the financial markets during the 1970s and 1980s, the revolution we have been describing would in all likelihood never have taken place; the ingenious journal articles would have stimulated more ingenious journal articles, but little change would have occurred on Wall Street. In any case, tax constraints and high transaction costs would have prevented individual investors from transforming their portfolios to accord with the new theories. Most individual investors work at the job only part-time and cannot undertake the long study and constant attention required by the application of innovative techniques.

Instead, the revolution was augmented by the rise of institutional investors such as pension funds, which were able to change as their size and investment goals changed. In the 1950s, financial institutions were far from performance-oriented. When I first came into the investment management business in 1951, buy-and-hold was the rule and turnover in institutional portfolios was slow. One reason for this complacency was rationalized laziness in an environment in which competition played a negligible role. But in another sense it was perfectly logical. In the 1950s most stocks were owned by taxable individuals who had bought them during the 1930s and 1940s at far lower prices. I remember how impressed I was by the profits in the portfolios managed by my father's investment counseling firm when I arrived on the scene in 1951. It made no sense to sell good companies and give Uncle Sam a disproportionate share of the winnings.

It was about this time that everything began to change. The early 1950s were a period of great prosperity across all income groups. Yearly savings by individuals nearly tripled between 1949 and 1957. As the depression-haunted generation faded away, common stocks once again became an acceptable asset, even for trust accounts; New York State led the way by discarding a long-standing statute that had limited stock ownership to 35 percent of the total of personal trust capital.

A great wave of new investors, with no share in the huge capital gains generated by the older portfolios, now acquired the habit of calling their brokers. Share-ownership doubled during the decade. By 1959, one in every eight adults owned stock, 75 percent of them with household incomes under $10,000 (the equivalent of about $40,000 in 1990 purchasing power). Individual savings flowed into the mutual funds even more rapidly than into the direct purchase of common stocks; mutual fund assets doubled between 1955 and 1960 and then doubled again over the next five years.

Corporate pension funds developed from a novelty to an institution and became the primary clients of the investment management profession. Their assets increased more than tenfold during the 1950s, giving them a powerful influence on portfolio turnover. Because pension funds are not subject to the capital gains taxes that hobble profit-taking by individuals, professional portfolio managers now began to have more fun.

This flood of new money, especially tax-free money, pouring into the marketplace soon transformed the traditional practices of comfortably ensconced trust officers and investment advisors. Competition goaded institutions into ever-higher levels of activity in their endless pursuit of rich returns. In 1967, my own organization, seeking a quick move into the big time, assented to being acquired by an aggressive young brokerage firm with a capital of only $1,000,000 that would keep on acquiring until one day it metamorphosed into one of the largest firms on Wall Street. Along with everyone else, we noticed that we were trading much more actively than in the old days, especially as more and more of the money we managed was exempt from taxation.

The process has been a constant joy to the investment advisory profession. Just during the 1980s the number of investment advisors registered with the S.E.C. tripled, while the number of mutual funds more than quadrupled. Dave Williams, chairman of one of the largest mutual fund organizations, recently quipped that "investment management is the only professional enterprise in America with more competitors than clients."[3]

There are giants among them. Nearly 100 portfolio management organizations now have over $10 billion each under management. The ten largest manage $800 billion of financial assets out of an institutional total of some $5 trillion in stocks, bonds, and real estate. Citibank, which was number one in 1977 with $26 billion, would barely have made the top 25 in 1989.

The tried-and-true methods of managing portfolios that my older partners taught me in the 1950s were ill suited to the management of the vast sums that accrued to institutions as the years went by. Everything had to be revised: investment objectives, diversification patterns, trading strategies, client contracts, definitions of risk, and standards of performance.

The merry game of just picking the best stocks and tucking them into a client's portfolio had worked well enough when portfolio management organizations were small. My firm, with less than $100 million under management when we were acquired, had no trouble running portfolios with less than twenty positions.

As organizations grew in size, that scale of operations was no longer practical. Managers with $5 billion under management and with only twenty holdings in a portfolio have to put $250 million into each position. To accumulate such large holdings and to liquidate them later on tends to move stock prices so far that the sheer cost of transacting cuts deeply into the portfolio's rate of return. Many of the go-go managers of the 1960s ignored that reality, and continued to act as though they were still managing small portfolios. Their innocent disregard of change helps explain what happened when stormy economic weather overwhelmed the optimistic markets of 1971 and 1972.

Before the revolution, the clients of our family-oriented business would come to us and say, "Here is my capital. Take care of me." As long as their losses were limited when the market fell, and as long as their portfolios rose as the market was rising, they had few complaints. They came to us and stayed with us because we understood their problems and the myriad kinds of contingent liabilities that all individuals must face. They recognized that we shared the delicate texture of their views about risk. We joked that we were nothing more than social workers to the rich—but skilled social workers to the rich, confident that our performance was being measured in human satisfaction rather than in comparative rates of return. We knew no more about the clients of other investment managers than they knew about ours.

But when corporate pension funds and university endowments

replace individuals as the dominant clientele, the manager/client relationship undergoes a transformation. Social work goes out of fashion: personal relationships, though still important, grow more tenuous. Usually the person with whom the advisor deals must report to some higher authority who has no direct relationship with the advisor. The shareholders in mutual funds seldom know the names of the people who manage their money. Anyone who is interested can find out how much the General Motors Pension fund has to invest, whether Yale is dissatisfied with the way XYZ Associates has been managing their endowment fund, or how well ABC Management performed last year.

As financial markets multiplied and as institutions and professional managers became the principal players, innovation was inevitable. But innovation must be preceded by theory. And the role of theory in the financial revolution took some surprising twists and turns.

The intellectual roots of most revolutions reach back to men and women who are also deeply involved in motivating what happens. Not so the makers of the revolution in finance. None of the pioneering work in either theory or practice was done in New York, the greatest financial market in the world. Most of the pioneers were professors with a taste for higher mathematics, strange bedfellows for the hard-nosed veterans of boom and bust. Few of them ever played the market with more than a few thousand dollars of their own. Nor did they shout their theories from the rooftops. With only a couple of exceptions, they were content to publish their ideas in academic journals and to debate them with their colleagues.

When their articles began to appear in the journals, adorned with fancy equations made up of Greek symbols, the few investors who were aware of them considered their ideas a joke dreamed up by a bunch of egg-heads who had never owned, much less managed, a portfolio. One distinguished practitioner, in an interview in 1977, dismissed their theorizing as "a lot of baloney."[4] Another referred to them as "academia nuts."[5]

When three of them were chosen to share the Nobel Prize in economic sciences in October 1990, few outsiders had the slightest idea of who they were, what they had done, or why they deserved the most coveted prize in economics, a discipline that itself was slow to claim them as its own. One of the laureates

*11*

remarked that their receiving the Nobel Prize was "sort of like the Chicago Cubs winning the World Series."[6]

For most of the scholars who pioneered the revolution, coincidence rather than any ideological passion determined the course of their work. One was a college varsity football star who had originally planned to teach French. Another was an astronomer. One dismissed his early fascination with finance as "a terrible mistake."[7] Others had settled on mathematics, engineering, and physics as their chosen fields. Such partiality may explain why most of them viewed the stock market as nothing more than a rich source of data and fascinating intellectual puzzles.

Another major player in the revolution was the computer itself. None of the theories we shall be describing here could have had any practical applications, or could even have been tested for its real-world relevance, had this revolutionary device not been available. Its extraordinary capabilities opened the way to theoretical frontiers that might otherwise have remained hidden. By transforming the sheer mechanics of financial transactions, the computer shaped their outcomes as well.

As theories about how capital markets function and how investors should manage their affairs are latecomers in the history of ideas, all but three of the principals in this story are still alive, and only four of them are over sixty years old. I sat with each of them for hours at a time, asking where their ideas had come from, how they developed and applied them, and what they had experienced during their unpredictable journey.

They told me that to conceive and develop a new theory is a high adventure. Though many of them were somewhat shy, none was faint-hearted. Moments of silent contemplation alternated with spirited disagreements with the views of colleagues and other theorists. If the answers they were seeking had been obvious, they explained, someone else would already have uncovered them. Francis Crick, a co-discoverer of the structure of DNA, once described the path of discovery this way:

> I think that's the nature of discoveries, many times: that the reason they're difficult is that you've got to take a series of steps, three or four steps, which if you don't make them you won't get there, and if you go wrong in any one of them you won't get there. It isn't a matter of one jump—that would be easy. You've got to make several successive jumps. And

usually the pennies drop one after another until eventually it all *clicks.* Otherwise it would be too easy![8]

Like all innovators who challenge accepted beliefs, the scholars who triggered the revolution in finance and investment were seldom welcomed with open arms. Some critics accused them of being incomprehensible; others complained that they had discovered nothing new. Stephen Jay Gould, the Harvard paleontologist and historian of science, has complained that "we modern scholars often treat our professions as fortresses and our spokespeople as archers on the parapets, searching the landscape for any incursion from an alien field."[9]

Like most adventurers, these scholars ended up someplace different from where they had expected to land. They had begun their exploration of the stock market as a way to solve some interesting hypothetical problems. Once having started down this path, they could not stop. In the end they succumbed to the fascination of the stock market and it conquered them. Most of the men in this book, prolific as theoreticians in finance, have at one time or another been associated with a Wall Street firm or a major investment organization.

I will also be telling the stories of six innovators who put the new theories into practice. Here we see the revolution in action. These adventurers, in search of financial reward, shared many of the experiences of the theoreticians. Self-doubt, reluctant colleagues, career risks, and uncertainty accompanied them all the way.

This book reflects my own adventures as an active participant in financial markets for over forty years. At first I found the new theories emerging from the universities during the 1950s and 1960s alien and unappealing, as did most other practitioners. What the scholars were saying seemed abstract and difficult to understand. And beyond that, it seemed both to demean my profession as I was practicing it and to prescribe radical changes in the way I should carry out my responsibilities.

Even if I could have convinced myself to turn my back on the theoretical structure that the academics were erecting, there was too much of it coming from major universities for me to accept the view of my colleagues that it was "a lot of baloney." Finally the market disaster of 1974 convinced me that there had to be a better way to manage investment portfolios.

It was in that year that I founded *The Journal of Portfolio Management* to help others to learn what the new theories were all about. My goal was to build a bridge between gown and town: to foster a dialogue between the academics and the practitioners in language they could both understand, and thereby to enrich the contributions of both.

The first issue of the *Journal* appeared within weeks after the collapse of the great bear market of 1973–74, which probably explains the *Journal*'s immediate acceptance. The time was right for opening minds that had been closed to unfamiliar ideas. The lead article alerted the investment management profession to the consequences of the appalling loss of wealth that had just taken place. The author, James Vertin, was chief investment officer for the trust accounts at Wells Fargo Bank in San Francisco and one of the earliest advocates of the use of the new theories. He warned: "Current and prospective customers are increasingly suspicious, hesitant, and downright skeptical that professional investment management can consistently provide benefits that justify its cost. . . . The dissatisfaction is pervasive. . . . [They] are afraid of us, and what our methods might produce in the way of further loss."[10] And yet, he pointed out, "It doesn't have to be that way."

This book celebrates the innovators and tinkerers who showed us how it ought to be, as well as the pioneers who brought about the improbable wedding between academia and Wall Street.

# PART
I

Setting the Scene

# Chapter

# 1

# Are Stock Prices Predictable?

*It is doubtful.*

**P**aul Samuelson, economist and Nobel laureate, once remarked that it is not easy to get rich in Las Vegas, at Churchill Downs, or at the local Merrill Lynch office. All investors, professionals as well as amateurs, acknowledge the truth of this observation. Even smart people have a hard time getting rich by predicting stock prices.

Some people never try to outguess the market: they simply hang on to the stocks they inherited, bought long ago, or acquired in some employer-sponsored savings program. Others buy and hold under the conviction that trading finances yachts only for brokers, not for customers.

Yet, in the face of admittedly high odds, enough people do try to predict stock prices to keep an entire industry humming. The demand for the wisdom produced by armies of security analysts, portfolio managers, television pundits, software peddlers, and newspaper columnists shows no sign of waning. Some of the wealthiest people on Wall Street are professionals whose bank accounts have been inflated by a constant flow of investment advisory fees. I have already pointed out that the number of investment management organizations tripled just during the 1980s. *Forbes, Barron's,* and *The Wall Street Journal* have subscribers that number in the millions. Index funds, which hold a diversified cross-section of the market and never sell one stock in order to buy another, account for less than 15 percent of all equity portfolios.

This appetite for predicting stock prices is all the more striking, because a huge volume of academic research demonstrates that it is a devilishly difficult job not likely to get any easier. While no one goes so far as to say that it is impossible to make good predictions or that all predictions are destined to be wrong, the abundant evidence and the robust character of the theories that explain the evidence confirm that the task of predicting stock prices is formidable by any measure.

The exploration into whether investors can successfully forecast stock prices has roots that reach all the way back to 1900, when Louis Bachelier, a young French mathematician, completed his dissertation for the degree of Doctor of Mathematical Sciences at the Sorbonne. The title of the dissertation was "The Theory of Speculation." This extraordinary piece of work, some seventy pages long, was the first effort ever to employ theory, including mathematical techniques, to explain why the stock market behaves as it does. Bachelier supported his novel theoretical analysis with a sophisticated study of the French capital markets at the turn of the century.

It is worth noting that Bachelier was an academic all the way. He employed his profound understanding of the markets for his intellectual exercise; we have no evidence that he ever speculated or invested in the markets he was analyzing. He set the style for many later theorists who, like him, refrained from putting their money where their minds were.

Bachelier was far ahead of his time. Paul Cootner, one of the leading finance scholars of the 1960s, once delivered this accolade: "So outstanding is his work that we can say that the study of speculative prices has its moment of glory at its moment of conception."[1]

Bachelier laid the groundwork on which later mathematicians constructed a full-fledged theory of probability. He derived a formula that anticipated Einstein's research into the behavior of particles subject to random shocks in space. And he developed the now universally used concept of stochastic processes, the analysis of random movements among statistical variables. Moreover, he made the first theoretical attempt to value such financial instruments as options and futures, which had active markets even in 1900. And he did all this in an effort to explain why prices in capital markets are impossible to predict!

Bachelier's opening paragraphs contain observations about

"fluctuations on the Exchange" that could have been written today. He recognizes that market movements are difficult to explain, even after the fact, and that they often generate a self-reinforcing momentum:

> Past, present, and even discounted future events are reflected in market price, but often show no apparent relation to price changes. . . . [A]rtificial causes also intervene: the Exchange reacts on itself, and the current fluctuation is a function, not only of the previous fluctuations, but also of the current state. The determination of these fluctuations depends on an infinite number of factors; it is, therefore, impossible to aspire to mathematical predictions of it. . . . [T]he dynamics of the Exchange will never be an exact science.[2]

Despite these demurrers, Bachelier sets himself an ambitious goal: to offer "a formula which expresses the likelihood of a market fluctuation"[3]—that is, a move upward or downward in stock prices. Recognizing that fluctuations over time are virtually impossible to interpret, he begins by concentrating on the market at a given instant, promising to establish "the law of probability of price changes consistent with the market at that instant."[4] This approach leads him into more profound investigations: the theory of probability and the analysis of particles in space subject to random shocks.

In view of the originality and brilliance of Bachelier's analysis of financial markets, we might expect him to have been a man of stature in his own time. It is easy to picture him as an inspiring professor at the Sorbonne, or perhaps lured from France to Harvard or Oxford. We can note his large following of students, who, having gleaned so much wisdom, will go on to make their own mark in the study of finance, uncertainty, and random behavior. Or perhaps we can visualize him as a fabulously successful investor, a forerunner of Keynes, combining financial acumen with theoretical innovation.

The truth is far different. Bachelier was a frustrated unknown in his own time. When he presented his dissertation to the committee at the Sorbonne, they awarded it merely *"mention honorable,"* a notch below the *"mention très honorable"* that was essential for anyone hoping to find a job in the academic world. It was long time before Bachelier finally won an appointment, and even then it was only at the provincial university at Besancon. Besancon is about as provincial as provincial France can get.

Some of the difficulty seems to have stemmed from a mathematical error in a paper he published in 1913—a slip that haunted him for many years. As late as 1929, when he applied for a position at the University at Geneva, a Professor Gevrey was still scandalized by the error, and, after consulting Paul Lévy, another expert in the field, Gevry had Bachelier blackballed from the University. Lévy later recognized the value of Bachelier's pioneering work, and the two became reconciled.

Bachelier's real problem, however, was that he had chosen an odd topic for his dissertation. He was convinced that the financial markets were a rich source of data for mathematicians and students of probability. Twenty years after writing his dissertation, he remarked that his analysis had embodied "images taken from natural phenomena . . . a strange and unexpected linkage and a starting point for great progress." His superiors did not agree. Although Poincaré, his teacher, wrote that "M. Bachelier has evidenced an original and precise mind," he also observed that "The topic is somewhat remote from those our candidates are in the habit of treating."[5]

Benoit Mandelbrot, the pioneer of fractal geometry and one of Bachelier's great admirers, recently suggested that no one knew where to pigeonhole Bachelier's findings. There was no ready means to retrieve them, assuming that someone wanted to. Sixty years were to pass before anyone took the slightest notice of his work.

The key to Bachelier's insight is his observation, expressed in a notably modern manner, that "contradictory opinions concerning [market] changes diverge so much that at the same instant buyers believe in a price increase and sellers believe in a price decrease."[6] Convinced that there is no basis for believing that—on the average—either sellers or buyers consistently know any more about the future than the other, he arrived at an astonishing conjecture: "It seems that the market, the aggregate of speculators, *at a given instant* can believe in neither a market rise nor a market fall, since, for each quoted price, there are as many buyers as sellers."[7] (emphasis added)

The fond hopes of home buyers in California during the 1980s provide a vivid example of Bachelier's perception. Those buyers were willing to pay higher and higher prices for houses "because values could only go up."[8] This myopic view implied that the people who were selling the houses were systematically ignorant or foolish. Clearly they were not.

Prices in markets that deal in bets on the future are, at any given instant, as likely to rise as they are to fall—as California real-estate prices have demonstrated. That means that a speculator has an equal chance of winning or losing at each moment in time. Now comes the real punch, in Bachelier's words and with his own emphasis: *The mathematical expectation of the speculator is zero.*"[9] He describes this condition as a "fair game."

Here Bachelier is not just playing a logical trick by setting unrealistic assumptions so tightly that no other result is possible. He knows too much about the marketplace to resort to something that deceitful. In a disarmingly simple but perceptive statement about the nature of security markets, he sums up his case: The probability of a rise in price at any moment is the same as the probability of a fall in price, because "Clearly the price considered most likely by the market is the true current price: if the market judged otherwise, it would quote not this price, but another price higher or lower."[10]

Under these conditions, prices will move, in either direction, only when the market has reason to change its mind about what the "price considered most likely"[11] is going to be. But no one knows which way the market will jump when it changes its mind; hence the probabilities are 50 percent for a rise and 50 percent for a fall.

This conclusion led Bachelier to another important insight. The size of a market fluctuation tends to grow larger as the time horizon stretches out. In the course of a minute, fluctuations will be small—less than a point in most instances. During a full day's trading, moves of a full point are not unusual. As the time horizon moves from a day to a week to a month to a year and then to a series of years, the range within which prices swing back and forth will grow ever wider.

But how rapidly will the range expand? Bachelier answered that question with a set of mathematical equations demonstrating that "this interval [will be] proportional to the square root of time."[12] This prediction has held up with stunning precision.

Stock prices in the United States over the past sixty-odd years have behaved almost exactly as Bachelier said they would. Two-thirds of the time, they have moved within a range of 5.9 percent on either side of their average level in the course of a month. But the range in the course of a year has not been 72 percent, or twelve times as much; rather, it has averaged around 20 percent, or about three and a half times the monthly range. The square root of 12 is 3.46!

If stock prices vary according to the square root of time, they bear a remarkable resemblance to molecules randomly colliding with one another as they move in space. An English physicist named Robert Brown discovered this phenomenon early in the nineteenth century, and it is generally known as Brownian motion. Brownian motion was a critical ingredient of Einstein's theory of the atom. The mathematical formula that describes this phenomenon was one of Bachelier's crowning achievements.

Over time, in the literature on finance, Brownian motion came to be called the random walk, which someone once described as the path a drunk might follow at night in the light of a lamppost. No one knows who first used this expression, but it became increasingly familiar among academics during the 1960s, much to the annoyance of financial practitioners. Eugene Fama of the University of Chicago, one of the first and most enthusiastic proponents of the concept, tells me that random walk "is an ancient statistical term; nobody alive can claim it."[13] In later years, the primary focus of research on capital markets was on determining whether or not the random walk is a valid description of security price movements.

Bachelier himself, hardly a modest man, ended his dissertation with this flat statement: "It is evident that the present theory resolves the majority of problems in the study of speculation by the calculus of probability."[14]

Despite its importance, Bachelier's thesis was lost until it was rediscovered quite by accident in the 1950s by Jimmie Savage, a mathematical statistician at Chicago. Savage himself is worth a story. Milton Friedman, after associating with Savage for twenty years, described him as ". . . one of the few really creative people I have met in the course of my intellectual life. . . . Here is one of those extraordinary people of whom there are only a handful in any university at any time."[15]

Savage's parents delayed in giving him a first name because his mother was seriously ill when he was born in 1917. They later named him Leonard, but a nurse in the hospital had called him

Jimmie and entered that name in the hospital records. Many years later, Savage arranged for a court order to make it official: His name became Leonard Jimmie Savage.

A child prodigy, Savage was afflicted with poor eyesight—he once confessed that "my eyes are too weak for much mischief."[16] When attending a public lecture, he was wont to walk up to the platform, examining the equations on the blackboard with a high-powered glass that he carried for the purpose. He once described himself this way: "I am a man of very many words. If I were to speak extemporaneously, I could probably hold myself spell-bound for an hour."[17]

Perhaps he was right to be spellbound: In the course of an out-standing career in various applied and theoretical areas of mathematics, Savage was offered faculty appointments by major universities in departments of biology, economics, management, and physics, in addition to mathematics.

Some time around 1954, while rummaging through a university library, Savage chanced upon a small book by Bachelier, published in 1914, on speculation and investment. Fascinated, he sent post-cards to his economist friends, asking "Ever heard of this guy?"[18] Paul Samuelson, who was just then beginning to explore theories of market behavior and valuation on his own, could not find the book in the MIT library, but he did discover a copy of Bachelier's Ph.D. thesis. Samuelson has remarked that "Bachelier seems to have had something of a one-track mind. But what a track!"[19] He immediately recognized the quality of Bachelier's work and spread the word throughout the economics profession. Bachelier's influence is apparent in Samuelson's early treatment of the behavior of speculative prices.

Even if Bachelier had been better known in his lifetime, few people would have paid much attention to what he had to say. Those who controlled the real world of finance in the United States had little interest in the inner workings of the stock market. Playing the market was just too much fun. Stock prices rose 60 percent from 1900 to 1916, declining in only four of those years. From 1921 to 1929, as the American industrial juggernaut linked itself to the nation's farms through the rapidly expanding railroad system, stock prices soared sixfold.

By 1900, Thomas Edison's stock tickers had been punching out prices for nearly thirty years. The streets of the financial district swarmed all day, and often into the night, with young boys rushing to deliver the latest news bulletins.

For many years those bulletins were inscribed by hand with a stylus on a sheaf of tissue and carbon paper that produced up to 24 copies at a time. Until the introduction of small, hand-cranked printing presses in the mid-1880s and then the Dow, Jones news ticker in 1897, these handwritten bulletins were the main source of information for Wall Street traders and investors. Dow, Jones & Co. continued to deliver bulletins by messenger up to the end of World War II.

Recipes for predicting stock prices were in urgent demand on Wall Street throughout these years. By far the most famous was the Dow Theory, developed by Charles Dow, co-founder of Dow, Jones & Co. in 1882 and the first editor of the company's flagship publication, *The Wall Street Journal,* launched in 1889.

Dow was born in a small town in Connecticut in 1851. He had had twenty jobs before he found his real love in journalism when he went to work as a reporter and part-time printer at the *Springfield* (Massachusetts) *Republican* in 1869. The editor, Samuel Bowles, a brilliant though difficult man, was one of the first editors to insist that the lead paragraph of an article should tell the whole story in brief: "who, what, when, where, and why."

In 1875, Dow left Springfield to join the *Providence Journal,* where he attracted national attention with a series of articles on the history of steam transportation. In those articles he concentrated on the efforts of the sailing freighters to withstand the inroads of the steamboat companies, many of which were forming joint ventures with the expanding railroad system.

In 1879, a group of eastern financiers, along with Senator Jerome Bonaparte Chaffee of Colorado, invited Dow to join them on a visit to Leadville, Colorado, the site of a huge silver strike. One of the mines, the Camp Bird mine, had been discovered by three Gallagher brothers—Irish laborers who on their arrival in Leadville had been refused credit for a few loaves of bread. The town had a population of 18,000 when Dow arrived; two years earlier, before the Gallaghers arrived on the scene, the mining camp had consisted of nothing but tents. There were numerous hotels and establishments when Dow arrived. And there were dancing houses where ladies charged 50 cents for a set of dances.

In Dow's words, those ladies had "descended to the very root of the soiled ladder."[20]

After three months, the Easterners had had enough. Dow's last article from Leadville to the *Providence Journal* quoted one member of the party, about to down a last glass of beer, who said, "Be it ever so humble, there's no place like Fifth Avenue."[21]

Dow returned home convinced that the economic future of America was almost unlimited. His experience in the mining country endowed him with an optimistic spirit that he never abandoned.

Deciding that Providence was now too small a town for him, Dow moved to New York City with an old newspaper friend, Eddie Jones. Lloyd Wendt, the historian of Dow, Jones & Co., describes Jones as "a tall, lean, red-haired man with smiling blue eyes and a dimpled chin," far more extroverted and sociable than Dow.[22] Dow also was tall and thin, but he had dark eyes and a full black beard. Slow to anger, he was a man of few words.

The two young men soon found positions at Kiernan's at 2 Broad Street, close to the site where the New York Stock Exchange would open its doors many years later. Kiernan, one of the publishers of the tissue-and-carbon news bulletins, owed his success to his friendship with many of the major players in Wall Street.

Kiernan was delighted to hire Dow and Jones. Jones had a nose for news and, according to Wendt, could read and understand a financial report faster than anyone else. Dow wrote the news bulletins with skill and clarity. He wanted to write a more analytical daily report as well, but Kiernan was not interested.

Dow, Jones, and a friend named Charles Milford Bergstrasser soon decided to go into the news-distributing business themselves. Bergstrasser, small, gregarious, and excitable, was working for Drexel, Morgan & Company, a banking house. Deciding that Bergstrasser's name was less than euphonious, they called their new company Dow, Jones & Co. (the comma did not disappear for almost fifty years). They opened for business in November 1882 at 15 Wall Street, down wooden stairs to a small, unpainted room next to a soda-water establishment.

Two years later they acquired their first hand-cranked printing press. By 1887, the company had grown so large that clients were complaining that deliveries were too slow and competitors were getting a jump on them. The partners responded by installing an electronic news ticker. Now known as "the broad tape," such tickers are still used on Wall Street.

Early in 1885, Dow, Jones converted its *Afternoon News Letter* into *The Wall Street Journal,* whose format and coverage have changed little over the years. As editor for thirteen years, Dow seldom missed writing the paper's daily editorial until his death in 1902. In his commentaries Dow expressed his ideas about the stock market and economic conditions and provided an original, sophisticated analysis of the business cycle, a field of study then in its infancy.

At heart Dow was a scholar rather than a speculator. He was more interested in interpreting the history of the stock market than in devising a system for predicting its future. The world has read his interpretation otherwise.

Underlying the so-called Dow Theory is the assumption that trends in stock prices, once under way, will tend to persist until the market itself sends out a signal that these trends are about to lose their momentum and go into reverse. Dow's best-known statement on the subject appeared in a *Journal* article in 1901:

> A person watching the tide coming in and who wishes to know the exact spot which marks the high tide, sets a stick in the sand at the points reached by the incoming waves until the stick reaches a position where the waves do not come up to it, and finally recede enough to show that the tide has turned.
>
> This method holds good in watching and determining the flood tide of the stock market. . . . The price-waves, like those of the sea, do not recede at once from the top. The force which moves them checks the inflow gradually and time elapses before it can be told with certainty whether the tide has been seen or not.[23]

Recognizing turns in the tide is less simple on Wall Street than it is on the beach. The market does fluctuate. Dow theorists boast that they can identify the very moment when what appears to be only a slight fluctuation is actually the first sign of the reversal of a major trend. They do not always agree among themselves, however. Disputes often arise over whether a slight fluctuation away from a trend is just a temporary setback—a "correction," in market patois—or the onset of a new trend. Sometimes the signal appears so late that the main trend has almost exhausted itself, and stock prices are about ready to turn around and start a new trend headed in the other direction.

Even people who have never heard of the Dow Theory are familiar with the Dow Jones Averages, Charles Dow's most lasting contribution to finance. This was the first attempt to create some sort of aggregate indicator of stock-market trends. Although other averages have since appeared, notably those from the Associated Press, the *New York Times,* and Standard & Poor's, the Dow Jones Averages are still what most people turn to when they want to know "How's the market doing?"

The first Dow Jones Average appeared in the *Afternoon News Letter* on July 3, 1884. It consisted of the closing prices of eleven companies: nine railroads and two industrials. Dow's idea was to provide an overall measure of the performance of active companies, at a time when an average day's activity on the New York Stock Exchange was about 250,000 shares. Although today's average volume is over 100,000,000 shares a day, 250,000 shares represented at the time a higher level of activity relative to the number of shares listed on the Stock Exchange and available for trading.

In 1882, Dow predicted that "The industrial market is destined to be the great speculative market of the United States."[24] He recognized that his list of companies would change as time passed. After twelve years of constant revision of the composition of the Dow Jones Average, he published the first strictly industrial list on May 26, 1896.

Of twelve industrials included in that list, only one still appears in the Industrial Average: General Electric. The other eleven were American Cotton Oil, American Sugar, American Tobacco, Chicago Gas, Distilling and Cattle Feeding, Laclede Gas, National Lead, North American, Tennessee Coal & Iron, US Leather preferred, and US Rubber. Later listings included such diverse items as Victor Talking Machine, Famous Players Lasky, and Baldwin Locomotive.

The twelve stocks in the first industrial list included all the industrial companies then traded on the New York Stock Exchange. The other companies listed consisted of fifty-three railroads and six utilities. Shares of banks and insurance companies then traded over-the-counter rather than on the floor of the New York Stock Exchange.

The term "industrial" is really a misnomer, because not all of the companies listed as industrials were industrial companies. They were simply all the companies that were neither railroads nor utilities.* Dow Jones published separate averages for the railroads and the utilities.

The sparseness of industrials relative to rails in the list is evidence of the boldness of Dow's foresight about the industrial market, as well as an indication of the importance of railroads to the American economy in the late nineteenth century. It reflects something else as well: Most industrial companies did not need as much capital as the rails, which required huge financing for their rolling stock and right-of-way.

In those days, industrial companies tended to rely on a combination of debt and their founders' wealth to finance their growth. This was partly a matter of choice, as incorporation did not offer major benefits to owners at that time. But it was partly because, as one historian of the period has noted, "the securities of industrial corporations were regarded as peculiar, unstable, and speculative. Even the largest and most visible firms were not 'public' corporations."[25] For example, two industrial giants of the period, the Singer Manufacturing Company and McCormick Harvesting Machine (later International Harvester), were still closely held corporations.

Dow died at his home in Brooklyn in 1902, just nine months after Dow, Jones & Co. had been sold to Clarence Barron for $130,000—only $2,000,000 in today's purchasing power. About a year later, Samuel Nelson, publisher of Nelson's Wall Street Library, published several of Dow's editorials in a book called *The ABC of Speculation*. Nelson is believed to be the first to use the expression "Dow Theory." Dow himself never used it.

In 1903, William Peter Hamilton took over as editor of *The Wall Street Journal*. Hamilton was a Scottish journalist who had joined the paper as a reporter in 1899, while Dow was still there. As editor, he followed Dow's practice of writing almost all the daily editorials himself and continued to do so until his death in December 1929.

Hamilton repeatedly stressed a central idea of Dow Theory that prices on the New York Stock Exchange are "sufficient in them-

---

*Today, the industrials include all stocks that are not utilities, railroads, airlines, or truckers.

selves" to reveal everything worth knowing about business conditions. Here Hamilton was anticipating a radical concept that was to appear long after his death. In the 1960s, a group of college professors would develop the Efficient Market Hypothesis, based on the notion that stock prices reflect all available information about individual companies and about the economy as a whole. The Efficient Market Hypothesis, however, also looks back to Bachelier, for it assumes that information is so rapidly reflected in stock prices that no single investor can consistently know more than the market as a whole knows. Hamilton, on the contrary, believed that the market itself revealed what stock prices would do in the future.

On October 21, 1929, just before he died, Hamilton predicted the end of the bull market of the 1920s in an editorial titled "The Turn in the Tide," a title that recalled Dow's view of market behavior. Hamilton had made similar predictions of impending disaster in January 1927, June 1928, and July 1928. So "The Turn in the Tide" was a lucky call. The worst day in the history of the Stock Exchange occurred just four days later. In the days ahead, values were to fall 90 percent from their 1929 peak before hitting bottom in 1932.

One of the victims of the crash was Alfred Cowles 3rd, a wealthy man whose father and grandfather had been major stockholders and executives of the Chicago Tribune Company. He was born in Chicago in 1891 and, following family tradition, attended Yale. He graduated in the class of 1913 and went to work as a reporter for the *Tribune* in Spokane.

Suddenly Cowles came down with tuberculosis. His family shipped him off to Colorado Springs for treatment, which, according to Cowles, "consisted mostly of resting in bed and hoping for the best."[26] The cure, uncertain as it may have been, ultimately succeeded. After ten years in Colorado Springs, he rejoined his family in Chicago. He was 93 years old when he died in 1985.

An interviewer who visited Cowles at his ten-room Palm Beach home in April 1970 described him as ". . . about six feet tall, and his thin gray hair is combed straight back. His skin is slightly splotchy and freckled, the neck crepey. . . . 'I'm getting along,' he said, 'and for a man with a plastic aorta in my heart and a game leg, I'm doing all right.'"[27]

Around 1926, while still in Colorado Springs, Cowles had begun to help his father with the management of the family's financial affairs. He kept in touch with what was happening in the market by subscribing to several investment services that carried tips and other information of varying degrees of reliability. The plethora of publications coming his way finally struck him as "a little wasteful."[28]

He decided to figure out which publication was the best and to subscribe to just that one. In 1928, he started to keep track records on the twenty-four most widely circulated services and continued to do so for four years. That period ran from the height of the great bull market of the 1920s, to the crash of 1929, to the cascading bear market of 1931–32. As the appalling drama unfolded, it seemed to come as a total surprise to the services Cowles was subscribing to. He decided to find out whether the failure was something endemic to the advisory business or just a reflection of the shortcomings of those services.

Ironically, a neighbor of Cowles in Colorado Springs, Robert Rhea, was in the process of reaching exactly the opposite conclusion from Cowles. Rhea, who had been permanently disabled while serving in the aviation branch of the Signal Corps during World War I, was later to emerge as the most famous exponent of Dow Theory. A diligent student of Hamilton's writings, he launched a market letter called "Dow Theory Comment" in mid-1932. The letter put Dow Theory on the map and became so popular that its subscription list reached 6,000, a large number in those days, particularly in view of the depressed state of the stock market and the economy.

Although Rhea made few original contributions to Dow Theory, he is generally credited with having transformed Hamilton's scattered observations into a structured set of ideas. He also traded successfully enough in the market to cover the large medical bills that had accrued during his many years of disability.

Rhea never pretended that market forecasting was simple. He wrote in 1935:

Those who try to profit from the advance and decline of security prices are perplexed perhaps 90% of the time. And it seems that perplexity increases with experience. . . .
[U]nvarying cocksureness on the part of traders or investors is a badge of incompetence. There is, nevertheless, a time and place for certainty where the market is concerned, but such times and places are few and far between.[29]

Rhea identified two "times and places for certainty." He called the bottom of the great bear market on the exact day it hit its low, on July 8, 1932, and then predicted the top of the market in 1937. We do not know whether his uncanny forecasting abilities would have continued into the future, because he died in Kansas City in 1939.

Meanwhile, in 1931, Alfred Cowles had set out on his own quest to determine whether stock prices are predictable. His achievements were noteworthy in his own time, and few scholars of any era have been as thorough, as creative, and as helpful to others. The amateur converted himself into a distinguished professional.

Cowles knew what he wanted to do but was uncertain about how to go about it. He consulted his friend Charles Boissevain, a Dutch biochemist with mathematical training who was chief of research at the Colorado Foundation for Research in Tuberculosis, where Cowles was a director and treasurer as well as a patient. Boissevain must have been a colorful and stimulating companion. At one time the champion sculler of Holland, he suffered from both tuberculosis and asthma and had come to Colorado for relief. A contemporary described Boissevain in these words: "He had a brilliant mind and knew what research was all about. Just one caveat though: Webb [the head of the foundation] would have to take care to keep Boissevain on the track. He had so many ideas, so much scientific curiosity, that he might be prone to start up too many hares and not all of them in the tuberculosis field."[30]

Boissevain referred Cowles to Harold Davis, a professor of mathematics at Indiana University who shared Cowle's interest in economics and statistics.

Cowles asked Davis whether it would be possible to compute a mathematical procedure called linear regression with twenty-four variables, an unusually large number. Davis replied that he could not imagine why anyone would want to perform a regression with that many variables, but he helped Cowles acquire a Hollerith machine, IBM's most advanced punch-card computer in the early 1930s. Despite Davis's skepticism, he helped Cowles to perform the necessary calculations.

Davis also urged Cowles to get in touch with the Econometric Society, an organization established two years earlier to encourage scholars interested in combining the science of mathematical statistics with economics. Davis was confident that Cowles would find the guidance he was seeking from among the society's membership of about a hundred distinguished economists and mathematicians. With Cowles's still ample fortune in mind, Davis mentioned that the society was short of funds and could afford only occasional small meetings and that the members were eager to publish a journal that would bring their work to the attention of other scholars in their own and related fields.

Cowles immediately wrote to Professor Irving Fisher of Yale, President of the Econometric Society and an old friend of Cowles's father from their undergraduate days at Yale. Like Cowles, Fisher had suffered from tuberculosis in his youth and managed to survive a long stay in a sanitarium. He emerged as a health fanatic and, in particular, as a passionate crusader against alcohol and tobacco.

Fisher had won worldwide reputation as a theoretician for his work on interest rates and statistical innovations. Despite his well-justified fame, his attempts to forecast the stock market had given him a different kind of reputation. On October 15, 1929, just a few days before the Great Crash, he made what John Kenneth Galbraith refers to as his "immortal estimate" that "Stock prices have reached what looks like a permanently higher plateau." That was not bad enough. Fisher went on to say, "I expect to see the stock market a good deal higher than it is today within a few months." On October 21, the day Hamilton published "The Turn in the Tide," Fisher welcomed the ominously weakening market, describing it as "a shaking out of the lunatic fringe."[31] Fisher subsequently lost his substantial fortune, which had been acquired partly from a wealthy wife and partly from an innovative filing system he had developed and marketed.

Fisher was overjoyed to receive Cowles's letter, in which Cowles offered to finance the publication of the Society's journal and the establishment of an organization to promote and publish econometric research. Fisher immediately telephoned Charles Roos, a Swedish economist who was another leader of the Econometric Society. Roos was so incredulous that he asked Fisher whether the letter might have been sent by a crank.

A short time later, Fisher, Roos, and Cowles met at Fisher's home in New Haven. Cowles proposed an initial budget of $12,000 a year—about $90,000 in 1990 purchasing power—and promised to provide more if the econometric research drew a response from people outside its immediate field of interest. In an interview many years later, Cowles described himself in his relationship to the Society as "I suppose, its main angel."[32]

In January 1932, Cowles established the Cowles Commission for Research in Economics in Colorado Springs. Its motto was "Science Is Measurement." The Commission, sponsored and supervised by an advisory council consisting of members of the Econometric Society, remained in Colorado Springs until it moved to Chicago in 1939; under Nobel laureate James Tobin's direction, it later moved to Yale. The Commission was home to Nobel laureate Harry Markowitz in the 1950s and is still home to many other famous scholars.

Plans were also made to establish the new journal, to be called *Econometrica*. That journal is now nearly sixty years old and commands wide respect among economists, statisticians, and mathematicians. The first issue of *Econometrica,* which appeared in January 1933, contained an introductory article by the famous Harvard economist and the first president of the Econometric Society, Joseph Schumpeter, as well as a timely paper by Irving Fisher titled "The Debt-Deflation Theory of Great Depressions."

The first fruit of Cowles's own research into market forecasting, an article titled "Can Stock Market Forecasters Forecast?," appeared in the July 1933 issue. A three-word abstract of the article concluded: "It is doubtful."

Cowles analyzed the track records of four sets of forecasters: sixteen leading financial services that furnished their subscribers with selected lists of common stocks; the purchases and sales of stocks made by twenty leading fire insurance companies; a test of the Dow Theory gleaned from Hamilton's editorials in *The Wall Street Journal;* and the twenty-four publications that had set Cowles off on his quest, including sixteen professional financial services, four financial weeklies, one bank letter, and one investment-house letter.

Cowles had set himself quite a job. He had to review 7,500 separate recommendations by the financial services, all transactions over four years by the insurance companies, 255 of Hamilton's editorials that contained definite market forecasts from 1903 to 1929, and 3,300 recommendations by the financial publications. Cowles's careful and thorough research methods are evident throughout the fifteen pages of the article. In each case, Cowles measured the percentage gain or loss against the gain or loss of the stock market as a whole over the same period.

Only six of the sixteen financial services had achieved any measure of success, and even the record of the best performer "could not be definitely attributed to skill"[33] rather than to pure chance. Performance for the group as a whole was negative relative to the performance of the market as a whole. Results for the fire insurance companies were no better and also "could have been achieved through a purely random selection of stocks."[34]

William Peter Hamilton called the top of the bull market in 1929, but apparently he was lucky to do so. True, the portfolio of an investor who had followed Hamilton's timing recommendations would have done all right in absolute terms: Cowles calculated that the portfolio would have grown nineteen-fold during the years from 1903 to 1929 when Hamilton was making his recommendations, a return that led Robert Rhea to remark, "I for one would not complain at such a gain."[35] But an investor who had simply bought into the market in 1903 and had held on for twenty-six years would have ended up twice as wealthy as an investor who had followed Hamilton's advice. Hamilton made twenty-nine bullish forecasts, of which sixteen turned out profitable, and twenty-three bearish forecasts, of which ten were profitable. These results are about what one could do calling heads or tails on the toss of a coin.

Cowles's conclusion on Hamilton's performance were not well received by his neighbor Rhea, whom Cowles had enlisted as one of five experts to judge each of Hamilton's editorials as a recommendation to buy, sell, or hold. Rhea's riposte in one of the issues of his *Dow Theory Comment* begins gently by referring to Cowles as ". . . long a friend of mine . . . doing a commendable job in proving up on the defects of advisory services generally. . . . The report is a clear-cut, concise, and masterly treatise, and I want to say here that I know that Mr. Cowles intended it to represent an impartial and scientific investigation of the theory."[36]

Then he takes off. He insists that Cowles's test of Hamilton's performance was less than fair. He maintains that Hamilton's editorials were intended to be taken as educational pieces, not as investment advice. Hamilton, Rhea insisted, would never have "incurred brokerage charges by closing his account [and going into cash] whenever he was in doubt about the trend."[37] Furthermore, Hamilton never claimed that forecasting was his occupation; he refrained from discussing the market over long periods and frequently traveled abroad. Rhea points out that Cowles chose to end his test of Hamilton's performance with the day Hamilton died, on December 9, 1929, when the Dow Jones Average was 260, already down by a third from its high but still far from its ultimate low. Hamilton had already announced that a bear market was imminent and had sold some stocks. Rhea declares: "Surely no Dow theory student saw anything resembling the termination of a bear market until June and July 1932, and it is inconceivable that Hamilton would have turned bullish before then."[38]

Rhea goes on to argue that, had Cowles continued his investigation beyond Hamilton's death, he would have found that the capital of the buy and hold investor would have suffered a shrinkage of more than 80 percent before the bear market hit bottom whereas the investor who had followed Hamilton's advice could have sat back comfortably with a pile of cash. On the other hand, an indefinite extension of the test period after 1933 might well have put the buy and hold investor back in the lead over the advice of a market-timing Dow theorist.

The financial publications that Cowles investigated fared no better than Hamilton: "We are enabled to conclude that the average forecasting agency fell [below] the average of all performances achievable by pure chance."[39] In 1928, when an investor in the market as a whole would have earned the enormous return of 44 percent, the ratio of bullish to bearish forecasts by this group was only four to three. In 1931, when the market fell 54 percent, the group made sixteen bullish forecasts to every three bearish forecasts.

In each test, Cowles found that the market as a whole had outperformed the practitioners. He also found that the best of a series of random forecasts made by drawing cards from an appropriate deck was just as good as the best series of actual forecasts. Even more depressing, the worst series of random forecasts was better than any of the worst series of actual forecasts.

In recalling this experience many years later, Cowles observed:

Of course, I got a lot of complaints. Who appointed me to keep track? Also, I had belittled the profession of investment adviser. I used to tell them that it isn't a profession, and of course that got them even madder.

Market advice for a fee is a paradox. Anybody who really knew just wouldn't share his knowledge. Why should he? In five years, he could be the richest man in the world. Why pass the word on?[40]

Cowles could not leave the matter alone. In 1944, he published a new study in *Econometrica* covering 6,904 forecasts over a period of fifteen and a half years. Once again the results failed "to disclose evidence of ability to predict successfully the future course of the stock market."[41] The bullish forecasts outnumbered the bearish forecast four-to-one, even though stock prices were falling more than half the time between 1929 and 1944. These were the grim conclusions from what Cowles characterized as "a very sober academic and professional report" that mentioned none of the services he analyzed by name: "We didn't want to get down to the level of nasty finger-pointing."[42]

Cowles was a compulsive score-keeper on many topics other than the stock market. His son was kind enough to show me a notebook Cowles had kept some time around 1960, which covered both facts and analysis on such varied topics as these:

Advertising, fraction of GNP
Blindness in US
Bridge Life Masters (Chicagoans, & Chicago women)
Death rates, Scheduled airlines—Domestic US
Dogs—most popular breeds
Health service manpower
Painting and rising prices
Palm Beach weather
Sharks
Yale, Admission to

He must have been a fiendish bridge player. Here is one passage from his notes on the game:

If each of 50 million bridge players in the US plays 200 sessions of 40 deals each, this adds up to 50 million × 200 × 40 = 400 billion hands dealt each year in US. The probabilities of any given hand being dealt with 13 cards of one suit are 0.00000000000156. The chances of a hand with 13 cards of one suit being dealt in the US in any given year, therefore are 400 billion times 0.00000000000156 = 0.624.

And so on, working though the chances of hands with 12 cards of the same suit all the way to hands with 7 cards of the same suit.

Cowles's comprehensive research on investment performance, carefully tested against the laws of chance and deeply respected by his academic colleagues, was to find solid confirmation thirty years later in similar studies carried out at a much higher level of sophistication. Like Cowles's analysis, these studies also were greeted by practitioners with deafening silence, especially as the studies appeared as the go-go years of the 1960s were just beginning to roll.

Cowles made other significant contributions to the field of finance. One of the Cowles Commission's goals was to establish an index "to portray the average experience of those investing in [stocks] in the United States."[43] In 1913, under Cowles's direction and inspired by Irving Fisher's pioneering work in developing such statistical tabulations, the Commission published an index purporting to show

> . . . what would have happened to an investor's funds if he had bought at the beginning of 1871 all stocks quoted on the New York Stock Exchange, allocating his purchases among the individual issues in proportion to their total monetary value, and each month up to 1938 had by the same criterion redistributed his holdings among all quoted stocks.[44]

This meticulous effort required over 1,500,000 worksheet entries and more than 25,000 hours on Cowles's primitive Hollerith computer. In addition to earnings, dividends, and composite monthly values based on the averages of high and low prices each month—monthly closing prices were unavailable at that time—the Commission provided 59 subcomponents classified by industry membership, dividend yields, and ratios of earnings to prices.

Conceptually, the Cowles Commission indexes are far superior to the Dow Jones Averages. The Dow Jones data are derived simply by adding up the prices of the individual components and dividing by the number of components—11 in the early days and now 30 for the Industrials, 20 for the Transportation Average, and 15 for the Utilities.

This scheme gives rise to many complications. The impact of any given stock on the average is dependent, not on the size of the company or its value on the exchange, but simply on the random chance that its price happens to be high or low. A 10 percent change of five points in a $50 stock would have five times as much effect as a 10 percent change of one point in a $10 stock.

*37*

When a stock splits and the price per share falls proportionately, the total value of the stock in the marketplace is unchanged, but the divisor in the average must be revised in order to maintain continuity. Finally, although the Dow Jones Averages have always been broadly representative of the market, they cover only a segment of it; the Cowles coverage in 1933 included about 97 percent of the market value of all stocks quoted on the New York Stock Exchange and is still, in its present-day incarnation as the Standard & Poor's Composite (also known as the S&P 500 index), much greater than the coverage represented by the Dow Jones Averages.

Why, then, in view of their statistical limitations, have the Dow Jones Averages survived as *the* measure of the market? Just about everyone was aware that the Dow Jones Industrial Average fell by 500 points on October 19, 1987, but who can recall the number of points lost on the S&P 500 index, assuming that anyone even bothered to notice at the time?

The answer lies in computing power. Until the arrival of high-speed, inexpensive computing in the 1960s, up-to-the-minute publication of the Cowles/Standard & Poor's indexes was impossible. Up to that time the cumbersome process of multiplying the latest prices of hundreds of stocks by the number of shares outstanding limited their publication to once a month. By contrast, the Dow Jones Averages require nothing more than adding a few prices and dividing by a preassigned number—a job that can be done on a scrap of paper in a minute or less. So, although today the Standard & Poor's data are in much wider use than they were in earlier times, the Dow Jones figures have been the only timely measures available throughout most of stock-market history. Habits die hard.

Investors cling to another stubborn habit: They continue to heed market forecasters, Bachelier and Cowles to the contrary. Cowles was wise enough to understand why this should be so—and sufficiently self-aware to recognize why he could not join in the fun:

> Even if I did my negative surveys every five years, or others continued them when I'm gone, it wouldn't matter. People are still going to subscribe to these services. They want to believe that somebody really knows. A world in which nobody really knows can be frightening.
>
> I don't come to belief easily. I'm an agnostic married to a Christian Scientist. She's tried to convert me, of course, and I want to believe. But I can't.[45]

# PART
# II

# The Whole
# and the Parts

# Chapter
# 2

# Fourteen Pages to Fame

*I was struck with the notion that you should be interested in risk as well as return.*

The most famous insight in the history of modern finance and investment appeared in a short paper titled "Portfolio Selection." It was published in the March 1952 issue of the *Journal of Finance,* the only journal then in existence for scholars in the field. Its author was an unknown 25-year-old graduate student from the University of Chicago named Harry Markowitz.

No one, including Markowitz, was aware that his paper would turn out to be a landmark in the history of ideas. Although his achievements would earn him a Nobel Prize in economic sciences 38 years later, the paper languished for nearly ten years after publication, attracting fewer than twenty citations in the academic literature until after 1960. By that time, Markowitz had written his dissertation on the subject and had converted it into a full-length book.

The simple title and the brevity of the article disguise its extraordinary intellectual density and originality. Only four of its fourteen pages are straight text without graphs or equations, while the seven graphs on the rest of the pages would readily qualify as the idle doodles of an absent-minded teenager or as designs for an archery target range. In contrast to most academic papers, "Portfolio Selection" lists merely three references to other works; Markowitz himself now admits that he was skimpy in his citations.

The article is remarkable for more than its originality. Investing in stocks was an odd topic for Markowitz to have chosen at that moment. Finance as a separate branch of economics was relatively young. The American Finance Association had spun off from the American Economic Association only twelve years earlier, and the *Journal of Finance* was only in its seventh year of publication.

Most of the articles the *Journal* published had to do with Federal Reserve policy, the impact of money on prices and business activity, taxation, and issues related to corporate finance, insurance, and accounting. The few articles that appeared under the rubric "Investments" dealt with topics like liquidity, dividend policy, and pension funding. In issues up to 1959, I was unable to find more than five articles that could be classified as theoretical rather than descriptive. The rest contain plenty of numbers but no mathematics. No other article in the issue that carried Markowitz's paper contains a single equation.

In the early 1950s, unhappy memories of the crash and the depression of the 1930s kept the stock market outside the purview of economics, or even of finance. Too little time had passed since the end of World War II to produce a crop of scholars free from the scars of those terrible years. Stocks in any case had never had more than a frail claim to legitimacy among prudent investors, and whatever claim they did have had been wiped out by recent history.

Widespread legal restrictions in the early 1950s limited to 50 percent or less the proportion of personal trusts and estates that could be invested in stocks. Only one in sixteen adults owned any shares, and the number of brokerage offices was still 20 percent below what it had been in 1929. After twenty-three years, stock prices were still one-third below their 1929 peak. Stock ownership was considered so risky that the stocks of some of the best companies were paying dividends nearly three times the interest being paid on savings accounts.

It was not just the disaster that turned people off; it was also the association of the market with wrong-doing by people in high places. After all, Richard Whitney, the President of the New York Stock Exchange and the brother of a Morgan partner, had gone to jail. J. P. Morgan himself, while testifying in defense of the community of bankers and brokers at Congressional hearings, had been pilloried by Committee Counsel Ferdinand Pecora. In short, the academic world and the general public both perceived the stock market as little more than a playground for speculators.

Markowitz himself was only incidentally interested in the stock market or investment when he wrote his paper. As a student, he had been wrestling with a broader and more abstract problem: how people can make the best possible decisions in dealing with the inescapable trade-offs in life. Economists insist that you can't have your cake and eat it too. If we want more of something, we have to give up something else—guns for butter, saving for consumption, employment for leisure.

Investors face an especially cruel trade-off, and that was what attracted Markowitz. Nobody gets rich squirreling money away in a savings account. So investors cannot hope to earn high returns unless they are willing to accept the risk involved, and risk means facing the possibility of losing rather than winning. As the old saw puts it, nothing ventured, nothing gained. But how much risk is necessary? Is there a method that can help an investor minimize risk while maximizing expected gains?

The answers Markowitz developed to these questions ultimately transformed the practice of investment management beyond recognition. They put some sense and some system into the haphazard manner in which most investors were assembling portfolios. Moreover, they formed the foundation for all subsequent theories on how financial markets work, how risk can be quantified, and even how corporations should finance themselves.

The very title Markowitz gave his paper reveals him as an innovator. It announces that the article will focus on how to select a *portfolio,* a collection of assets, rather than on how to select individual stocks and bonds.

The word "portfolio" always brings back memories of how my father used it in connection with his clients' accounts after he started his investment counseling firm in 1934. My idea of a portfolio was a fancy leather folder with a sheaf of papers inside. In the world of investing, a portfolio has no physical existence. Rather, it represents the investor's total capital.

Though the most ordinary of subjects today, the analysis of portfolio selection was uncharted territory in 1952, even among practicing investment advisors. An index of articles published from 1945 to 1966 in the *Financial Analysts Journal,* the official publication of the investment profession, has an entry for "Portfolio Management" but does not deem the subject important enough for a separate classification. Rather, the index suggests that the reader "See: Investing, Investment Management, and Various Institutions.'' Even there the pickings are sparse, with fewer than a dozen articles relating to Markowitz's theories. In contrast, the index devotes four pages of listings to "Security Analysis" and includes 41 articles on growth stocks and even 24 articles on the subject of gold.[1]

In the early 1950s, most popular books and articles on investing, overwhelmingly of the "how to" variety, featured ways to find the best buys in the market or to tell when stocks were about to crash. There was also a modest amount of homey material on how to deal with risk—off limits for the very old and the very young, more appropriate for the businessman on his way up.

Despite its formidable appearance, the true meaning of Markowitz's article is also homey. It boils down to nothing more than a formal confirmation of two old rules for investing: Nothing ventured, nothing gained. Don't put all your eggs in one basket.

Markowitz defined these familiar rules with scientific precision, using mathematics to solve the puzzle of the investor's trade-off. His analysis shows precisely how investors can combine their hopes of realizing the largest possible gain with exposure to the least possible risk.

Sandy-haired and tall, Markowitz looks at you blandly, speaks quietly, even hesitantly, and interrupts his conversation with chuckles inspired by secret jokes. He was born in 1927 and grew up as an only child in a middle-class neighborhood in Chicago, nine miles from downtown. When he reminisced with me about his boyhood, he confessed that today he would be classified as a "nerd."[2] He read a lot, played chess, was a member of the violin section in the school orchestra, and joined a national club for amateur cryptographers—but he never tried out for school sports.

The summer he became fourteen, Markowitz read Darwin's *Origin of Species.* He was impressed by Darwin's ability to marshal evidence for his revolutionary hypothesis and "the care with which he presented his arguments and considered counter-arguments which might be or had been presented to his views. . . . I liked his tone; his style. I was really moved."[3]

Then philosophy caught his fancy. Here his hero was the English philosopher, David Hume, who died in 1776. Hume's essay titled "Skeptical Doubts Concerning the Operations of the Understanding" had a profound influence on Markowitz. In it Hume exalts "propositions . . . discoverable by the mere operation of thought," such as the truths demonstrated by Euclid, that are "without dependence on what is anywhere existent in the universe." He contrasts these leaps of the imagination with empirical work or "arguments from experience" and warns about the dangers of paying too much attention to facts.[4]

When it came time to go to college, Markowitz applied only to the University of Chicago. The University was less than satisfied with his high-school grades but was sufficiently impressed with what he had studied on his own to let him take the entrance exam anyway. He was accepted. And college made a difference: he gave up the violin ("The world was better for it," he concedes), studied hard, did well, and earned scholarships.

Markowitz had read enough on his own to be excused from the undergraduate science survey course, but he was required to take the survey course in social sciences. He found economics particularly appealing, because it combined mathematics with the social sciences.

The intellectual environment at the University of Chicago in the late 1940s and early 1950s was exhilarating. The University had always been a center for innovative scholars in both philosophy and economics. The big attraction for Markowitz was the Cowles Commission for Research in Economics. Nearly all the U.S. winners of the Nobel Prize in economic sciences have spent time at the Cowles Commission.

After earning an undergraduate degree in economics, Markowitz managed to do his graduate work while serving as a Research Associate at the Cowles Commission. This assignment gave him the opportunity to pursue his own research, write papers, give seminars, and attend seminars offered by distinguished scholars in residence or by visiting scholars.

The Director of Research of the Cowles Commission at the time was Tjalling Koopmans, Professor of Economics at the University. A Dutch economist, originally trained as a theoretical physicist, Koopmans later turned to the application to economics of complex statistical techniques; he shared the Nobel Prize in economic sciences in 1975 for his work in this area. Koopmans developed an analytic method known as linear programming or activity analysis that falls under the general heading of operations research.

Linear programming solves problems that involve combinations of inputs and outputs. Assume, for example, that an airline has a limited number of airplanes, hours of flying time, crew availabilities, and gates at airports along its routes. How many flights a day to how many locations can the airline make? If it aims to make, say, 200 flights a day, how can it minimize the necessary amount of flying time and crew time and number of airplanes? How would the answers to these questions differ if the airline wanted to make economizing on crew time its most important objective? Or if it wanted to make as many landings as possible in the New York City area? Linear programming identifies the combinations of inputs and outputs that are achievable, defines the combinations that minimize the inputs and maximize the outputs, and then identifies the trade-offs required if one element is increased or decreased relative to the others.

When the time came to choose a topic for his doctoral dissertation, Markowitz went to see Jacob Marschak, who had preceded Koopmans as director of the Cowles Commission. While waiting outside Marschak's office, he fell into conversation with an older man who identified himself as a stockbroker. Unaware of the ultimate consequences of his advice for the world of investing, the man suggested that Markowitz write his thesis about the stock market. When Markowitz mentioned this suggestion to Marschak, he was surprised to find that Marschak was enthusiastic about this unorthodox proposal, pointing out that Alfred Cowles himself had done major research in that area.

Marschak admitted, however, that he did not feel qualified to guide Markowitz in what was then an offbeat topic for a mathematically inclined economist. When professors have no advice of their own to give a student, they usually send the student to another professor. Marschak sent Markowitz to Marshall Ketchum, then Dean of the Graduate School of Business and co-editor of the *Journal of Finance.* In 1957, Ketchum would be elected president of the American Finance Association.

At most universities, the business school and economics faculties barely greeted each other on the street. (The same is true today.) At Chicago, however, and later at MIT and a few other universities, the two faculties cooperated closely. That unique degree of cooperation had a lot to do with many of the most exciting developments we will be exploring later.

Ketchum sent Markowitz to the library to read what was then—and in many ways still is—the authoritative work on how to value financial assets. *The Theory of Investment Value,* itself a Ph.D.

thesis, was written in 1937 by John Burr Williams, a Harvard graduate student. In that book Williams combined original theoretical concepts with enlightening and entertaining commentary based on his own experiences in the rough-and-tumble world of investment. Markowitz found the book fascinating.

Williams's model for valuing a security calls for the investor to make a long-run projection of a company's future dividend payments and then to test that projection against his own confidence in its accuracy. Forecasting future dividends for a public utility, for example, is easier than forecasting dividends for General Motors, and forecasting the long-run outlook for General Motors is easier than forecasting the outlook for a start-up company in a highly competitive business. Williams then shows how to combine the long-run projection of dividends with the expected degree of accuracy of that forecast to estimate the intrinsic value of the stock. Williams called his model the Dividend Discount Model.

It was the deeper implications of what Williams had to say that attracted Markowitz. He realized that Williams's analysis led to a curious paradox.

Williams seemed to be recommending that the investor should buy the one stock that had the highest expected return—*and then shun all the rest*. If you are in love with IBM, why own Apple Computer or Digital Equipment too? Why, in fact, own General Electric or Consolidated Edison at the same time you own IBM?

This is not the way investors behave in the real world. Only crazy people and gamblers invest their entire fortune in just one stock. Moreover, most investors own other kinds of assets, such as cash, bonds, and real estate, at the same time they own stocks.

"That afternoon in the library," Markowitz said in a conversation with me, "I was struck with the notion that you should be interested in risk as well as return."[5] The reason people do not put all their eggs in one basket is that they know they would run the risk of being wiped out if the basket dropped.

Markowitz's key insight was that risk is central to the whole process of investing. Elroy Dimson, a British finance theorist, once remarked, "If projects were riskless, there would be no problem. . . . Risk means that more things can happen than will happen."[6] We do not expect our house to burn down, but it might, so we insure against the risk of fire. We do not expect a stock we like to decline in price, but it might, so we do not put all our money into that one stock.

Most human beings are naturally risk-averse. They prefer known outcomes to uncertainty no matter how confident they may be about their skills at security analysis and even though they are eager to see their wealth increase. They know that nothing will be gained if nothing is ventured, but they also know that venturing inevitably involves the risk of loss.

The perception that human beings are naturally risk-averse seems obvious enough. Nevertheless, the literature on investing up to 1952 had either ignored the interplay between risk and return or had treated it in the most casual manner.

John Maynard Keynes, perhaps the most influential economist of the twentieth century, is a case in point. For many years Keynes managed the portfolio of a major British insurance company as well as the endowment funds of Kings College, Cambridge. Although he wrote that "the management of stock exchange investments of any kind is a low pursuit . . . from which it is a good thing for most members of our Society to be free,"[7] Keynes invested with zest. He was convinced that concentration was the only way to invest and that diversification was a flawed strategy:

> I am in favor of having as large a unit as market conditions will allow. . . . To suppose that safety-first consists in having a small gamble in a large number of different [companies] where I have no information to reach a good judgment, as compared with a substantial stake in a company where one's information is adequate, strikes me as a travesty of investment policy.[8]

One of the books that influenced me when I first became an investment counselor in the early 1950s was a bestseller with the catchy title *The Battle for Investment Survival*. Its author was Gerald Loeb, a leading broker and pundit on Wall Street, whose photograph on the book jacket glared fiercely at prospective readers. The book was first published in 1935 and went through several editions, the last in 1965. I doubt whether a busy broker like Loeb had ever heard of Harry Markowitz, nor would he have paid Markowitz much heed if he had.

Loeb's confidence in his ability to pick winners led him to take a view of diversification that matched Keynes's. "Once you obtain confidence, diversification is undesirable," he wrote, adding that "Diversification [is] an admission of not knowing what to do and an effort to strike an average."[9]

That attitude was typical of Wall Street thinking, and in some quarters still is, in large part because its error is not readily visible: A single-minded focus on return, without regard to risk, leads to portfolio selection that is less than optimal. Investors can do better than that. Markowitz recognized that error and developed a systematic means to avoid it.

Markowitz's reflections on diversification and risk led him to explore the subject more thoroughly in a linear programming course he was taking under Koopmans. Koopmans had asked the class to describe a resource allocation problem and state whether or not it was a linear programming problem. Markowitz took the occasion to analyze the choices facing an investor who must decide between seeking high returns and attempting to hold down risk at the same time. He concluded that the solution to this problem was even more complex than linear programming. Koopmans gave him an A on his paper and noted, "The problem does not seem that hard. Why don't you solve it?"[10] That assignment was a trial run for what later developed into "Portfolio Selection" and Markowitz's doctoral dissertation.

The more Markowitz thought about the behavior of risk-averse investors trying to make their fortune in the stock market, the more he sensed that he was just beginning to scratch the surface. Why do most people put their eggs in more than one basket? They do so in order to reduce risk. But how does diversification reduce risk?

Diversification works because owning more than one asset protects the investor from the contingency that everything will be lost at one fell swoop. As Antonio, the merchant of Venice, tells us:

> My ventures are not in one bottom trusted,
> Nor to one place; nor is my whole estate
> Upon the fortune of this present year;
> Therefore my merchandise makes me not sad.

That's the good news. The bad news is that not all assets go through the roof at the same time either. Diversification may reduce risk, but it also tends to reduce the opportunity to earn the high rewards that an investor *might* achieve by following

Keynes's advice: Put all your eggs in the one basket that looks like the best basket of all.

The tension between risk and return, between diversification and concentration, was just the beginning of Markowitz's breakthrough. He then followed the idea down two separate tracks.

The first track tells the investor how to apply the trade-off between risk and reward in selecting a portfolio; this is the subject matter of his 1952 article and is closely related to the techniques of linear programming that Markowitz learned from Koopmans.

The second track tells how each investor should go about selecting the single portfolio that most closely conforms to the investor's goals. A much fuller treatment of this aspect appears in Markowitz's book, *Portfolio Selection: Efficient Diversification of Investment,* which was essentially completed in 1955 as his Ph.D. thesis but was not published until 1959.

Because Markowitz sees risk as an equal partner with expected gain in the investment process, he puts primary emphasis on diversification. If diversification is to work, he insists, it must be what he calls the "right" kind of diversification "and for the right reason":

A portfolio with sixty different railway securities, for
example, would not be as well diversified as the same size
portfolio with some railroad, some public utility, mining,
various sort [sic] of manufacturing, etc. The reason is that it
is generally more likely for firms within the same industry to
do poorly at the same time than for firms in dissimilar
industries.[11]

Aside from the quaint suggestion that anyone might want to own sixty railway securities, or that sixty railroad securities were even available, the argument here is central to Markowitz's whole thesis. Diversification depends more on the way individual assets perform relative to one another than it does on how many assets the investor owns. In Markowitz's terminology, "It is necessary to avoid investing in securities with high covariances among themselves."[12] Assets have high covariances when they move up and down in sympathy with one another; the baskets in which the investor has distributed his eggs all bear a strong family resemblance. When a portfolio has assets with low covariance, on the other hand, the eggs are distributed among baskets that have different designs and are made from different materials. That is the only sure way to minimize risk.

The technical term for the risk that diversification aims to reduce is "variance." Variance means distance from an average. When property owners want to deviate from accepted building standards in their community, they must obtain a permit known as a "variance." Statisticians like to tell about the man who had his feet in the oven and his head in the refrigerator, but who on the average felt pretty well. This was a case of high variance. Start-up companies and General Motors have high variance; utilities and companies that produce consumer staples have low variance.

Stocks in general have high variance. A tax-free investor who stayed in the stock market from the end of 1925 to the end of 1989, reinvesting all dividends, would have enjoyed an average annual return of 12.4 percent a year. And yet the variations around that average were extraordinarily wide. In addition to many swings of as much as 20 percent a year around the average, there were nine super years with returns in excess of 33 percent and twelve dismal years with returns below −8 percent. In five of those bad years, investors lost 40 percent of their capital. Such variability explains why stocks are considered risky investments and why people have such a hard time predicting the stock market.

A charitable foundation I know would have done well to have listened to Markowitz on how to use the right kind of diversification to keep portfolio variability within tolerable bounds. This foundation had been funded with a large block of shares of one of the famous Favorite Fifty stocks of the late 1960s. The Favorite Fifty were so-called because they were the top group of the most stable, glamorous, and respected companies in the United States at that time, companies like Procter & Gamble, IBM, Merck, and Avon. The popularity of this group of stocks reflected the fascination with growth in that most growth-oriented of all decades.

Institutional portfolio managers like bank trust departments and mutual funds were so enamored with the future of these companies that they bid the prices of their stocks into the stratosphere. Meanwhile, the stocks of the old-line, cyclical industrial companies fell out of favor and languished at depressed values.

I do not use the word "stratosphere" lightly. At the peak in 1972, for example, Eastman Kodak with sales of $3.5 billion was valued in the market at $24 billion, the same as General Motors with sales of $30 billion. International Flavors and Fragrances was valued at $1.6 billion, only slightly below U.S. Steel, although IFF had sales of only $138 million while US Steel's sales exceeded $5 billion. Avon's sales were only a third of Union Carbide's, but investors set Avon's value nearly three times higher than Union Carbide's. These were not exceptions: they were the rule. On November 15, 1972, Heinz Biel, a much-quoted market columnist writing in *Forbes* magazine, stated flatly: "[T]he high-quality growth stocks . . . have been, and apparently still are, the favorites of the banks, trusts and pension funds, and the insurance companies. That's where the money is, and it is quite pointless for the individual investor to argue that the price/earnings ratios of the super-blue chips are too high."[13]

The trustees of the charitable foundation I referred to recognized the extraordinary levels to which their own Favorite Fifty stock had risen. They decided that diversification would be a better strategy than keeping all their eggs in the one basket the founders had bequeathed to them. Immune from capital gains taxes, they sold 75 percent of their Favorite Fifty stock at close to its all-time high price.

The trustees then took the conventional route and turned the proceeds of the sale over to two major bank trust departments and a large, well-established investment counseling organization. The managers of all three had identical investment styles and were extraordinarily naive about diversification. So they all went out and bought other Favorite Fifty stocks! These managers shared a conviction that the high prices they had to pay were justified and that an investment in such powerful, growing companies carried relatively little risk.

At the time, their appraisal of the *companies* may have been fair, but their appraisal of the *stocks* was extraordinarily bad. Actually, they were not buying a group of stocks; they were buying the equivalent of one stock, and overpaying for it. Four years later (1976), when the market as a whole was at just about the same level as in 1972, Eastman Kodak was selling for only 80 percent of its 1972 value, IFF was down 40 percent, and Avon had fallen more than 60 percent. Meanwhile, unglamorous US Steel and Union Carbide had more than doubled, while General Motors was down less than 10 percent.

Nevertheless, as Keynes and Loeb insisted, diversification takes a lot of the fun out of investing, especially if it is diversification of the "right" kind, because the investor must resist the temptation to put the entire pot of money into the one or two stocks that look most promising. How can investors find their way out of this dilemma?

"There is a rule," Markowitz tells us, "which implies both that the investor should diversify and that he should maximize expected return. The rule states that the investor does (or should) diversify his funds among all those securities which give maximum expected return . . . and commends this portfolio to the investor."[14]

At first glance, this rule sounds like nothing more than a variation of Keynes or Loeb. But it is far more than that. Markowitz's obsession is with systematic solutions rather than with rules-of-thumb.

In setting forth a paradigm for discovering the portfolio that his rule commends to investors, Markowitz borrowed a concept he had learned from Koopmans: efficiency. Efficiency means maximum output for a given input, or minimum input for a given output. The output is the return the investor expects from owning an asset. Nothing ventured, nothing gained, however: A higher expected return means assuming additional risk. Risk is the unavoidable *input* needed to generate the return.

As a result, the portfolio that conforms to Markowitz's rule and that he "commends" to the investor is an *efficient* portfolio. It is a portfolio that offers the highest expected return for any given degree of risk, or that has the lowest degree of risk for any given expected return.

This sounds good. But how does an investor go about selecting the most efficient combinations from the whole long list of possible candidates for the portfolio? The longer the list the better, because a longer list makes possible more different combinations from the available universe. Two separate calculations are necessary.

The first step is to estimate the return the investor can expect. Markowitz recommends using Williams's Dividend Discount Model for this purpose. This model is handy when you have the numbers to plug into it, but, as a practical matter, generating reliable long-run estimates of dividend payments is something else again.

How certain can the investor be about the future earning power of a company like General Motors? Earnings might be high under some circumstances and devastatingly low under others. The most one can say about predicting the earning power of General Motors is that there is much more uncertainty about the outlook for automobiles than there is for a soap, diaper, and toothpaste company like Procter & Gamble. As Will Rogers said after visiting the gold rush in the Klondike, "There is a big difference between prospecting for gold and prospecting for spinach." A young company trying to make it in biotechnology might end up as the Hoffman-LaRoche of tomorrow with a new Valium to conquer the market, but it also might end up going nowhere except out of business.

In effect, explicitly or implicitly, investors arrive at judgments about the riskiness of individual stocks by considering the range of outcomes that may lie ahead. The range will be wide for GM, wider for the biotechnology start-up company, narrower for Procter & Gamble.

Markowitz's most original contribution was his insistence on distinguishing between the riskiness of an individual stock and the riskiness of an entire portfolio. *The riskiness of a portfolio depends on the covariance of its holdings, not on the average riskiness of the separate investments.* A combination of very risky holdings may still comprise a low-risk portfolio so long as they do not move in lockstep with one another—that is, so long as they have low covariance. For example, the managers of the charitable foundation's portfolio would have done better to mix automobile stocks, utilities, and even bonds with their glamour stocks, instead of concentrating on forty or fifty holdings with only one dominant characteristic: growth.

Even a little diversification goes a long way to reduce volatility. A portfolio consisting of just one stock will be twice as variable as the market on the average, but a portfolio consisting of just fifteen stocks selected at random will be only about 5 percent more variable than a portfolio consisting of a hundred randomly selected stocks. Markowitz's article provides a formula for calculating the variance of a portfolio; the critical ingredient in that formula is covariance.

Now we know what Markowitz meant when he used the expression "Mean-Variance Analysis" in the title of a book he published in 1987 to update his thinking. This hyphenated expression, which uses "mean" in the statistical sense of average, has become the byword not just for Markowitz's theories but for portfolio theory in general.*

Mean variance, a theory of investing that includes risk as well as return, had been an unexplored area before Markowitz's work in the 1950s. Only a few scholars had even mentioned the subject in passing. Among them were Irving Fisher of Yale, who had guided Alfred Cowles in establishing the Cowles Commission in 1932; John Hicks of Cambridge, one of Keynes's most distinguished interpreters and a Nobel Prize-winner; and Dickson Leavens, who was at the Cowles Commission from 1936 to 1947. None of these scholars, however, had provided the systematic treatment subsequently developed by Markowitz.

Markowitz reports a curious twist to this story. In his 1987 book, *Mean-Variance Analysis in Portfolio Choice and Capital Markets,* he devotes only one paragraph to the sparse history of these ideas. Referring to himself in the third person, he remarks, "The era of modern portfolio theory opened with two papers published in 1952. [One was by] Roy (1952) [and] Markowitz (1952) [was] the other paper opening the era of modern portfolio theory. . . ."[15]

A. D. Roy, who was seven years older than Markowitz in 1952, was teaching at Sidney Sussex College at Cambridge. He had the misfortune of publishing an article titled "Safety First and the Holding of Assets" just three months after Markowitz's article had appeared in the *Journal of Finance.* It is an odd coincidence that Roy's paper appeared in *Econometrica,* a journal established by Alfred Cowles, and that Markowitz had been working at the Cowles Commission when he developed his ideas on portfolio selection.

"Portfolio Selection" and "Safety First" are similar in their lines of argument, and I am at a loss to explain why Roy's paper failed to cut the swath that Markowitz's paper did. Roy's approach is more limited in scope, in that it focuses only on how individuals can minimize the probability that their wealth will fall below some disaster level—hence the title of his article. And yet he comes to essentially the same conclusions as Markowitz does.

---

*Mathematicians and statisticians will be amused to learn that Markowitz put the dependent variable, expected return, on the horizontal axis of his charts and the independent variable, risk, on the vertical—a device he insists on using to this very day.

To my surprise, few of the practitioners and academics I approached during my investigation had even heard of Roy. Markowitz himself responded abruptly to my query: "I know nothing about Roy. I never met him. I would have to look up his article to recall his affiliation. I do not know of anything else he wrote."[16]

Thanks to Richard Brealey, a member of the faculty at London Business School, I was finally able to locate Roy in the spring of 1990. He was alive and well at the age of 70, retired, and living in the London suburb of Putney.

Roy studied mathematics and physics while he was still in secondary school and then went on to study mathematics at Cambridge. After service overseas in the Royal Artillery during World War II, he returned to Cambridge to "read" economics and began teaching at Sidney Sussex in 1950. He left the academic world in the early 1960s to join the civil service, where he enjoyed a distinguished career at the Treasury, the Department of Trade & Industry, the Ministry of Defense, and finally the Department of Health & Social Security. He published a follow-up article to "Safety First" in 1956 and four or five papers on probability and uncertainty theory, but investment and finance were never his main interests. That may be the real reason why he faded into anonymity among the scholars in the field.

I asked Roy what had induced him to write "Safety First," suggesting that perhaps it was some unhappy investment experience. He said no. Like Markowitz, he was motivated by an "interaction of curiosity and elementary analytical explorations," but, also like Markowitz, he was "reacting against a straight expected gain." In a letter to me later, he added an odd suggestion: "The practical experience of gunnery may also have played a part."[17]

Some experts I consulted pointed out weaknesses in Roy's analytical structure that Markowitz managed to avoid. One wit suggested that Roy was too mathematical for the masses and but used too little mathematics for the elite. Another criticism was that Roy had put too much emphasis on avoiding disaster and not enough on the full range of possibilities from maximum gain all the way down to the worst case.

But the most convincing explanation was just plain bad timing. As Darwin narrowly predated Wallace, as Leibnitz and Newton were following the same scent (Newton won out), so Markowitz simply beat out Roy in getting into print.

Whatever the similarities and differences in content, Roy is the more colorful writer. For example, seeking to discover "the rules of behavior in an uncertain and ruthless world," he argues:

Theory should take account of the often close resemblance between economic life and navigation in poorly charted waters or maneuvers in a hostile jungle. Decisions taken in practice are less concerned with whether a little more of this or of that will yield the largest net increase in satisfaction, than with avoiding known rocks of uncertain position or with deploying forces so that, if there is an ambush around the next corner, total disaster is avoided.[18]

Rewarding as it may be in concept, Markowitz's rule sets a difficult task for the investor in practice. In order to follow Markowitz's prescriptions, investors must analyze every possible combination of assets, searching for the efficient portfolios among them.

This analytical procedure is complicated and time-consuming, to put it mildly. Investors not only have to make reliable estimates of variability for each individual security—itself a difficult chore. They also have to estimate the expected return for each individual security, a challenging task under any circumstances. But that is the easy part. They must then determine how each of the many securities under consideration will vary in relation to every one of the others. This is not something you can figure out on the back of an envelope.

The task is simpler if you have access to a computer. Markowitz combined his skill with the computer with Koopmans's achievements in linear programming to make the task at least manageable. Still, the audience for such technical matters was still limited in the 1950s. The *Naval Research Logistics Quarterly* was the only outlet Markowitz could find for a 1956 paper balefully titled "The Optimization of a Quadratic Function Subject to Linear Constraints."

Moreover, computers at the time were both slow and expensive. One of Markowitz's students, William Sharpe, who was to share the Nobel Prize with Markowitz in 1990, reported in 1961 that the best commercially available IBM computer required 33 minutes to solve a 100-security problem. The cost of that modest experiment in terms of today's purchasing power would be over $300. Sharpe subsequently developed a method that greatly simplified the elaborate procedure.

Even today, however, the investor has only just begun to fight after calculating the expected returns and covariances and after identifying all the efficient portfolios among the universe of assets under analysis. The next step is to rank these portfolios in order of their expected returns or, if preferred, in order of their riskiness. Each portfolio that is efficient will either have a higher expected rate of return than any other portfolio of equal risk or will be less risky than any other portfolio with the same expected return.

With a good sense of metaphor, Markowitz dubbed the resulting group of efficient portfolios "the Efficient Frontier." As we go up the scale of expected returns, we find that risk also is increasing; and as we go up the scale of riskiness, we find that the expected rate of return is going up at the same time.

Once the Efficient Frontier has been identified, the investor must turn to Markowitz's second track of investigation: How does one choose among the portfolios on the Efficient Frontier? Which portfolio is most appropriate for young Mr. Jones? Should elderly Mrs. Smith consider a different one? Is there a way to tackle this question systematically?

The answer rests on a simple but pervasive feature of human behavior that I will illustrate with a true story.

Some time in the late 1950s, a shabby-looking man about fifty years old came to my investment counseling firm accompanied by his wife, who was clearly in a state of high nervousness. He offered us his portfolio to manage. When we examined it, we discovered it was much larger than we had expected, judging from his appearance. It consisted of only three stocks: AT&T, US Steel, and an obscure company called Thiokol that made fuel for space rockets. He owned all three at huge profits—AT&T and US Steel were hot stocks in the late 1950s, and space exploration has always lured investors.

We looked at our visitor in amazement. What in the world did he think we could do for for him? Then he told us his story.

He had been a reporter on the *Brooklyn Eagle* until it failed a few years earlier. At that time, he had a total wealth of about $15,000 and his wife was earning a modest income teaching in the public school system. Fifteen thousand dollars was what he had earned the last year he was employed. He figured that if he gambled with the $15,000 and lost, his family would be broke one year sooner than if he kept the money in a savings account. If he struck it rich, however, their future would be secure.

He had obviously struck it rich. He did not want us to make him any richer. His wife had calmly accepted his original decision, but she had become increasingly anxious as the portfolio grew and grew. Now we understood why she was so tense during the interview. Our role was clearly to help this man preserve his good fortune and to protect him from growing poor.

Economists associate such shifts in attitude with the marginal utility of wealth. An extra dollar of wealth has higher marginal utility to poor people than to rich people. In extremis, poor people will even beg, borrow, or steal to acquire an extra dollar. Meanwhile, wealthy people are content with the interest on their tax-exempt bonds and the dividends on their well-balanced port-folios of blue-chip stocks.

Markowitz once pointed out to me how someone with "patho-logical risk aversion" would behave. Suppose such a person were offered a choice between a certain gain of 5 percent and a 50-50 gamble of coming out with either nothing or infinite wealth. The pathologically risk-averse person would choose the 5 percent cer-tain, while most people would gladly risk giving up that modest gain for the opportunity to own the world.

If taking on more risk is the price we have to pay for the oppor-tunity to become richer, then the investor can use the concept of marginal utility in deciding which of the portfolios on the Effi-cient Frontier to select. The investor goes up the line toward higher expected returns to the point where the additional risk required to gain an extra dollar of wealth is just too high a price to pay. Wealthy people will take risks only if the expected return is big; people with limited funds will accept huge risks even if the possible return is slight.

The investor's sensitivity to changing wealth and risk is known as the utility function, and the elements that determine the shape of the utility function are obscure. As Roy put it, "A man who seeks advice about his actions will not be grateful for the sugges-tion that he maximize his expected utility."[19] The complexity of the subject has attracted the attention of some of the best thinkers of our time, including Kenneth Arrow, a Nobel Prize-winner, and Oskar Morgenstern and John von Neumann, famous for having invented game theory.

But this is not the only feature of the Markowitz paradigm with controversial implications. The calculation of the Efficient Fron-tier is a task that would defy the abilities and capabilities of many investors, and even the capacities of many computers. so it is fair to ask whether the relationship between risk and return is as neat as Markowitz postulates.

Market prices, investor expectations, and the riskiness of assets do not stand still. They are dynamic, not static. Moreover, they constantly interact as new information arrives in the marketplace. The consequence is that the necessary conditions for an accurate calculation of risk may not prevail.

Markowitz was aware of these problems and subsequently made efforts to deal with them himself. But his great leap forward that afternoon in the library was to inspire a flood of new ideas and theoretical discoveries by others.

Despite the cogitations that led to the fourteen-page article he published in 1952 and the book he published in 1959, Markowitz's progress to his doctorate was not as smooth as he had anticipated. When he arrived at the conference room to defend his dissertation, he had been telling himself, "I know this deal cold. Not even Milton Friedman can give me a hard time."[20] Friedman, fifteen years Markowitz's senior, would become one of the titans among American economists in the years ahead and was already a shining star on the Chicago faculty. And Friedman was on Markowitz's examining committee.

A couple of minutes into the defense, Friedman turned to Markowitz and declared, "Harry, I don't see anything wrong with the math here, but I have a problem. This isn't a dissertation in economics, and we can't give you a Ph.D. in economics for a dissertation that's not economics. It's not math, it's not economics, it's not even business administration."[21]

Markowitz sat grimly through the next hour and a half listening to the same complaint over and over. In a state of black frustration, he finally went out to the hall to await the verdict. After about five minutes, Marschak appeared, looked him in the eye, and said, "Congratulations, Dr. Markowitz!"[22]

# Chapter
# 3

# The Interior
# Decorator Fallacy

*. . . that one of the available assets in the model . . . was
riskless turned out to have interesting consequences.*

In 1961, one of our friends, a woman in her early 40s, came
into a modest inheritance and asked me to manage a small portfolio for her. She was married to a clergyman, a man with a logical
mind and a strong dose of intellectual curiosity. We used to joke
about his writing my market letters and my delivering his sermons.

He enjoyed his profession, but he had no illusions about his
earnings prospects. His wife's inheritance was a real windfall, and
they wanted it invested for maximum income.

Shortly after they became clients, my investment counseling
firm began to recommend a strategy based on demographics. We
called it "investing in the puberty boom." We bought heavy positions in Gillette and Tampax (then a highly controversial stock to
own, and awkward even to suggest to a client of either sex), and
in Georgia Pacific Lumber for the new homes being built for
growing families. For reasons unrelated to demography, we were
also accumulating large holdings of IBM, because of our convictions about the dynamic future for computers.

I had a hard time deciding whether our new clients should participate in what looked like—and turned out to be—an exciting
investment program. Whenever I called them with a suggestion,
they inevitably asked, "Does it pay a good dividend?" None of
these companies paid a "good dividend" at that time. We wanted

to own them because we believed that their explosive growth would bring good dividends in the future, and because the value of the stocks would rise as dividends rose.

Even though these stocks seemed inappropriate for people who were investing for current income, I was reluctant to deny this couple the opportunity to benefit from what we considered to be the best idea we had had in a long time. So I took the plunge and called them to make my recommendation. It took a lot of arm-twisting, but we finally bought them small positions in each of the four stocks. No one was sorry afterward.

I had just the opposite problem with some of our more aggressive clients. I can still hear the young business executive who told me on his first visit that "The one thing I can't stand is more income." In the mid-1950s, we thought the electric utilities were irresistible, with safe and growing dividends that yielded at least double what an investor could earn on high-grade bonds. My client's distaste for paying taxes on current income made me hesitate for a long time before I finally recommended the utilities to him. He was more stubborn than the clergyman and his wife, and he missed out on some handsome capital gains as a result.

Although our philosophy is now more widely accepted than it was in the 1960s, our willingness to recommend growth stocks to conservative investors and income stocks to aggressive investors was an unorthodox approach for its time. Rejecting the gospel of the tailor-made approach to portfolio selection, we were motivated by the simple thought that every client was entitled to benefit from our best ideas. We could vary the character of the portfolio by buying more or less of this stock or that, or by limiting or expanding a client's exposure to stocks in general, but we could find no good reason why each client's list of stocks had to be unique.

When I say that our approach is no longer regarded as unorthodox, I do not mean to suggest that it is now the *only* method. The old way is still in use, especially when the clients are individual investors, endowment funds, or foundations, whose particular circumstances and tax positions differ much more widely than is the case with pension funds.

Managers responsible for the portfolio of an elderly widow, for example, emphasize income and avoid taking risks. A widow who was obliged to "eat principal," even when that principal included substantial capital gains, was once considered to be committing a mortal sin. For many years the quintessential stock for widows and orphans was AT&T, which faithfully paid a dividend of $9, through bad times and good, from 1922 to 1958. In April 1959, the leopard changed its spots. AT&T split 2:1, increased its dividend 5 percent, set out to convert itself into a growth stock, and was no longer the *ne plus ultra* for widows.

Selecting stocks for business executives on the rise is an entirely different matter. These executives are trying to build an estate and focus more on the future than on the present. Unlike the widow, they are willing and able to live with unavoidable short-term risks and variability if their portfolios are to grow in the long run. Such clients are in search of the next Xerox, as the saying goes. Managers will therefore buy them a collection of young, adventuresome companies, many of which may not be paying dividends at all.

Richard Brealey, professor of finance at the London Business School, once described portfolio managers who use such long-established approaches as "interior decorators" who see each client as a distinct entity with unique requirements. They view the widow's holdings in AT&T as inappropriate for the executive eager to build an estate; they consider the executive's exotic stocks equally inappropriate for the widow with shorter life expectancy and with no earning power outside the portfolio. Presumably, the living-room decor of two such clients would be equally revealing about their lifestyles.

Although my investment counseling organization had the right intuition about how to manage the affairs of our clients, we had never heard of Harry Markowitz or the Efficient Frontier when we were developing our methodology. Neither had the orthodox management organizations. Yet Markowitz's ideas about efficient portfolios that maximized expected return while minimizing risk were breathing mathematical precision into the practical problems we were trying to solve.

Even if we had mastered Markowitz's message, there was no way we could have applied it as he had designed it. A. D. Roy himself, reviewing Markowitz's book in 1959, cautioned his readers:

> While Dr. Markowitz warns that past experience is unlikely
> to be a very good guide to future performance, he gives us
> no clear indication of how either we, or our investment

advisers, can provide ourselves with sufficiently precise or generally agreed expectations to merit their processing in an elaborate way. . . .

Dr. Markowitz presses for a precision in the specification of both motives and of expectations which it seems unlikely that any existing investor can reasonably be expected to possess or to express coherently.[1]

Consider the task that Markowitz asks the investor to perform. First, the investor has to calculate the expected returns and the covariances for all the securities under analysis. To analyze only 50 securities, as many as 1,225 separate calculations are required; by the time the universe of stocks to be analyzed reaches 2,000—not an unrealistic number for large bank trust departments or major investment advisory organizations—the calculations required reach 2,003,000.

And that is only the beginning. Now the Efficient Frontier must be ferreted out from the mass of numbers already accumulated. That means that the investor must examine all possible combinations of the securities under consideration, rank them in order of their riskiness, and then identify those portfolios that have the highest expected return for each level of risk. This procedure is hardly an inviting prospect, even for an organization equipped with the latest computing equipment.

That is not the end of the story—it is only the end of the calculating part of the job. Now comes the moment to make the decision that matters. The calculations may end up with many different portfolios perched on the Efficient Frontier, some with high risk, some more conservative. Which of these many portfolios should the investor select?

Traditional managers who follow the interior decorator approach will have an easy time of it. Managers who want both the clergyman's wife and the aggressive businessman to hold the single best combination out of all possible combinations will have a much harder time.

An ingenious method of simplifying this intimidating task appeared in the February 1958 issue of an academic journal called *The Review of Economic Studies*. Titled "Liquidity Preference as Behavior Toward Risk," its author was James Tobin, Sterling Professor of Economics at Yale. Then forty years old, Tobin was widely recognized as an outstanding economic theorist in the field of macroeconomics, the analysis of the forces that determine the overall levels of unemployment, production, and inflation. Although investments and finance were not Tobin's main focus, the paper was a major consideration in his winning the Nobel Prize in economic sciences in 1981.

Tobin is a tall, quiet man. He was born in 1918 in Champaign, Illinois. His maternal grandfather lost his entire fortune during the Depression, as president of a bank that failed. The very prototype of the scholar, Tobin has always been as interested in economic policy as in economic theory—a consequence of his having grown up during the 1930s in a family that was unshakably enthusiastic about Franklin Roosevelt's New Deal. The family's liberal views were considered highly eccentric in the home territory of what was then among the most conservative of newspapers (and the source of the Cowles family's fortune), the *Chicago Tribune*. In a straw poll taken in 1932 among the thirty students in his sophomore high-school class, which consisted largely of the children of university faculty, Tobin alone voted for Roosevelt.

Tobin went to Harvard under a scholarship program designed to diversify its eastern-establishment student body and graduated in 1939. At that time, most wealthy people still considered Roosevelt a traitor to his class: On the day Tobin received his degree in economics, with highest honors, the alumni celebrating their 25th reunion appeared in the commencement parade wearing only suspended barrels bearing the legend "A Harvard Man Did This to Us."

Economics appealed to Tobin for two reasons. First, he is a mathematics enthusiast who considers high-school algebra "about the most exciting intellectual experience of life."[2] He did not realize until later how useful math would be in economics— that was a bonus—but economics attracted him because it suited his taste for logical argument.

Second, and surely as important, economics offered an opportunity to understand and perhaps do something about the burning issues of the Great Depression. His mother's experiences as a social worker during the Depression and the failure of his grandfather's bank were close-up views of problems that cried out for practical solutions.

In those days, the introductory economics course at Harvard was considered too difficult for freshmen. Tobin got more than elementary material in his sophomore year, however. Spencer Pollard, an advanced graduate student who served as his instructor and as his advisor out of the classroom, gave him the opportunity to cut his teeth on John Maynard Keynes's *General Theory of Employment, Interest, and Money*. The most influential work in economics of the twentieth century, the book had only just been published. Even the most senior members of the Harvard faculty were trying to comprehend and interpret Keynes's revolutionary concepts.

Tobin was hooked. Keynes was made to order for him—a difficult, novel theoretical structure combined with persuasive prescriptions for overcoming the massive unemployment of the 1930s. Tobin made his mark in economics by putting both features to good use.

After two years of graduate work at Harvard, he did a brief stint of war work in Washington and then served with the Navy for the next four years as a line officer on a destroyer. He refers to those years as being "on leave" from economics.[3]

Tobin returned to Harvard after the war to complete work for his doctorate, which he received in 1947. In 1950, Yale made him a handsome offer that he felt he could not refuse. He went to Yale as an associate professor, was promoted to full professor in 1955, and was appointed Sterling Professor of Economics in 1957. When Harvard tried to lure him back in 1957, Tobin replied that Yale had completely won his allegiance. New Haven has been home base for the Tobin family ever since.

The year 1955 was a high point in Tobin's career for another reason as well. It was in that year that the American Economic Association awarded him the John Bates Clark Medal, given annually to an outstanding economist under forty years of age.

That year also saw the consummation of a flirtation that had been going on for seven years. In 1948, only a year after receiving his Ph.D., Tobin had been invited to discuss a paper on statistics and economics written by Jacob Marschak, one of the stars of the Cowles Commission in Chicago. The Cowles Commission, which Tobin has described as "one of the most productive research centers in history,"[4] was where Harry Markowitz would develop his ideas on portfolio selection, in part under Marschak's guidance.

Tobin was flattered and put all his efforts into the task. Although Marschak's elegant paper was highly intricate, Tobin found a conceptual flaw in it—a flaw that he describes as the kind an economist would find but a straight mathematician might not.

Marschak and his colleague Koopmans, later to be a Nobel laureate, were impressed by Tobin's critique. A warm friendship developed, and Marschak and Koopmans urged Tobin to join them in Chicago. Finally, in 1953–54, when they were looking for a new director, they invited Tobin to accept the post. He was honored by the invitation, but, he recalls, "I liked Yale, and my wife and I thought it was a better place for our family."[5] He turned them down.

In 1954–1955, Koopmans spent a sabbatical year at Yale as a visiting professor. He was deeply concerned about what was happening at the Cowles Commission back at Chicago. The primary focus of the work at Cowles was on the application of complex mathematical and statistical methods to the problems of economics. This approach is what had fascinated Markowitz, but it was also the approach that had irked Milton Friedman at Markowitz's doctoral examination. The Chicago economics department was never completely convinced that the work being done at Cowles was "economics," but that department in turn had left Harry Markowitz with a lifelong conviction that economists may not be worth their salt.

In any case, the leaders of the Cowles Commission were eager to leave Chicago because of the deteriorating neighborhood in which the University was located. The area has been significantly upgraded since that time, but it was then a major obstacle to recruiting topflight scholars. As Alfred Cowles himself was a Yale graduate, a permanent home in New Haven seemed a fitting choice.

Together, these considerations led Koopmans to negotiate the transfer of the Cowles Commission from Chicago to Yale. Yale president Griswold wanted the organization to have a new name to go with its new location, so the Commission became the Cowles Foundation for Research in Economics at Yale University, with Tobin as its director. Thus, Tobin was able to remain at Yale and to become Director of the Cowles Foundation as well.

Tobin's only excursion into full-time employment outside academia was a year and a half in Washington serving on John F. Kennedy's Council of Economic Advisers in 1961–62. When Tobin answered the telephone one day in December 1960 and heard President-elect Kennedy's voice at the other end, he recalls saying, "I'm afraid you got the wrong guy, Mr. President. I'm an ivory-tower economist." Kennedy responded, "That's the best kind. I'll be an ivory-tower president." Tobin: "That's the best kind."[6]

As this conversation might suggest, managing personal wealth—portfolio theory and the stock market—has never been among Tobin's primary interests. His powerful contribution to portfolio theory was a fortuitous outgrowth of his concerns over economic policy and the ravages caused by depressions and inflations.

That is precisely what Keynesian theory is all about. When Keynes wrote *The General Theory* in the 1930s, he was particularly concerned about getting interest rates low enough to stimulate a sustained revival in business activity. He predicted that the economy would be doomed to an intolerable level of unemployment as long as interest rates remained too high to encourage corporate capital investment. The only escape from this dilemma, he insisted, was through government intervention.

Keynes's emphasis on the dominating influence of interest rates on unemployment was one of the more controversial ideas introduced by that most controversial of economists. It was also a made-to-order problem for Tobin to tackle in his 1958 article, both because of its controversial nature and its implications for economic policy.

Tobin's innovation to portfolio theory was a major simplification of Markowitz's methodology. That simplification triggered a direct attack on the interior decorator approach to portfolio management. An exploration into economic policy and the Keynesian theory of interest seems a long way from my decision to buy Gillette and Tampax for the clergyman's wife, but, though the path is circuitous, there is a direct connection between them.

Keynes had argued that older economists were wrong when they espoused the established notion that interest is a reward for saving and that the interest rate is the price that equates the flow of saving with the flow of investment. People do not have to put their savings out at interest. If they choose, they can keep their savings in the form of cash, which earns no interest at all. The opposite is also true. People do not have to save in order to lend money if they happen to be holding some cash when the lending opportunities appear. The notion that saving and the management of liquidity are two distinct and often unrelated decisions was one of Keynes's most important contributions to economic theory.

Keynes uses the expression "Liquidity Preference" to describe the idea that investors will not part with their cash unless they perceive the reward for doing so as adequate. Interest, in other words, is not only a reward for saving; it is a reward for taking the risk of owning assets that fluctuate in value and are costly to buy and sell.

Money, the basic liquid asset, cannot fluctuate in price, because it itself defines price. Moreover the cost of using money to pay for things is minimal, most often zero. If other assets shared these unique attributes, stocks and bonds and even real estate could circulate as money. Other assets do not share these attributes, however. Their future prices are uncertain, and buying and selling them is costly. All other things being equal, therefore, people prefer liquidity. Anticipating Markowitz's ideas, Keynes argued that investors will move from money to assets that are risky and less liquid only if they expect to earn a reward for doing so.

Tobin points out that Keynes built two bizarre features into his theory of Liquidity Preference. For one thing, Keynes assumed that investors' expectations of interest rates in the future are extremely slow to change: ". . . the rate of interest is a highly conventional, rather than a highly psychological phenomenon. . . . *Any* level of interest which is accepted with sufficient conviction as *likely* to be durable *will* be durable. . . . [I]t may fluctuate for decades about a level which is chronically too high for full employment."[7]

Although Keynes fails to provide a convincing explanation of why interest rates have to be so stable, even for decades, economic theorists tend to draw on their own experience and the history they learned at school. Keynes's memory bank in the early 1930s undoubtedly explains why he wrote that particular paragraph. For nearly sixty years, from 1861 to 1929, interest rates on high-grade long-term bonds never deviated by more than two percentage points from their average level of 4.8 percent. During Keynes's lifetime up to 1935, the year he finished writing his book at the age of 52 (he was born in 1883, the same year Karl Marx died), interest rates had averaged 4 percent a year and had varied at the extremes by only one percentage point in either direction. During the 1940s, the variation was less than half a percentage point around the average level of 2.6 percent.

When Keynes died in 1946, he had no sense of the extraordinary changes that lay ahead. By 1957, as Tobin was drafting his own paper on liquidity preference, long-term interest rates were already more than 50 percent above the lows of the 1930s while short-term rates had more than tripled. Over the next thirty-three years, long-term rates would average 7.3 percent but they ranged from a high of 13.6 percent to a low of 3.8 percent. Investors' perceptions of where the rate of interest "should be" became much more variable as a result. As anxieties about volatility gradually dominated memories of familiar interest rate levels, the rate of interest has developed into more of a "highly psychological" than the "highly conventional" phenomenon with which Keynes was familiar.

Keynes also failed to explain why interest rates should stay where they were if investors considered the current level to be a temporary divergence from the normal, or conventional, level. Would it make sense for an investor to sell a bond at 95 when its "normal" level was 100? Keynes made clear that investors would note and would be concerned about any such divergence, but precisely what would happen as a result remained obscure.

Keynes's second unrealistic assumption was that each investor would choose between cash and risky assets in an either-or manner, holding only one asset at a time. Investors who expected interest rates to rise would want to hold all their capital in cash; investors who expected rates to fall would want to hold only bonds—risky because they fluctuate in price. He did not contemplate portfolios that would consist of some combination of the two.

Tobin's contribution to economic theory was to demonstrate how the Keynesian system would work even if these two arbitrary assumptions about the behavior of interest rates and the responses of investors were replaced by something more realistic. In this paper he rejects the view that people expect interest rates to fluctuate around some constant long-run normal level. That would be the case only under the highly restrictive assumption that everything in the economy is in equilibrium. Under those conditions, he points out, no one would see any need to hold cash at all. But he adds, "So stationary a state is of very little interest."[8]

Instead, investors recognize the truth of Mark Twain's remark that forecasting is very difficult, especially when it concerns the future! They may have opinions about the outlook for interest rates, but only plungers are certain that their opinions are correct. Once uncertainty becomes part of the picture, most investors tend to avoid all-out wagers. They prefer to hold their wealth in mixed form—some cash, some risky assets. Because nobody likes unpleasant surprises, in other words, risk-averse investors hedge their bets.

Tobin's paper also emphasizes that people in the real world will not wait indefinitely until the reward is high enough to persuade them to part with 100 percent of their liquidity. So investors make their decisions on some kind of continuum: they want to have at least some exposure to risky assets on the chance that things might turn out better than they expect. Diversification— an asset mix that includes both liquid and risky assets—is the most effective way to deal with outcomes that cannot be known in advance.

This focus on asset diversification brought Tobin to the same subject matter that had concerned Markowitz. Tobin had been working in this area before he became familiar with Markowitz's work. He invited Markowitz to spend 1955–56 at the Cowles Foundation, by which time Markowitz had completed the book that was to appear in 1959. Tobin, in a footnote to his article, cites Markowitz's forthcoming book but distinguishes between their aims:* "Markowitz's main interest is prescription of rules of rational behavior for investors; the main concern of this paper is the implications for economic theory . . . that can be derived from assuming that investors do in fact follow such rules."[9]

As Tobin had discerned weaknesses in Keynes's model, he also detects a weakness in Markowitz's model. Markowitz assumes that investors select securities for their portfolios from a universe consisting totally of risky assets. He pays no attention to investors who might control risk by expanding the universe to include cash or other assets of very low risk. His only suggestion for controlling risk is to diversify the selections from the universe of risky assets. This narrow approach is unnecessary: Investors have a wide range of choice, and most people modulate the riskiness of

---

*It is pleasant to record that Tobin and his wife were in Tokyo in October 1990, where Markowitz was working when his Nobel Prize was announced several weeks before the Tobins arrived. The Tobins and the Markowitzes dined together to celebrate.

their portfolios by holding some share of their wealth in cash, or in cash equivalents like Treasury bills.

But Tobin went further. Portfolio selection is not simply a two-asset choice—bonds versus cash, or risk versus no risk. There are always many risky assets to choose from. There is always a spectrum of interest rates and of assets with varying degrees of risk. There are bonds due in two years and bonds due in thirty years, bonds issued by takeover artists and bonds issued by the government, stocks that hold the promise of becoming the next Xerox and stocks like AT&T. That is what makes the whole procedure so complicated, and so fascinating.

"The fact that one of the available assets in [Markowitz's] model . . . was riskless turned out to have interesting consequences,"[10] Tobin wrote in 1986 after winning the Nobel Prize. The most interesting of those consequences led him to place the portfolio-selection problem into a richer setting. And that setting led him to the concept that explains his fame in investment theory:

> The convenient fact that has just been proved is that the proportionate composition of the non-cash [i.e., risky] assets is independent of their aggregate share of the investment balance.[11]

This concept has come to be known as the Separation Theorem, because it argues that *the Markowitzian process of selecting securities for the most efficient risky portfolio is completely separate from the decision of how to divide up the total portfolio between risky and risk-free assets.* Two levels of decisions are required.

The investor's first and most important decision is how much overall exposure to risk is appropriate—how much to hold in risky securities like stocks and how much to hold in more stable assets like bonds and cash. The portfolio's tilt, or asset mix, should be sensitive to considerations of personality, financial circumstances, other sources of capital or income, the nature of the investor's liabilities, and so on. Widows will accept less risk and aggressive business executives will accept more; a pension fund that reinvests its income will be more venturesome than the endowment fund of a college that is pressing to make ends meet. It is likely that no two investors will come out at exactly the same degree of risk-aversion.

Having determined the appropriate exposure to risk, the investor's next task is to select the securities that will comprise the risky part of the portfolio. This selection will be made from among the whole universe of risky assets that are available for investment.

When combined with some relatively simple mathematics, Tobin's model enables the investor to identify the single portfolio of risky securities on Markowitz's Efficient Frontier that dominates all the other possible combinations of efficient portfolios. This will be the portfolio that, among all possible combinations of available risky assets, offers the highest expected return relative to the risks involved. As this super-efficient portfolio dominates all other portfolios on the Efficient Frontier, the choice should be identical whether the investor is a widow, an aggressive business executive, or someone in between.

The logic of Tobin's Separation Theorem rejects the interior decorator approach and puts a cap of respectability on the intuitive approach to investing in the puberty boom that I took with the clergyman and his wife. Why settle for less than the best?

The Separation Theorem suggests that a manager's zeal for avoiding risk in a widow's portfolio of stocks will lead to disappointing results. A portfolio that contains too many supposedly "safe" stocks is badly diversified; its holdings will all decline in price together when some commonly adverse influence strikes them. Even worse, the companies it contains will probably be so conservative that the total portfolio will have too low an expected return to justify the risks of being in the stock market in the first place.

The obsession with high expected returns in the executive's stock portfolio produces similar errors. The concentration in companies that are expected to be the next Xerox also defies the elementary principles of diversification. So-called emerging growth company stocks have a habit of moving in and out of fashion as a group, and consequently move up and down in price together. From the end of 1983 to the end of 1989, the stocks with the smallest dollar capitalization on the New York Stock Exchange rose in value by only 50% while those with the largest capitalization soared 167 percent; the prices of the small stocks were more variable to boot. Even though investors may have high hopes when they invest in such companies, the expected return may not be big enough to compensate for the extremely risky character of this undiversified portfolio.

73

If the optimal portfolio identified by Tobin's model happens to be too volatile for the elderly widow, she can keep some of her wealth in savings accounts or in the form of Treasury obligations; then the fluctuations in her total portfolio will be smaller than the fluctuations in the risky assets she holds. If this portfolio is not enterprising enough for the aggressive executive, he can borrow and invest more than 100 percent of his wealth, amplifying the impact of even small fluctuations.

Tobin sums up his approach as "the theory of risk-avoiding behavior." Although his paper is heavy going for a casual reader, it brings abstract ideas into a realistic setting in which both analysis and policymaking can be more effective. It sets Keynesian principles on a firmer footing; it gives portfolio theory broader relevance; and it raises portfolio practice to a new level of sophistication and elegance.

Tobin makes a wry joke about this accomplishment. His advice has been good enough for presidents of the United States, the Board of Governors of the Federal Reserve System, the Congressional Budget Office, and even the City of New Haven, making him, in his words, "in some sense a contributor to finance and portfolio theory." On the other hand, he observes, "I am unique in that no real world financial enterprise has ever asked me for any advice whatsoever."[12]

Despite the advance that Tobin's innovation made possible, it did nothing to ease the awful chore of those thousands, perhaps millions, of calculations prescribed by Markowitz. Tobin helped the investor to make the strategic choice from the Efficient Frontier, but he did nothing to make defining the frontier any easier.

Five years were to pass before that problem could be solved. The reverberations from the solution were every bit as great as those from the Separation Theorem.

# Chapter

# 4

# The Most Important Single Influence

*It is more than likely that United States Steel will do well when Sweets Company does well.*

One day in the spring of 1969, a book editor I knew arranged for me to have lunch with a young Stanford professor named William Sharpe. She told me that he was someone I "just had to meet." Sharpe was then in his early thirties, an attractive man and easy to be with.

The charm made the shock even greater when, after the usual pleasantries and banter about the weather, he turned to me and asked "Do you beat the market?" No one had ever asked me that question before. In my world of investment counseling, it was taken for granted that investors always turned to a professional for guidance, for they knew they would do better in our hands than if they tried to manage their investments on their own. The only room for argument was over which professional manager's returns were furthest above average. It was unthinkable that any of us would ever deliver below-average returns.

I replied that I thought the answer was obvious. But Sharpe was not satisfied with that. Nor did he seem satisfied with any of the answers I managed to come up with (needless to say, I never got to put any questions to him) in the course of what turned out to be a less congenial lunch than I had anticipated. He was scornful when I defined "the market" we were beating as the Dow Jones Industrial Average, a messy porridge of only thirty stocks that was increasingly unrepresentative of the broad market.

75

Sharpe's grilling made a greater impression on me than I realized at the time. It prompted me, for the first time, to question my antagonism to the way academics were converting the art of portfolio management into an array of incomprehensible equations. Perhaps those mysterious mathematical symbols did mean something after all. I began to worry, and then to learn, and finally to change my ways.

It was high time. Sharpe was already a leading pioneer of investment theories who would go on to share the 1990 Nobel Prize in economic sciences with Harry Markowitz. He was also deeply involved in applications of the new theories and was on a consulting assignment with Merrill Lynch on the day we had lunch in New York.

Sharpe had developed an effective method for overcoming the difficulties inherent in the day-to-day application of Markowitz's theories of diversification and efficient portfolios. Tobin's Separation Theorem was an important step forward, but it still required the investor to perform the statistical high-wire acts of the Markowitz system. The computers of the late 1950s made the task less formidable but, even if they had sufficient capacity, the cost of using them was prohibitive for all but the very largest investment organizations.

As late as 1966, in an article on the Markowitz-Tobin system, William Baumol of Princeton reported that even a simplified version for selecting efficient portfolios from among 1,500 securities could cost between $150 and $350 for a single run, and that the complete Markowitz computations could cost as much as fifty times more. And the whole exercise would be worth nothing unless analysts could provide consistently accurate estimates of the expected returns, the risks, and the covariances of all the available candidates for selection in the efficient portfolios.

Markowitz was aware of the obstacles to the routine use of his approach, and he was genuinely concerned that its theoretical significance should not be lost to the real world of investing. He was convinced there had to be some way to cut the calculations down to an acceptable number and, at the same time, to reduce the number of errors analysts inevitably made in their estimates.

In the book he published in 1959, he sketches out a promising variation for making the job more manageable. Markowitz's style at this point is remarkable for its down-to-earth tone. His language is straightforward. He enlivens his proposal with vivid descriptions, including eccentric rich uncles with odd ideas about how to bequeath their wealth. In discussing how investors form their beliefs about the probability of differing outcomes—a topic he had explicitly excluded from his 1952 article—he gets into meteorology and observes that "a higher probability of 'right' weather conditions is required before proceeding with a nuclear weapons test than with a picnic excursion," and for a picnic than for hanging out the family wash.[1]

His discussion of probability leads him to an analysis of how investors arrive at their predictions of future rates of returns and the convictions they hold about the probable accuracy of those estimates. He introduces an imaginary security analyst and describes each of the forecasts and judgments the analyst has to produce. His objective is to make the portfolio selection system operable, so that its results can be portrayed "by means of an electronic computer."[2] His idea is simple:

> The returns on most securities are correlated. If the Standard & Poor Index rose substantially, we would expect United States Steel (Common) to rise. If the Standard & Poor Index rose substantially, we would also expect Sweets Company of America (Common) to rise. For this reason, it is more than likely that United States Steel will do well when Sweets Company does well.[3]

Estimates of such correlations are easy to make. They are also relatively stable, because in many instances past history is a reliable guide.

All the analyst has to do is determine whether each stock under consideration is more or less volatile than the market as a whole. The analyst should also consider whether a stock's behavior is subject to any influences beyond the dominating influence of the market as whole, such as the industry it happens to belong to. These judgments are readily quantifiable and, when added up and averaged, will yield a good picture of the projected portfolio.

Having progressed to this point, Markowitz did not carry his idea much further. His notion that "The returns on most stocks are correlated" was suggestive but by no means complete. He even relegated the underlying equations to a footnote, although the mathematics involved was much simpler than the mathematics in his 1952 article.

Instead of working out the details himself, Markowitz played the role of mentor in the development of his revolutionary short-cut. At his suggestion, that project was undertaken by William Sharpe, who had been doing his graduate work under Markowitz's supervision.

Sharpe had fallen into economics and finance by default. He started his college education at the University of California in Berkeley in 1951, aiming to become a physician. But he discovered that he hated science and switched to business. He also transferred to the University of California in Los Angeles. But then he found that he hated accounting as much as he hated science. Economics attracted him because it combined the discipline of science with a broader view of the world than the dead hand of accounting had revealed. Discovering an obscure regulation at UCLA that made it possible for him to take finance courses as he was working for an advanced degree in economics, he became the first person at UCLA to study in both fields at the same time. He earned his B.A. in economics at UCLA in 1955 and his M.A. in economics the following year.

Sharpe began work on Markowitz's project in 1960, when he was 26 years old and Markowitz was 33. He completed a paper containing the full development of the idea during 1961, the same year he was awarded his doctorate. He titled the paper, appropriately, "A Simplified Model for Portfolio Analysis."

He submitted the paper in December 1961 to *Management Science,* and it appeared in the issue of January 1963. *Management Science* was one of only two main journals at the time that published articles on operations research, the analysis of the relationships between input and output that Koopmans had pioneered at the Cowles Commission and that had also attracted Markowitz's attention. Unaware that Markowitz had used the same word in describing himself to me, Sharpe told me that he submitted the paper to *Management Science,* "because I was then (and am now) a computer nerd, so it seemed a reasonable target."[4]

Sharpe's arrangement with Markowitz was unusual. Sharpe was working for his doctorate at UCLA, where Markowitz was not a member of the faculty. Markowitz had just moved from the Cowles Commission in New Haven to take up residence in the Los Angeles area at a think tank called RAND—an acronym for R&D, or research-and-development—to work on linear programming applications for industrial firms. RAND had been established during World War II, primarily to do research for the armed forces. Its sphere of interest has broadened considerably over the years and now covers political, social, and economic issues as well as military and technological ones.

Sharpe was a busy young man when Markowitz put him to work on the simplified model He was taking graduate courses at UCLA and was also serving as a teaching assistant in graduate courses. In addition, he was carrying on his own line of research at RAND. J. Fred Weston, a distinguished professor on the UCLA faculty, had Sharpe taking one of his seminar courses and simultaneously teaching part of another of Weston's courses on the basis of what had he had learned in the first.

The work Sharpe was doing at RAND in 1960 was in an area known as transfer prices, the prices that one division of a corporation charges another division. When General Motors buys radios from its wholly owned subsidiary Delco to install in its automobiles, the price charged by Delco is a transfer price. And when Exxon moves crude oil from the well to the refinery, the refinery pays the drilling organization an appropriate transfer price. Without transfer prices, integrated corporations would never be able to arrive at a rational appraisal of the profitability of the assets they devote to their individual segments.

Sharpe has happy memories of his days at RAND: "We operated under very loose instructions there—basically, we played around with ideas until we found one that could save the Air Force some money. We then did a study, and returned to playing around with other ideas. The good old days."[5]

There seems to have been no shortage of "other ideas," and Sharpe began his career as an author of articles on subjects quite unrelated to investment. He published his first article in 1959, with three co-authors, on "A Proposal for a Smog Tax." His next effort, "Aircraft Compartment Design Criteria for the Army Deployment Mission," appeared in the *Naval Research Logistics Quarterly,* the same journal that had carried Markowitz's "The Optimization of a Quadratic Function Subject to Linear Constraints" three years earlier. The article on the simplified model in *Management Science* was only the third time Sharpe had appeared in print.

For reasons that he now finds difficult to reconstruct, Sharpe became fascinated by the subject of transfer pricing in 1960, so much so that he decided to write his Ph.D. thesis about it. After writing some 60 pages of what he thought was "earth-shattering stuff," he showed his work to Jack Hirshleifer, a newly arrived economist to whom Sharpe had just been assigned.[6] Hirshleifer came back to him a week later and declared flatly that there was absolutely no thesis there.

Although Sharpe now admits that Hirshleifer's rejection had a profound effect on the course of his career, he was shattered by the bad news. He recalls "singing a sad tune" to Weston, who suggested that he talk with Harry Markowitz.[7]

Weston had long been an enthusiastic supporter of Markowitz's work. As editor of the *Journal of Finance,* he had helped make possible the publication of Markowitz's "Portfolio Selection" in 1952. As early as May 1955, Weston had written an article about it for the *Financial Analysts Journal,* which is the official journal of the profession and is distributed to the members of the local professional societies around the country. In that article—one of the few on portfolio selection published up to that time—Weston admits that Markowitz's hypothesis "will seem strange and impractical to many investment executives [and] many may think that a high level of technical and mathematical skill is required to employ portfolio programming."[8] Nevertheless, Weston insists, it is simply another version of the techniques of operations research, "which have already secured wide acceptance in production and marketing" and which can be handled "relatively inexpensively . . . by modern electronic computing machines."[9]

Weston's suggestion that Sharpe talk with Markowitz was inspired counsel because the talk produced an immediate community of interest between them. UCLA approved their request that Sharpe continue his graduate work under Markowitz's guidance.

Although Sharpe uses the term "diagonal model" to describe his simplification of Markowitz's approach, it is generally referred to as the single-index model. Taking his cue from the analysis in Markowitz's book, Sharpe declares: "The major characteristic of the diagonal model is the assumption that the returns of various securities are related only through common relationships with some basic underlying factor."[10]

That underlying factor, which Sharpe refers to as an index, could be "the level of the stock market as a whole, the Gross

National Product, some price index," but it must be a "factor thought to be the most important single influence on the return from securities."[11]

The procedure Sharpe recommends eliminates the tedious chore of calculating the covariances between each pair of securities. The analyst need only calculate the relationship of each of the securities to the dominant factor. If the price of a security is more volatile than the movements of the dominant factor, that security will make the portfolio more variable, and therefore more risky, than it would have been otherwise; if the price of the security is less volatile, it will make the portfolio less risky. In well-diversified portfolios, the simple average of these relationships will then serve as an estimate of the volatility of the portfolio as a whole.

What is the "basic underlying factor" to which Sharpe refers? There is no doubt that individual stocks respond most directly to the stock market as a whole. About one-third of the variability of the average stock is simply a reflection of moves in the "index"—or "the most important single influence." The rest of its variability is split about evenly between the influence of other stocks to which it has a family resemblance, such as the auto stock group or the public utility group, and the unique characteristics of the stock itself. Even those influences disappear when as few as a dozen individual stocks are combined into a portfolio. Then the power of diversification obliterates the individual attributes of the stocks, and more than 90 percent of the portfolio's variability is explained by the index.

The simplicity of all this should not obscure its profound importance. If investors are going to buy any stocks at all, they cannot avoid accepting the risk of owning stocks in general. An investor who buys even one stock is buying an investment in the index as well as an investment in that stock. Wall Street is fond of the old adage that says when the paddy wagon pulls up to a house of pleasure, the cops take away the nice girls along with the bad ones. When the stock market goes down, only a tiny number of stocks will fail to go down with it. The same is true when the market goes up.

Sharpe's simplified model was a giant step forward in bringing Markowitz's ideas on portfolio selection closer to real-world applications. In a talk given to the Econometric Society in 1962, before the article had appeared in *Management Science,* Sharpe reported that the efficient portfolios selected by his model closely resembled portfolios developed by the full Markowitz system. More important, he pointed out that his model was consistent with the views of practicing security analysts, who normally classify securities according to how they respond to overall movements in the economy or the market.

Sharpe went on to describe a test of the model carried out with the help of a practicing security analyst who was a friend of Weston's and who had an enviable record of picking winners in the stock market. Sharpe took this analyst's subjective judgments about which stocks were attractive, put them through the program he had written for the computer, and came out with portfolios that purported to be efficient portfolios.

An annoying problem cropped up during the test: The computer kept turning out portfolios with 40 percent or more invested in just one stock. That stock was Haloid Xerox, the predecessor company to the Xerox Corporation, which was just then in the process of developing the office copier. Sharpe kept asking the analyst, "Do you really like that stock that much?"[12] The analyst said he did.

When Sharpe came home after conducting this experiment, his mother bugged him, as usual, for tips on the market that he must have picked up from his work on investments. He had always pleaded ignorance about picking individual stocks, but this time he gave her the Haloid Xerox tip—which she failed to follow. Had she followed it, an investment of $5,000 would have grown to $1,718,000 by the time Xerox stock reached its peak in 1971. Even in 1990, well after the stock had fallen from grace and Xerox had made the unfortunate decision to diversify into financial services, that $5,000 investment would have been worth nearly $500,000.

Early empirical tests of Sharpe's simplified model by other researchers demonstrated that it worked well as a tool in selecting efficient portfolios. Later refinements of the procedure have worked even better. Even so, no procedure, no matter how ingenious, can overcome the need for developing high-quality inputs—expected returns and estimates of covariances. That applies to all models: garbage-in-garbage-out is one of the most enduring of rules.

The big attraction of the single-index model was the computing time it saved. Sharpe disclosed in his article that the time needed to solve a 100-security example on a state-of-the-art mainframe IBM computer was reduced from 33 minutes with the full Markowitz program to 30 seconds with the simplified model.* Moreover the old model used so much of the computer's memory that it could handle a maximum of 249 securities; the new model could handle up to 2,000. Sharpe pointed out to me that today's IBM personal computer, equipped with an 80386 chip and math-coprocessor, would take less than a minute to perform the full Markowitz run that took 33 minutes. The 30-second run with Sharpe's simplified model would take only an instant.

Sharpe's article gives us the first indication of his headlong rush to become a virtuoso at the computer. When the IBM PC appeared on the scene in the early 1980s and knocked the old Apple IIs out of the box, Sharpe immediately recognized what the PC could do in solving portfolio management problems. The software he produced for the purpose and the enthusiasm with which he proseltyzed the use of the PC made him a driving force in the rapid proliferation of desktop computing among professional investors.

Sharpe was convinced that the benefits for investors in balancing risk against expected return demanded further refinements of his simplified model to save even more computer time: "Although the diagonal code allows the total computing time to be greatly reduced, the cost of a large analysis is still far from insignificant. Thus there is every incentive to limit the computations to those essential for the final selection of a portfolio."[13]

Sharpe was not alone in his fascination with ways to apply the computer to investment. The belief in science in the early 1960s was running strong, in part inspired by the space age, in part by the computer's power to solve problems that had been beyond solution up to that time. Robert McNamara, the whiz kid from Ford who became John Kennedy's Secretary of Defense, set the style by running his department according to operations research methodologies that turned out rigorous cost/benefit choices. As

---

*Milton Friedman has described how computing fifty years ago combined what now seems primitive capability with what must have seemed a miracle then. An experimental Mark I computer at Harvard based on card-sorting machines in an enormous air-conditioned gymnasium performed in 40 hours, not counting data insertion, a job that would have required three months on an electric calculator; today's desktop PC could do the job in less than 30 seconds. (See Friedman and Schwartz [1991])

students of operations research poured out of MIT, Carnegie Tech, Stanford, and Chicago, the commercial banks hired them in increasing numbers to systematize the business of record-keeping and data-processing. Soon they were moving into the trust area and experimenting with mean-variance applications like Sharpe's.

Richard Brealey of the London Business School related an incident to me that reflects the spirit of the times, even before the introduction of Sharpe's diagonal code. Martin Beale, a mathematical computer programmer, had just written a quadratic programming code for which there was no potential user in sight. At that very time, Brealey was looking for a good code with no idea of where to find one. He happened to meet Beale, quite by chance; Brealey found his code, and Beale found his user. In the end, Beale's code failed to work out as hoped, because computing time was still too expensive and because users plugged in wildly exaggerated numbers for expected returns. But the ball was rolling.

Sharpe's paper on the simplified model introduces another advance that also reflects his eagerness to reduce computation time. He adopts Tobin's Separation Theorem by incorporating borrowing and lending into his model, pointing out that "there is some interest rate at which money can be lent with virtual assurance that both principal and interest will be returned; at the least, money can be buried in the ground."[14] He recommends lending—buying bonds—for conservative investors who do not want to put all their wealth into risky assets like stocks. On the other hand, "In some cases an investor may be able to borrow funds in order to purchase even greater amounts of a portfolio than his own funds will allow."[15] This procedure is appropriate for aggressive investors who want to take on more risk than any combination of stocks would provide.

Like Tobin, Sharpe demonstrates that, when investors have the choice of lending or borrowing, there is one portfolio on the Efficient Frontier whose trade-off between risk and expected return will dominate all other portfolios. This portfolio, because it is optimal, is the one portfolio that all investors should hold, regardless of their appetite for risk. When an analyst inserts the current interest rate for lending and borrowing into the diagonal code, the model will identify that super-efficient portfolio. At the same time, it will restrict the computations "to those absolutely necessary for determination of the final set of efficient portfolios. . . . [T]he results of the analysis . . . [are] not an insignificant saving."[16]

How much of Sharpe's paper on the simplified model was due to Markowitz, one can only guess. Markowitz told me that "I do not think it is quite accurate to say that I supervised Bill. He supervised himself."[17] Sharpe, on the other hand, is always generous when the talk turns to Markowitz. He told me he considers Markowitz "the most truly gentle man I know."[18] In his article in *Management Science* Sharpe begins with a note acknowledging computer assistance at UCLA and the University of Washington and goes on:

> [The author's] greatest debt is to Dr. Harry Markowitz of the RAND Corporation. . . . It is no longer possible to segregate the ideas in this paper into those which were his, those which were the author's, and those which were developed jointly. Suffice it to say that the only accomplishments which are unquestionably the property of the author are those of authorship—first of the computer program and then of this article.[19]

Nineteen sixty-one, the year in which Sharpe wrote "A Simplified Model for Portfolio Analysis," was also the year in which an American astronaut, Alan Shepard, first rode a missile in space, for a thrilling fifteen minutes. Harry Markowitz had launched William Sharpe, unaware that he would soon rise so high that he, too, would go into orbit. Within a short time after the publication of the paper in 1963, Sharpe transformed his simplified model into a major breakthrough whose theoretical ingenuity and practical importance would rival that of Markowitz himself.

Sharpe's achievements in combining theoretical innovations with practical applications have made him a hero in the world of investment professionals. On the morning in October 1990 when the news arrived that Sharpe had been awarded the Nobel Prize, he was attending a meeting of the Institute for Quantitative Analysis in Finance, a club whose members are the elite among practitioners in the area and who like to refer to their organization as the "Q Group." Champagne was served at the morning session to celebrate the award. Martin Leibowitz, one of the most distinguished members of the group and a managing director of the investment firm of Salomon Brothers, rose to give a toast "to one of Q's favorite sons."[20]

Leibowitz used the word that Jews recite at Passover, "Dayenu!," which means "what God has done for us already would have been more than enough, even if He had never helped us again." At Passover services the singers exclaim "Dayenu!" after each verse as they recall how God had liberated the Jews from bondage, led them across the desert, parted the waters of the Red Sea, and so on. Leibowitz expressed the group's admiration for Sharpe with this variation on the theme:

> If he had only discovered the central building
> blocks of capital market theory—dayenu!
>
> If he had only written the best books on
> investments—dayenu!
>
> If he had only shown how these theories can
> be applied to real life problems that
> confound the daily workings of the financial
> system—dayenu!
>
> If he had only shown how wonderful
> academic research can survive, and indeed
> thrive, beyond the walls of academia—
> dayenu!
>
> If he had only been, as he is, one of the most
> fundamentally deserving and unassuming
> individuals in this field—dayenu!

Sharpe's major breakthrough came in 1964, with what is known as the Capital Asset Pricing Model, which the cognoscenti call CAPM, pronounced "CAP-EM." CAPM starts out from the basic idea of the single-index model that returns are related "only through common relationships with some basic underlying factor."[21] But it ends up a long way from there.

The model concludes with the startling but inescapable conclusion that Tobin's super-efficient portfolio is the stock market itself. No other portfolio with equal risk can offer a higher expected return; no other portfolio with equal expected return will be less risky. This controversial view was what had prompted Sharpe's disturbing interrogation of me at that lunch meeting in

New York. If the market itself is the super-efficient portfolio, no one can beat it without taking on an unwarranted amount of risk.

Heresy. Totally inadmissible. Most investors believe they can read the tea leaves that stock prices leave in the cup of fortune. They ask one another, over and over, "How's the market? How do you like the market?" They call their brokers, sometimes every day, even every hour. They hang on the news reports, study the stock listings in the daily papers, and faithfully watch the TV show, Wall $treet Week. They act on the notion that knowing what happened today will somehow tell them what will happen tomorrow. And if they do not themselves know what is going to happen, there must be somebody, somewhere, who does know and who will share that information with them, or will sell it to them.

It is ironic that Sharpe was arguing that the optimal investment strategy was simply to buy and hold as widely diversified a basket of stocks as possible just as the performance cult was taking hold. In the mid-1960s, the investing public's faith in the capabilities of professional investment managers was leading to a degree of hero worship comparable to the general public's adulation of the Beatles and the Jet's quarterback Joe Namath. In the winter of 1968, John Hartwell, one of the towering figures in the world of professional investing at that time, declared: "It is a basic fact that we should look upon performance as something that is attainable, has been attainable and can be attained with a great deal of consistency if one organizes to do it."[22]

In his introduction to *The Money Managers,* a book published in 1969, "Adam Smith," television's best-known commentator in economic and financial matters, reflected the mood of the heady, performance-oriented environment:

We live in the Age of Performance. Performance means, quite simply, that your portfolio does better than others. . . . The managers of the Age of Performance are . . . Stars. . . . And a star can earn a million dollars a year.

Are these stars really smarter than all the rest of us? . . . They do work at it all day long, but it doesn't seem like work, because the quest for the new and fresh idea—the stock that will outperform all the others—is an exciting game. "Oh, beautiful, baby, beautiful," says David Meid [one of the stars], as someone reads some nubile bewitching numbers to him over the phone. . . . In short, [the star] is really at his job seven days a week because he thinks about the market all the time. It turns him on.[23]

That the stars would fall—that their apparent outperformance would turn out to be nothing more than fluff—was preordained by the very nature of how they went about their business. But in 1969 the stars were blissfully unaware of the inevitability of this outcome or of how the logic of Sharpe's analysis would make it inevitable.

Sharpe's work was not all they were unaware of. An impressive body of research on the predictability of stock prices was readily available to anyone who wanted to look at it—but few people did.

The researchers who carried out this research and the theorists who explained its findings built a powerful structure on the foundations that Louis Bachelier and Alfred Cowles had prepared for them. They include a famous columnist on *Newsweek* magazine, a college football star who majored in French and never took a course in math, a compulsive marathon-runner, and an economist at MIT whose gloomy conclusions led him to observe, "I must confess that the fun has gone out of it somehow."

We will now let them state their case.

# PART
# III

# The Demon
# of Chance

# Chapter
## 5

# Illusions, Molecules, and Trends

*. . . the epitome of unrelieved bedlam.*

When the *Journal of Finance* published Harry Markowitz's article on portfolio selection in June 1952, the Dow Jones Industrials stood at 280. The market had nearly quintupled since Alfred Cowles's article on investment performance had appeared in *Econometrica* in January 1933. Even so, after twenty-three long and painful years, prices were still about 25 percent shy of the record high scored in 1929. They had taken a tumble in the fall of 1946 and had recovered only moderately by mid-1952.

It was a sleepy time. Daily volume on the New York Stock Exchange averaged well below one million shares during much of the 1940s and below two million shares during the 1950s. At a daily turnover of two million shares, less than one in five shares listed on the Exchange changed hands in the course of a year. Not until well into the 1960s would daily turnover exceed one in five.

Change in this dreary market came slowly. In many brokerage offices the "board" showing the prices of the more active and widely held stocks was still an old-fashioned blackboard. A boy chalked up the latest prices as he received them on a headset from someone at the Exchange who read them off the ticker tape. A ticker continued to tick away under its glass dome in the corner of the brokerage office so that traders could run the tape through their fingers and catch up on the action. There was usually another ticker that recorded the latest business news on the Dow Jones broad tape; as the tape reached the floor, a boy would cut

*91*

it off and clip it up where customers and the "customers' men" could peruse it at their leisure.

Some time in the late 1940s, the more progressive brokerage firms began to replace the blackboard with a new kind of board that recorded the prices on the board in response to electrical impulses. The numbers were still shown in white, however, against a dark background—a reminder that automation is always more welcome in a familiar setting. In addition, these offices often had a "Trans-Lux," a lighted reproduction of the tape in pale chartreuse moving across a screen just over the black-and-white quote board.

It is little wonder that no one paid much attention to Cowles's research into the predictability of stock prices, despite the academic recognition he had earned for setting up the Commission and establishing *Econometrica*. People in the stock market turned a deaf ear to his devastating conclusions about the pathetic track records of professional investors and advisors.

Those who had pulled through the crash, as well as those who had gone under, knew more about that wretched performance than they wanted to know. The individual investors who had fled the market in droves during the 1930s had, as yet, little taste for another go at it. Distaste for Wall Street and the stock market was so strong that only those who had survived the crash remained there, joined by only a trickle of newcomers. As a result, the financial community was more in-grown than it had ever been before.

Even good news was greeted with anxiety. When 1954 turned out to be one of the great bull market years of history, with prices rising over 40 percent and finally surpassing the 1929 high, Senator William Fulbright, then Chairman of the Senate Committee on Banking and Currency, launched an investigation into the party underway on Wall Street. Among the witnesses he called was Professor John Kenneth Galbraith of Harvard, who had just completed a book titled *The Great Crash*—destined to become a long-run bestseller. This vivid memoir of the 1929 debacle and its immediate aftermath started Galbraith on the high-visibility career that he has pursued with boundless enthusiasm ever since.

In his introduction to a later edition, Galbraith recalled that he was holding the proofs of the book in his hand as he testified about what had happened twenty-five years before: "Toward the end I suggested that history *could* repeat itself, although I successfully resisted all invitations to predict when. I did urge a stiff tightening of margin requirements as a precautionary step."[1]

Questions from the full roster of Senators came fast and furious. "You do not think we are faced with a bust, do you?" asked Senator Ives of New York. Photographers and newsreel cameras crowded the hearing room. Galbraith confesses that he was the only person there who failed to realize that his grim prognosis would drive stock prices into a "nasty plunge." The market fell about 1.5 percent that day, a disturbing decline at the time.[2]

The indifference of investors to Cowles's work is less surprising than the silence of the academics. Cowles's research had provided a mother lode of statistical evidence for economists, including the precious gift of a comprehensive data base. It had also uncovered a wealth of data that analysts could use to study how expectations are formed, how markets digest new information, and how speculative prices behave.

True, many academics still regarded the stock market as a sideshow in the economic system, not worthy of serious attention. But another explanation for their apathy may be more compelling: Most people who studied economics before the mid-1950s had little or no exposure to mathematics or sophisticated statistical techniques. A few people had ventured into mathematical economics, including Keynes (who wrote an authoritative treatise on probability in the 1920s), but none of the great works in economics up to that time used anything more than high-school algebra, relegating concepts of greater complexity to footnotes or small-print appendixes. In my own work as both economist and investment manager, at least until the mid-1970s, I felt no need to use anything fancier than an electric (not electronic) calculating machine and a slide rule.

Computer literacy also was extremely rare, and the equipment needed to perform data processing was still prohibitively expensive, slow, and cumbersome. Few scholars had much taste for the disagreeable job of entering thousands of numbers, performing the necessary calculations, and summarizing the results in a fashion that would support some kind of hypothesis about market behavior.

I had never even set my fingers onto a computer keyboard until I attended a 1969 summer workshop at Harvard Business School. PCs with video screens were not yet a gleam in an inventor's eye; we sat at terminals hooked into a mainframe located somewhere else and waited patiently while a clattering printer produced our results in hard copy. I now realize that we were using the computer to compose diversified portfolios, but I had little idea at the time of what that clattering was all about.

Only two analyses of any note had appeared during the twenty years following Cowles's 1933 article, one in 1934 and the other long afterward in 1953. Neither paper was by an economist. The authors in each case were statisticians who used the data base of the financial markets to prove a point about statistical methods. The bean-counting procedures they employed, and the statistical theories they came up with, make less than fascinating reading. Their papers are technically impressive, however, because of the mechanical hurdles they had overcome in manipulating such huge masses of numbers.

Despite the tedious character of the papers, they provided the first confirmation that Bachelier may well have been on the right track when he concluded that "The mathematical expectation of the speculator is zero." Cowles had shown that the performance of the professional investors he investigated had been less than noteworthy; the statisticians raised the unpleasant possibility that the professionals never had a chance to begin with.

The 1934 study was the work of Holbrook Working of Stanford. Working was hardly a dynamic personality. Paul Samuelson, who classes Working among the greats, described him to me as "a dry stick . . . not a sparkling expositor"[3] and recalled seeing Holbrook, his economist brother, and his father ". . . all three paper-thin and from the same DNA mold, standing together at the 1940 Colorado Springs Cowles Commission conference (and looking to my 25-year-old eyes old as sin)."*

Working's paper appeared in the *Journal of the American Statistical Association* with the unpoetic title, "A Random Difference Series for Use in the Analysis of Time Series." Samuelson believes that the paper deserved far more attention than it received at the time and that it would have won applause if Working had been at Harvard or Chicago. Stanford in those days "was in the boondocks."[4]

*Samuelson makes this comment about the Cowles Commission conferences: "You drank well, unless by bad luck Irving Fisher was also a guest, in which case all was dry."

94

Working focused on commodity prices, a rich source of statistics with a long historical record. His study turned into a detective story, with the unusual twist that the obvious suspect turned out to be guilty.

When he plotted his commodity price data on graphs, he observed that their trends and fluctuations showed identifiable and repetitive patterns rather than "a completely hit or miss character."[5] This was about what he had expected to find, because traders in commodity markets have always believed that prices follow certain rhythms and trends. Analysts see in those rhythms and trends more intricate structures that can be used to predict the future. Even today, forecasts of commodity prices are dominated by past price behavior rather than by fundamental information about demand and supply.

Working then tried another approach. He plotted the *changes* in prices from one transaction to the next. Now he saw something radically different: Although price *levels* do not follow a random pattern, price *changes* tend to be "largely random."[6] Random changes, by definition, are unpredictable.

Good statisticians trust facts more than they trust their eyes. Working decided to compare his results with changes in a sequence of truly random numbers. In a series of random numbers the sequence is completely unsystematic; no number bears any predictable relationship to the numbers that precede or follow it. A hundred spins of a roulette wheel (honestly balanced) would produce a series of random numbers, as would the draw of cards from a well-shuffled deck. The experiment worked: Working found that he could not tell the difference between his graphs of commodity price changes and his graphs of changes in the sequence of random numbers.

Concerned that he might still have missed something, Working wondered whether a professional commodities trader might be aware of a pattern that his untutored eye had overlooked, some critical signal buried in what seemed to be a meaningless jumble of price changes. Working took both sets of graphs down to the traders in the commodity trading pits in Chicago and asked them to tell him which were the graphs of commodity prices and which were the graphs of random numbers. Like art critics who occasionally cannot differentiate between the scrawls of a child and the work of some modern master, the traders were unable to distinguish the prices of the commodities in which they were trading every day of the week from the random series.

Working's discoveries were revolutionary. Someone engaged in a more glamorous pursuit than explicating statistical methodology and analysis might have sought out the widest possible audience for his message. An economist would at least have asked *why* changes in commodity prices so consistently resembled random fluctuations. But Working was a statistician, and he simply offered his findings "for Use in the Analysis of Time Series." He never completely let go of the problem, however. He continued to make tests into the 1950s, and he did try to explain the uniformity of the results his tests produced; here and there an exception popped up, but exceptions were few and far between.

After the publication of Working's paper in 1934, almost complete silence reigned until 1953. In that year, the *Journal of the Royal Statistical Society* in London published a paper by Maurice Kendall, a professor of statistics at the London School of Economics and the author of a monumental two-volume work, *The Advanced Theory of Statistics*. The title of Kendall's 1953 paper, "The Analysis of Economic Time Series," was no more inviting than Working's, though his writing style was livelier. Like Working, he was a statistician not familiar with economics or economists. Like Working and Bachelier—but unlike Dow and Hamilton—his research was research for its own sake, rather than an effort to uncover a strategy for making money in the market. Yet Kendall's drab title belied the significance—even the drama—of his findings.

The question he asked was relevant to the interpretation of data in many fields: How can we distinguish short-term ripples from longer-term trends? Do two unusually warm winters in a row signify the onset of global warming, or are they a normal variation that will be succeeded by bitterly cold winters in the future? When the championship baseball team loses three games in a row, is that the beginning of the end of their league dominance, or just a brief interruption in their string of victories? Dow Theory claims that these are precisely the questions it answers for the stock market—that it can tell whether the tide is turning or just churning. Its methodology for doing so, however, falls far short of the high-powered statistical analysis Kendall used in his search for a scientific basis for making such distinctions.

His results took him by surprise. In an example of British understatement, he declares at the outset that, "the pattern of events in the price series was much less systematic than is generally believed."[7] He then provides overwhelming evidence to support that conclusion.

Kendall analyzed weekly data for nineteen different stock groupings, covering the years 1928 to 1938 and ranging from the stocks of financial companies to industrials, rails, breweries (always big in the British stock market), oils, and utilities. He also analyzed the monthly average price of wheat in the Chicago commodity markets from 1883 to 1934 and of cotton on the New York Mercantile Exchange from 1816 to 1951.*

Kendall's findings confirmed Working's. He found no structure of any sort in this wide variety and long history of price patterns. Here is a typical comment, this one about 2,387 weekly price changes in wheat for the fifty-year period 1883–1934 (excluding 1915–1920):

> The series looks like a "wandering" one, almost as if once a week the Demon of Chance drew a random number from a symmetrical population of fixed dispersion and added it to the current price to determine next week's price. And this, we may recall, is not the behavior in some small backwater market. . . . The best estimate of the change in price between now and next week is that there is no change.[8]

Lest anyone count on the possibility that there is hope here for stock-market investors, I must point out that the behavior of wheat prices was typical of Kendall's findings, not an exception. In the case of the stock prices, Kendall found some scattered evidence of brief trends but concluded that the prices were "virtually wandering," and that such trends as were present were "so weak as to dispose at once of any possibility of being able to use them for prediction. The Stock Exchange, it would appear, has a memory lasting less than a week."[9]

All of this led him to offer some unwelcome advice for investors: "Investors can, perhaps, make money on the Stock Exchange, but not, apparently, by watching price movements and

---

*So voluminous were his statistical materials that he was obliged to violate "the golden rule in publishing work on time-series [which] is to give the original data." As that would have required thirty pages in the Society's journal, he offered to make the data themselves or his computer punch cards available on request.

coming in on what looks like a good thing. . . . But it is unlikely that anything I say or demonstrate will destroy the illusion that the outside investor can make money by playing the markets, so let us leave him to his own devices."[10]

Toward the end of the paper Kendall admits, "I am well aware that this paper raises more difficulties than it resolves."[11] He was right: his findings, together with the harshness of his presentation, created an uproar when he delivered his paper to the members of the Royal Statistical Society. The members were more than just angry and incredulous. As one observer put it, "Such nihilism seemed to strike at the very heart of economic science."[12]

Despite this experience, Kendall dominated British statistics well into the 1970s. In 1974, he received the ultimate accolade for an English scholar: He became Sir Maurice George Kendall. His *Advanced Statistics* is still a standard reference work. Richard Brealey tells the story that someone who was looking for the well-known and highly successful software company called CEIR stopped Kendall in the street and asked him whether he knew the way to CEIR. Kendall replied, "You are talking to CEIR."*[13]

Kendall's message did pique curiosity in certain academic circles. Two important papers on price behavior appeared in 1959, though silence persisted in the economics and finance fraternity.

In March 1959, the *Journal of Finance* published "Stock Market 'Patterns' and Financial Analysis," by Harry Roberts, a statistician at the Graduate School of Business at the University of Chicago and among the first of many talented scholars there to focus on the puzzling behavior of financial markets.

Roberts was then in his mid-40s and a fitness freak. At this writing, more than thirty years later, he has lost none of his fervor for strenuous exercise. He is, to the best of my knowledge, the only character in this history of ideas to have run a 26-mile marathon, and he has run it on more than one occasion. His slightly younger colleague at Chicago, Nobel Laureate Merton Miller, likes to say that he and Roberts run an average of five miles a day: "Harry runs ten."[14]

Even though his article appeared in an academic journal, Roberts was the first researcher in this area to address himself directly

*US CEIR was one of the hot stocks of the late 1960s and a highly volatile one. The company merged into Control Data in 1968.

to financial analysts rather than to fellow academics. I do not know whether he really expected any Wall Street practitioners to find their way to a journal of this kind, or whether any of them did, but he was clear about the audience he wanted to reach.

Roberts cites both Working and Kendall and takes his cue from the statistical approach Kendall had used to prove his point about the Demon of Chance—and to horrify his fellow statisticians. Roberts proposes to bring to the attention of analysts empirical results that "seem to have been ignored in the past, for whatever reason."[15]

His target was a group of market analysts then known as chartists; today we call them by the more impressive title of technicians. Dow, Hamilton, and Rhea are their spiritual forefathers. Their credo is Hamilton's statement that stock prices, which record the history of where transactions have actually taken place, are therefore "sufficient in themselves" to reveal everything the profit-seeking investor needs to know.

The technicians have a theory of their own. When stock prices move, the argument goes, they do so primarily in response to decisions made by big investors; small investors play with too little money to make any noticeable impact on prices. The big investors have the really valuable information about individual companies and the economy, and they reveal that information as they drive prices up or down.

Price movements are all that matters to the technicians. The study of corporate balance sheets and income flows or broad economic data is worse than a waste of effort, they insist, because it can be positively misleading if certain investors know more than the data reveal. The late John Magee, a leading authority on technical analysis in the 1950s, habitually read the daily newspapers two weeks after the fact, just to be certain that current news would not color his view of the patterns of stock price movements over time.

Following the footprints of the big investors, the technicians search their charts for evidence of future price movements. An upswing on strong volume, a new low or a higher high, a small decline followed by a larger rise, and more arcane price patterns are the signals they seek.

Like Working, Roberts used a series of random numbers. He set up the series to be consistent with normal weekly stock market changes at the time. To do so, he instructed his computer to select random numbers whose individual changes would average +0.5 percent, with about two-thirds of the changes within −4.5 percent and +5.5 percent. He assumed, arbitrarily, that Week #1 would start at a level of 450, which is where the Dow Jones Industrial Average was at the moment. He then cumulated his "weekly" changes, adding Week #1's change to 450, adding Week #2's change to that result, and so on until he had a record for 52 "weeks."

Figure 1 shows the results. As Roberts commented, "To even a casual observer of the stock market, [this graph] is hauntingly realistic, even to the 'head-and-shoulders' top."[16]

By the "head-and-shoulders top" Roberts meant the peak reached around Week #30 at 475 and the two lower peaks that lie to its right and left. These are skinny shoulders, but such a formation is a sheer delight to a technician. Technicians believe that the market will be weak when prices break the neckline of the formation, which happened in this particular random sequence after "prices" broke down through 455 in Week #37; the market will be strong if prices break the neckline of an inverted

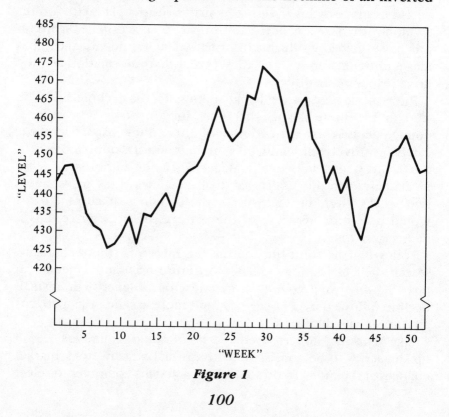

*Figure 1*

head-and-shoulders. William Scheinman, a well-known technician, recently remarked: "Even though the Dow Jones Industrial Average is having difficulty exceeding the 2650–2675 area, which is defined by the neckline of the inverted head-and-shoulders formation . . . we believe that market is ready to vault above these levels."[17]

Roberts suggests that just about all of the classical patterns of technical analysis could be generated by chance—"artificially by a suitable roulette wheel or random-number table."[18]

Carefully following the scheme laid out by Working, Roberts next plotted the weekly *changes* in his random series. When he did so, any resemblance to regularity or systematic patterns vanished, as shown in Figure 2. Roberts admits that "intensive and imaginative scrutiny would undoubtedly suggest some [patterns],"[19] but that scrutiny would have to be unusually imaginative. The graph shows a succession of wiggles.

Then Roberts plotted the weekly changes in the Dow Jones Industrial Average for the year 1956. The graph that emerged, shown in Figure 3, bears an arresting resemblance to the graph of the random series of weekly changes, despite somewhat greater dispersion between the big upward moves and the big downward moves. The graph of the weekly levels of the Dow Jones Average also bears a strong family resemblance to the weekly levels of the random numbers, even to the head-and-shoulders that developed between Week #10 and Week #20, shown in Figures 3 and 4.

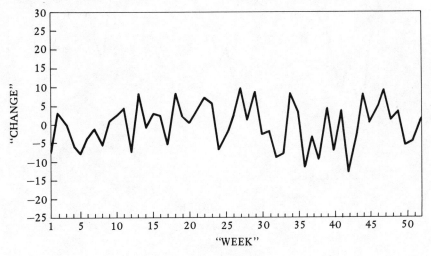

*Figure 2*

101

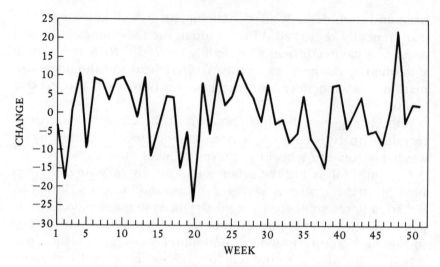

**Figure 3**

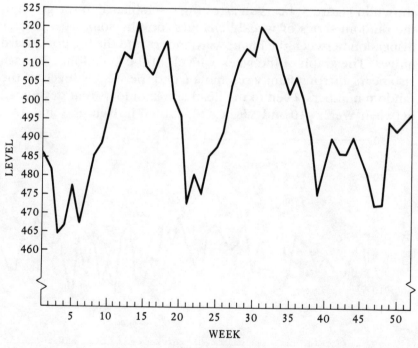

**Figure 4**

The results of Roberts's adherence to Working's methods were the same as Working's results. The weekly changes in stock prices—the very stuff from which technical analysts create their predictions of future price levels—were indistinguishable from the changes in the random series.

The second important article that appeared in 1959 was by M. F. M. Osborne, an eminent astrophysicist at the U.S. Naval Research Laboratory in Washington. Osborne's paper, "Brownian Motion in the Stock Market," appeared in the March-April 1959 issue of a highly technical Navy Department journal called *Operations Research*.

What was an astrophysicist up to in analyzing the behavior of stock market prices? And why did he present his findings in a journal that few if any stock market enthusiasts would be likely to see?

Osborne had begun his professional career in 1941 doing graduate work in astronomy and physics at the University of California at Berkeley. When war threatened, he moved to the Naval Research Laboratory in Washington to work on antisubmarine warfare and underwater explosions. Then, after the atomic bombs were dropped in 1945, Osborne found that "physicists could do no wrong" in selecting problems to work on—"a privilege which I enjoyed to the utmost."[20] His interest in the stock market was simply a byproduct of his interest in statistical techniques: "It occurred to me that it would be nice to examine a real 'slow motion' random process in detail, so you could see in detail what was going on. Stock market prices . . . were an obvious candidate, but I was quite surprised at the interest stirred up when I published that first article."[21]

It never occurred to Osborne to publish his paper in a financial journal: "I didn't know anything about them," he told me, "whereas at NRL there were groups involved in war games and submarine hunting strategies that involved operations research, so I think it [*Operations Research*] was a natural choice."[22] (This observation may help explain why Arthur Roy's experience as a gunnery officer led him to look into "safety first" in the process of selecting portfolios.)

Osborne's article is some thirty pages long. Believing that he was exploring uncharted territory, he includes only two references to other works, one a book on statistical astronomy and the other a book titled *The Mathematical Theory of Non-Uniform*

*Gases.* That paucity of references reveals his unfamiliarity with the limited research into stock market behavior that had already been done. Despite his attention to Brownian motion, he had never heard of Bachelier; and despite his focus on the random character of stock prices, Working, Kendall, and Roberts were strangers to him.

After the publication of his paper, Osborne received substantial feedback that broadened his knowledge of the subject. He published a related short piece about a year and a half later that included twenty-one citations to other writers. He lists Bachelier, Kendall, and Roberts, as well as works by two well-known Wall Street figures, the reporter Burton Crane and the technician John Magee. He also refers to Einstein's work of 1905 and later.

The declared purpose of Osborne's 1959 article was to show that percentage changes in stock prices have "a close analogy with the ensemble of coordinates of a large number of molecules."[23] Actually, his goal was a little more ambitious than that. He demonstrates that the statistical analysis normally applied to the study of an ensemble of molecules will be equally effective when applied to stock prices.

He begins by describing "a statistician, trained perhaps in astronomy and totally unfamiliar with finance."[24] His imaginary statistician studies a day's transactions in the *Wall Street Journal* and arrives at five important findings.

First, absolute stock prices—100, 52 3/4, 4 7/8—have no meaning in and of themselves. The amount investors want to invest is independent of the price of the stock; they simply buy fewer shares when the price is high than when it is low. *Changes* in prices do have meaning, however, because they represent variations in wealth. Osborne's statistician also reasoned that investors make decisions in terms of the *percentage* changes in prices rather than in terms of absolute prices.

Here Osborne's approach differs in an important way from Bachelier's. Bachelier had hypothesized that a stock was as likely to move up by five points as down by five points. Osborne concludes that "the sensation of profit (or loss) . . . between a $10 and an $11 price for a given stock, is equal to that for a change from $100 to $110."[25] Therefore, prices are as likely to rise by five *percent* as to fall by five *percent*.

Second, again unaware that he was echoing Bachelier, Osborne argues that prices represent decisions at those moments—and only at those moments—when the buyer expects a stock to rise in price and the seller expects it to fall: Transactions take place only when there is a difference of opinion. This means that, for the market as a whole, the expected price change is zero. The market is as likely to go up $x$ percent as down $x$ percent.

Third, Osborne's mathematical manipulations show that the range within which prices tend to fluctuate will "increase as the square root of the time interval"[26]—Brownian motion, precisely as Bachelier had prophesied.

Fourth, in a set of experiments with actual stock market data, Osborne confirms the hypothesis of Brownian motion, including percentage price changes over intervals of a day, a week, a month, two months, up to twelve years. He also finds that Cowles's long history of stock prices follows " . . . the square root of time diffusion law very nicely indeed."[27] Finally, he finds that distributions of the monthly changes in the Dow Jones Industrial Average from 1925 to 1956 "are quite comparable."[28]

The fifth finding made by Osborne's imaginary statistician is another example of how Osborne, working all by himself, confirmed the research conclusions of others.

In order to analyze the probabilities of outcomes under the random conditions of Brownian motion, Osborne describes a set of coin-tossing experiments. First he repeatedly tosses 2,000 pennies grouped in 1,000 pairs and analyzes the results to see how frequently two heads, two tails, or one of each turn up. Then he tries a second "ensemble," consisting of 1,000 pennies and one gold piece, and flips the gold piece with each of the 1,000 pennies.

The payoffs in terms of heads and tails are identical in the two experiments. The outcomes in terms of *money,* however, are entirely different. The results with the gold coin dominate the results with the pennies alone. Furthermore, ". . . we put forth the hypothesis, and we believe the data will support it, that [this] Model will represent the behavior of our ensemble of stock-market prices."[29]

Here Osborne anticipates in striking manner the concept developed by Markowitz and Sharpe of "the most important single influence" on the return from stock prices. When I asked Sharpe about this, he replied, "The Osborne piece definitely had the same idea and was, I presume, arrived at independently."[30]

By the time Osborne had published two follow-up articles, one in late 1959 and other in 1962, the astrophysicist had been converted into an enthusiastic researcher into "what appears superficially to be the epitome of unrelieved bedlam."[31] More than thirty years later, and now more than seventy years old, Osborne the astrophysicist is still investigating and reporting on Brownian motion in security prices. He is still convinced that the movements of stock prices are no more predictable than the movements of an "ensemble" of molecules.

He concludes his 1962 article with this stunning paragraph:

> The stock market is a gigantic decision-making phenomenon. It deserves scientific attention from those who would like to understand how decision making occurs, naturally, and in the large. As an economic phenomenon, we believe the market can reproduce in a few weeks a scaled version of supply-demand relations that would take many years to complete in a different setting.[32]

In the late 1950s Osborne stood as a lonely investigator into the behavior of the stock market. In the late 1950s, as I pointed out earlier, most economists were still ignorant of sophisticated statistical techniques, and the equipment to handle masses of data easily and inexpensively was not yet available. Cowles was a rare bird whose wealth put virtually unlimited resources at his disposal. Working, Kendall, and Osborne were mathematicians and statisticians, not economists.

Yet even Kendall, who was never dismayed by the quantity of material he had to process, observes at the end of his 1953 article that the computations involved in his research were "severe." He gives a hint of what the job was like when he acknowledges the help of two women who "carried [the computations] out with zeal and gratifying cheerfulness."[33] And a reference to punch cards tells us that he had a computer to do the grunt work.

By the end of the 1950s, rapid advances in computer technology were making data manipulation faster, cheaper, and more effective. This development was stimulating for younger faculty members though troublesome for their older colleagues. Economist Eugene Fama, who earned his doctorate at Chicago in 1964, recalls those days with a gleam in his eye. The IBM 709, which he characterizes as "the first serious machine," had just become available. Fama claims that for a long time he and a member of the physics department were the only people at the university who knew how to use it. "We could just pop the data in," he told me. "We were like kids in a candy store."[34]

A pioneering study in the analysis of large quantities of statistical data appeared in 1961 in the *Industrial Management Review,* a journal published by the Sloan School of Business at Massachusetts Institute of Technology. The author of this paper, Sidney Alexander, describes an effort he made to find a winning strategy for a speculator, investor, or economist who is convinced that stock prices do *not* fluctuate randomly.

Alexander was an economist, the first we have encountered in the research into the predictability of stock prices. In the late 1930s, when he was in his mid-forties, he had enjoyed the unusual opportunity of studying with Keynes at Cambridge. Unlike the mathematicians who had perceived the stock market as nothing more than a case study to prove some unrelated point, Alexander was interested in the stock market for its own sake.

The title of Alexander's article, "Price Movements in Speculative Markets: Trends or Random Walks," sums up its subject matter. His aim was to discover whether stock prices display trends that investors can identify in advance. After the fact, investors can readily see that the market has moved broadly in both direction. Before the fact, however, they are always uncertain whether an observed trend is likely to continue or go into reverse, or whether a price movement counter to a trend is just a twitch or the beginning of a new trend in the opposite direction. This is the same dilemma that Kendall sought to resolve.

In short, asks Alexander, are stock prices predictable, or are they ruled by the Demon of Chance? How investors answer that question determines whether they will choose to buy and hold for the long pull, or will try to swing between cash and stocks as the market fluctuates.

Investors who opt for buy-and-hold say that all they can forecast is that stocks are a good investment over the long run. This attitude is typical among many individual investors. Some simply have no taste for shifting their holdings around. They see no advantage in doing so. Others have inherited their stocks and feel sentimental about them, or else they have old holdings with big unrealized gains and are reluctant to incur the capital gains taxes involved in selling.

Swingers take an entirely different approach. They must be able to spot the very moment when a trend begins, when a trend is continuing in force, and when a trend is about to go into reverse. Otherwise they will have no chance of outperforming buy-and-hold.

Alexander asserts that investors can accomplish this feat only if other investors have "imperfect knowledge of these facts"[35] —if they are what today we call "noise traders." No one can win if everyone receives all the necessary information, understands it completely, and acts on it at once. When a given piece of information prompts an almost simultaneous response by investors—as when a bank announces a huge write-off for loan losses or an oil company comes up with a big drilling hit in an unexploited area— even the cleverest analyst of balance sheets or with the keenest eye for the charts will fail to do as well as the investor who simply buys and holds. At least, that is how a perfect market operates.

Profitable trading depends on imperfections, which develop only when other investors are slower than the swinger to receive information, draw erroneous conclusions from it, or delay acting on it. Gradual recognition and understanding of the facts is what makes for trends instead of bedlam.

Professionals insist that they can win when they invest actively, as opposed to buying and holding a broadly diversified portfolio, because they can distinguish trends from noise and make better sense than amateurs out of new information. Moreover, because they are full-time players tuned in to all the smart brokers and analysts, professionals are confident that they can act fast enough to beat the others to the gun.

Alexander contrasts this view with the view of the academics who hold that the best way to anticipate future price movements is to toss a coin. A zero expectation of gain means that prices are likely to move in random fashion. But such prices are unpredictable.

Alexander focuses on what he defines as filter strategies. In a filter strategy, the investor buys after stock prices have moved up by some predetermined amount and then sells after they have fallen by some predetermined amount. If a trend persists strongly enough, investors should be able make consistent profits by buying in after they see that stocks have started to move up and by selling off after they see that stocks have started to move down.

Alexander examined daily data for the Standard & Poor's Industrial Average from 1897 to 1959 and recorded the outcomes of acting after the onset of various combinations of trends, long and short, such as moves up and down of 1 percent, 3 percent, 5 percent, and so on, all the way up to 50 percent. He then compared those outcomes with the return the investor would have earned by just buying stocks at the beginning of the period and holding them until the end.

Alexander came up with positive results: "[A] move, once initiated, tends to persist."[36] Bravo! Was this a ray of hope for professional investors? Did Alexander provide the evidence to consign Bachelier and his successors to oblivion?

Alas, this is not the end of the story. If it were, this would be THE END, with Alexander as the unquestioned hero. But criticisms of Alexander's procedure, and some second thoughts of his own, led him to go back to the drawing board and try again. In 1964, he published a second article on the subject, with the same title but with addendum "No. 2." Here his conclusions are much sadder:

> The big bold profits of Paper I must be replaced with rather puny ones. The question still remains whether even these profits could plausibly be the result of a random walk. But I must confess that the fun has gone out of it somehow. . . .
>
> I should advise any reader who is interested only in practical results, and who is not a floor trader and so must pay commissions, to turn to other sources on how to beat buy and hold.[37]

By the end of the 1950s, a huge collection of facts about the behavior of stock prices had been gathered. Those facts demonstrated consistently that changes in stock prices appear so irregular that they defy the forecasters who are so intent on predicting them. With this ammunition, the investigators of market behavior shot a gaping hole into the fabric of Wall Street lore. Yet it was not a shot heard around the world.

Wall Street paid no heed. Between Kendall's research in 1953 and Alexander's in 1959, stock prices more than doubled, insurance company holdings of stocks tripled, pension fund holdings went from less than $1 billion to nearly $12 billion, college endowments and foundations about quadrupled their positions, and individual holdings of shares in mutual funds and investment companies rose more than sixfold. The number of individual shareholders grew from 6.5 million to 12.5 million over these years, or from about one out of every sixteen adults in the United States to more than one out of every ten.

All these investors were coming into the market in the expectation of getting rich. No one was likely to listen to strange tales spun by a bunch of academic mathematicians and economists with no investment experience.

If the research provided by the academics was going to have any impact at all on the real world of investing, somebody would have to go beyond Bachelier's obscure mathematics and the bare statistical cases laid out by researchers from Cowles to Alexander. Only then would investors be able to make sense of the seemingly senseless patterns cut by stock prices. Only then would it become clear why the stock market can defy the efforts of so many forecasters, professional as well as amateur.

The shift from mathematicians and statisticians to economists and finance specialists was by no means inevitable. Most courses in finance up to the late 1950s to early 1960s had had nothing to do with the behavior of the stock price. Roberts himself refers to "the traditional academic suspicion about the stock market as an object of scholarly research."[38] Instead, the emphasis had been on the effectiveness of security analysis and the use of accounting data, capital budgeting, and proper methods for valuing corporate assets and earning power.

This was hardly exciting stuff. Arnold Sametz, one of the senior members of the faculty at New York University's School of Business, who started teaching in 1957 fresh from the Princeton economics department, has commented that "If I had known how 1920s-like the contents of the finance courses were, I might have been scared off!"[39]

The investment course at Harvard Business School in the 1950s had so few takers that it was taught at noontime so that it would not take up precious classroom space at prime time. In a reference to Arthur Koestler's gloomy novel about political prisoners in Stalinist Russia, the course became known as "Darkness at Noon."

Professors teaching investment had not begun to ask the question about accounting data and corporate valuation techniques that really counted: *Even if you had this information, could you use it to achieve superior investment results?*

During the 1960s, answers to this question proliferated. It took a new group of scholars with more interest in economic theory than in statistical bean-counting to supply the answers. Wall Street was still reluctant to listen, but by the end of the decade the sound of the distant drummers on the campuses had become so loud that investors could no longer ignore it.

# Chapter
# 6

# Anticipating Prices
# Properly

*Future events . . . cast their shadows before them.*

How can we make sense of the obstreperous behavior of stock prices that Bachelier, Working, Kendall, and others discovered? To answer that question, we would need someone who can bring rich theoretical insights into the forces that determine prices in competitive markets—the whole gamut of concepts that fall under the rubric of the laws of supply and demand. That scholar would also need a feel for the rowdy world of Wall Street and the commodity exchanges, and the ability to adjust, reformulate, and qualify the neat theorems in the economics textbooks to fit the realities of the financial markets.

Fortunately, the right man showed up for the job: Paul Samuelson of MIT, whom a student once described as "a human mainframe." So compelling were the prospects of a theory of capital markets—and the impact of those markets on the world of output, employment, and prices—that they attracted years of intellectual effort from this most famous economist of our time. Cowles, Working, and Kendall are Samuelson's heroes, and to them he swears undying allegiance. The theory he developed, with Bachelier's powerful inspiration, illuminated their masses of numbers and turned out to be a thing of clarity and beauty. It also sent shockwaves through the world of professional investors.

Most people know Samuelson through his textbook, *Economics,* first published in 1948 and now in its thirteenth edition. Though he has written countless books and articles, Samuelson particularly enjoys the fame, influence—and revenue—this book has brought him. Amending Shelley's boast, "Poets are the unacknowledged legislatures of the world," Samuelson once observed, "Let those who will, write the nation's laws, if I can write its textbooks."[1]

Samuelson classifies himself as a theorist, but he has been busy in the work-a-day world too. He has, in his own words, given "economic tutorials" to the likes of Adlai Stevenson, Averill Harriman, and, especially, John F. Kennedy. Although he recalls that, "Moses-like, I did not pass into the promised land beyond the Potomac"[2] during the Kennedy administration, he admits to serving as its *éminence grise.* His column in *Newsweek* from 1966 to 1981 kept him in the public eye. In 1970, he was the first United States economist to win the Nobel Prize in economic sciences. He served for many years as a trustee and member of the Finance Committee of the College Retirement Equities Fund, a huge college teacher's pension fund also known by its acronym CREF.

Samuelson takes a dim view of most portfolio managers. He has only scorn for those who claim that their skill in selecting stocks enables them to outperform investors who simply buy and hold a well-diversified portfolio of equities. In the first issue of the *Journal of Portfolio Management* in the fall of 1974, he minced no words:

> They also serve who only sit and hold; but I suppose the fees to be earned by such sensible and prosaic behavior are less than from essaying to give it that old post-college try. . . .
>
> But a respect for evidence compels me to incline toward the hypothesis that most portfolio decision makers should go out of business—take up plumbing, teach Greek, or help produce the annual GNP by serving as corporate executives. Even if this advice to drop dead is good advice, it obviously is not counsel that will be eagerly followed. Few people will commit suicide without a push.[3]

Samuelson was born in Gary, Indiana, in 1915. His father was a druggist who prospered as Gary's steel mills roared through World War I. Samuelson did his undergraduate work at the University of Chicago, following in the footsteps of "all the bright people in that area during the Hoover depression."[4] It was there that he discovered economics: "The first drink from the economic textbooks [was] like the Prince's kiss to Sleeping Beauty. . . . The terrain was strewn with beautiful theorems begging to be picked up and arranged in unified order."[5]

Although Samuelson loved Chicago, he left that Olympus "for a few pieces of silver" in September 1935 after winning a generous graduate fellowship with the unusual requirement that the recipient leave home. His professors urged him to go to Columbia, which was then heavy in mathematics and statistics, but he chose to go to Harvard "in search of ivy."[6]

By the time he was 25, he was already famous for having published more articles than he was years old. Being prolific seems to have come easily to him. (He is the father of six children, including triplets.) His *Collected Scientific Papers,* which include his work from 1937 to 1986, run to five volumes. They include 388 articles filling 4,665 pages—and a sixth volume is on its way. *Paul Samuelson and Modern Economic Theory,* a celebration of his contribution to economic theory written in 1983 by his contemporaries, extols his accomplishments in ten fields of economics: welfare, consumption, international trade, money, capital theory, policy, Ricardo, Marx, and finance. *Paul A. Samuelson: Critical Reassessments,* published in 1989, contains over a hundred appraisals of his contributions to economics.

Samuelson came to love Harvard almost as much as he loved Chicago. Nevertheless, in 1940, he gave up the "princely post of instructor in the Department of Economics . . . packed up his pencil, and moved three miles down the Charles River to MIT, where he lived happily ever after."[7] Samuelson has flourished at MIT and has helped its economics department flourish as well.

During World War II he moved over to MIT's Radiation Laboratory to work on radar-servomechanisms for fire control against aircraft, primarily for the Navy. (This was a switch: Arthur Roy and M. F. M. Osborne had gone from gunnery to finance!) In his usual succinct tone of self admiration, Samuelson informed me that "the Rad Lab won the war."[8]

How could Samuelson have left the Harvard economics department, which was nearing its zenith of talent and influence, for MIT, where economics was held in much lower esteem? Samuelson says he made the move for two reasons,

First, "I got a better offer."[9]

There was a deeper reason. Although no one, least of all himself, thought that any lack of merit would keep him from a chair in economic theory at Harvard, he felt that his departure "would not cause irreparable grief." Why? Was it anti-Semitism? Samuelson's reply to that question in 1983 was: "I suppose that would be the *simplest* explanation . . . but if a simple hypothesis cannot explain all the facts, I don't think it mandatory to embrace it." He points out that, even though American universities before World War II were anti-Semitic to a degree that would hardly seem possible today, a distinguished non-Jewish contemporary who suffered only from "the disability of being from Kansas" failed to receive tenure at Harvard at the time. Samuelson sums up the matter by citing "the failure of any one factor to account for the richness of reality."[10]

Samuelson dabbled for a time in the stock market and recalls that that experience was important to his subsequent theoretical work. Around 1950, he subscribed to a service called "The RHM Warrant and Low-Price Stock Survey." Warrants are securities that give the investor the right to buy a specified number of shares of a stock at a stated price and to hold those rights for a stated period of time or in perpetuity.

The mathematics that determines the price of a warrant sometimes makes the appreciation potential of the warrant greater than the appreciation potential of the stock itself and at the same time makes the downside risk of the warrant less than the downside risk of the stock. The RHM service Samuelson subscribed to made a specialty of touting such advantages, and at first he thought he had found a free lunch. And the subscription cost only $125 a year! "All I wanted," he recalls, "was one good idea net of the bad ones."[11]

He soon realized that if the service was making its subscribers rich, the subscription would cost many times $125. Moreover, he could not figure out why the owner of a warrant would sell it at a price that would give the buyer a free lunch. Somehow the price of a warrant would have to bring equal benefits to both sides, or no transaction would take place.

Samuelson's interest in the theoretical aspects of capital markets was further stimulated by a doctoral thesis he had suggested to one of his students, Richard Kruizenga, on the pricing of contracts on options. Options are financial instruments, also known as puts and calls, that are almost identical to warrants. In 1956, when Kruizenga was just about to wrap up three years of work on his dissertation, Jimmie Savage stumbled across Bachelier's work, brought it to Samuelson's attention, and torpedoed poor Kruizenga's claim to originality. As I have mentioned, Bachelier's idea of the random character of price movements in financial markets had a profound influence on Samuelson.

Samuelson did spot something that Bachelier had missed. Bachelier had hypothesized that security prices were as likely to go up as they were to go down and that, with the passage of time, the range over which they fluctuated would expand according to the square root of time. Samuelson describes such views of random movements as "ridiculous . . . absurdities"[12] because security prices cannot fall below zero.

The zero downside limit exists because the owners of corporations—that is, the stockholders—have limited liability. By law, they cannot lose more than they have invested, and they have no obligation to pay off the company's debts. That is why securities can be traded in markets where buyers and sellers know absolutely nothing about each other: neither buyer nor seller assumes any unlimited or unspecified liabilities when buying the other's assets. The system would grind to a halt if every seller had to run a credit check on every interested buyer. A stock selling for $15 a share can go down by no more than fifteen points, but it can go up to infinity. There can be no symmetry of expectations when the upside is infinity and the downside is zero.

Samuelson's solution to Bachelier's oversight is closely related to Osborne's emphasis on using percentages rather than absolute changes. (The papers were published at almost the same moment.) Osborne had little familiarity with the financial literature when he wrote his first article in 1959. So he knew nothing about either Bachelier or Samuelson at the time. Until Osborne published his article, Samuelson had known nothing about him either.

Samuelson's serious interest in the behavior of security prices was triggered by the news of Kendall's tumultuous reception at the Royal Statistical Society in 1953. He learned of the event from a young Dutch colleague, Henry Houthakker, who had attended the session with his fellow Cantabridgian, S. J. Prais. When I wrote to Prais in London and asked him to tell me more about what had happened, he returned my letter with a barely legible pencil scribble at the bottom: "I do not remember anything about this." When I showed the response to Samuelson, he remarked that this was "like the case of the guard at the Crucifixion who could remember only the bracelet that the Thief wore!"[13]

Samuelson was enthralled by Houtthakker's description of pandemonium provoked by Kendall's statement that the behavior of speculative prices looked as though the Demon of Chance had drawn a series of random numbers. He took heart at the way the economists and statisticians had reacted to Kendall as an upstart invader of their turf and an enemy agnostic. Delighted, Samuelson said to himself: "Work the other side of the street! The nonpredictability of future prices from past and present prices is the sign, not of failure of economic law, but the triumph of economic law after competition has done its best."[14]

He recognized the jumble that stock prices presented as an unexplored variation on a theme that runs throughout economic theory—the difference between price and value. From Adam Smith onward (not the fellow on TV who puts the name in quotation marks, but the eighteenth-century author of *The Wealth of Nations*), all the great economists have wrestled with this problem in one form or another; it plays a central role in Karl Marx's model of capitalism.

Economists agree that "value" refers to something that lies behind, or beneath, the prices observed in the marketplace; prices gyrate around "true value." But what is this "true value"? The question is not unlike the exchange between three baseball umpires trying to describe how they distinguish between a ball and a strike: "I call them as I see them," said the first. "I call them as they are," replied the second. "They ain't nothing till I call them," declared the third. Is value a subjective quantity? Or is it a quantity that cannot be measured except by some objective standard? Or does value emerge only when a transaction takes place in which buyers and sellers agree on a price?[15]

In theory, competition is always driving the price of a commodity to the point where price and value are identical. If wheat is selling for $2.50 a bushel and costs only $1.50 to produce, consumers obviously value wheat so highly that it is relatively scarce. As a result, wheat farming will be so profitable that farmers will start planting marginal land that produces less wheat per acre, pushing the cost of production toward $2.50 a bushel. On the other hand, if consumer taste shifts from wheat to corn and the price of wheat falls to $1.00, many farmers will give up wheat farming and the supply will decline until the only survivors are the farmers with the lowest costs of production.

The reason stock prices jump around so much, and the reason stocks are considered such a risky investment, is that *there is nothing clear-cut about their value.* Is General Motors worth $50 a share because the accountants, in their wisdom, add up GM's assets, deduct its liabilities, divide by the number of shares outstanding, and find that the difference is $50? Or is it worth only $40 because a security analyst applying John Burr Williams's model finds $40 to be the discounted present value of GM's future cash flows? Or is it worth perhaps $60, because there is a rumor that the hot mutual fund manager or the latest takeover artist is buying it, and everyone knows that what they buy is bound to go higher?

The most pessimistic and disturbing, and the most amusing, answer to these questions came from Keynes, who was no mean speculator in his own right. Published in 1936, Keynes's sarcastic indictment of the stock market appears in a chapter in *The General Theory of Employment, Interest, and Money,* in which he uses the phrase "prospective yield" to refer to the intrinsic value of an asset:

> It is not sensible to pay 25 for an investment of which you believe the prospective yield to justify a value of 30, if you also believe that the market will value it at 20 three months hence. . . . Human nature desires quick results, there is a peculiar zest in making money quickly, and remoter gains are discounted by the average man at a very high rate.
> It is, so to speak, a game of Snap, of Old Maid, of Musical Chairs—a pastime in which he is victor who says Snap neither too soon nor too late, who passes the Old Maid to his neighbor before the game is over, who secures a chair for himself when the music stops.[16]

Although Samuelson is probably Keynes's most distinguished disciple, he rejected Keynes's sour view of the market as little more than a casino. He found more substance in the market process. His two most important papers on the subject appeared in 1957, in a German scholarly journal, and in 1965. The title of the 1965 paper, which appeared in MIT's *Industrial Management*

*Review,* reveals its message: "Proof That Properly Anticipated Prices Fluctuate Randomly."

Samuelson begins by introducing the expression "shadow prices" to characterize so-called true values, or what Keynes refers to as "prospective yield." He admits that these are theoretical prices—"prices never seen on land or sea outside of economics libraries." Nevertheless, even though they cannot be observed or calculated, Samuelson insists we must assume that they exist: there is such a thing as intrinsic value.[17]

But if value hides in the shadows, how can we bring it to light? Echoing Bachelier, Samuelson suggests a startling answer: Perhaps the best estimates of shadow prices are the prices set in the marketplace, every minute of every trading day. Those prices may not be precisely equal to the shadow prices, but no other estimate of intrinsic value is likely to be more accurate than what buyers and sellers agree on in the marketplace.

This is a strong statement—the sort of statement that has turned many professional investors away from academic theories of capital markets. Those professionals remain convinced that persistent differences between intrinsic value and market prices do exist and that they can be identified by skilled managers. They cite the enormous premiums over market prices produced by takeovers during the 1980s, or Polaroid's fall from a high of 150 in 1972 to 14 in the crash of 1974.

Samuelson points to what Bachelier, Working, and Kendall had discovered about the behavior of prices in the markets for commodities and for stocks and bonds. In these markets, buyers and sellers are engaged in constant, intense competition, each trying to make a more accurate bet on the future than the others. If they have reason to expect General Motors to sell at a higher price in the future, the price will go up today. If the guru on Wall $treet Week says that mortgage rates will soon fall to 9 percent, the young couple buying a new home will refuse to take out a mortgage currently offered at 10 percent. Farmers will not sell their winter wheat for delivery next summer at $2.00 if they hear that the crop has been poor and that the price next summer is expected to be $2.25.

Echoing Bachelier, Samuelson wrote:

> We would expect people in the marketplace, in pursuit of avid and intelligent self-interest, to take account of those

elements of future events that in a probabililty sense may be discerned to be casting their shadows before them. (Because past events cast "their" shadows after them, future events can be said to cast their shadows before them.)[18]

Or, as he put it to me in an interview, "When the broker calls to say 'Hurry, hurry, hurry!' that's nonsense. If the stock were sure to go up, it would already be up."[19]

Samuelson puts great stress on the importance of information. No investor in stocks, no buyer of commodities for future delivery, and no lender or borrower can possibly arrive at a decision without information of some kind. It was the hunger for information in the 1880s that kept the boys rushing around Wall Street to deliver their tissue-and carbon reports, making handsome fortunes for Kiernan, Dow, Jones, and Bergstrasser. Today, whether it be a car buyer looking at the new-model Chevrolet truck, a takeover by China of Hong Kong textile supplies, or the downgrading of New York State's credit, no participants in a speculative market will buy or sell without what they perceive to be the relevant facts. Jack Treynor, long-time editor of the *Financial Analysts Journal,* once said that you may not get rich by using all the available information, but you surely will get poor if you don't.

When information dries up and gives way to uncertainty, the markets go dead. But just drop a hint about a company that some conglomerate is eyeing, or about the weather in Peru, or about the mindset of Japan's new finance minister, and volume will pick up and prices will move. Like a pebble dropped in a still pond, a scrap of information will send ripples in every direction.

Although new information is what triggers a change in prices, it arrives with no predictable pattern. One day the papers are bulging with it. Another day there seems to be nothing interesting to report. Some information is world-shattering. Some is trifling. No wonder properly anticipated prices fluctuate randomly.

Under these conditions, what can an investor expect to earn by buying an asset? The answer, to repeat the conclusion reached by Bachelier and Osborne, is—zero! Or, as Samuelson puts it, "No easy pickings, no sure-thing gains."[20]

That is something of an oversimplification. Samuelson recognizes that people will not invest without hope of at least some minimum return on their investment—higher on risky securities, lower on safer ones. It has to be a positive-sum game to some extent, or else no one would play. The issue is not whether the positive sum exists, but whether we can predict who is going to end up possessing it. Samuelson maintains that its ultimate ownership is a random outcome.

But where does that positive sum come from in the first place? From the growth of the economy itself, whose fruits must accrue to someone, somewhere, some time. In subsequent elaborations of Samuelson's ideas by others, the expected minimum return to investors becomes an integral part of the theory of how financial markets work and how investors should balance their decisions between risk and return. When Samuelson echoes Bachelier in stipulating that the expected return will be zero, he is careful to emphasize that it is the excess return over the minimum that is likely to be zero; it is the allocation of the excess return that is likely to be random.

Moreover, by "No sure pickings" Samuelson does not mean that the excess return in speculative markets is going to be zero, or even negative, every day or every decade, or that some players may not earn and keep a fat profit. He means that the excess return is going to be zero on the average and over the long run. In markets as savagely competitive as the financial and commodity markets, outguessing all the other players with any degree of consistency is truly a challenging task. The unpredictability of speculative prices is proof that they are predictions of themselves!

Samuelson has returned to the riddle of speculative price behavior many times over the years. He says he always has an inventory of questions in his mind, some of which "slumber in that limbo for two decades. There is no hurry; they will keep."[21] He remarks:

> Finance was my Sunday painting. . . . Sunday painters are not quite in the Club. They publish in unrefereed journals and are not read much. However, by word of mouth and letter, through visiting lectures and distributed blue ditto [a primitive form of copy] manuscripts, I kept . . . the Club informed and honest. Like Frank Sinatra, I did it my way.[22]

In lectures and graduate seminars at MIT, Yale, and Carnegie Tech, Samuelson has explored how human behavior shapes expectations and how expectations shape speculative prices. He has shared his thoughts with hundreds of economists, many of whom have built other theoretical constructs on the foundations he laid out.

One of the most important of these theoretical innovations is known as the Rational Expectations Hypothesis. The concept of rational expectations derives from the great nineteenth-century classical economic theories of Adam Smith, David Ricardo, John Stuart Mill, and Alfred Marshall. These theories share the assumption that most human beings have stable, well-defined preferences, and that they make rational choices consistent with those preferences. Rational expectations theory puts another layer on the classical view of human behavior by assuming that the Darwinian survivors who win out typically take a view of the future that is thoughtful rather than visceral, even if not necessarily accurate.

Though this hypothesis was developed by others during the 1960s, Samuelson gave it its embryonic prologue in his 1957 paper on the theory of speculation. He mentioned the idea again, calling it "Balanced Ignorance," upon becoming a member of the American Philosophical Society. "My pearls were well received," he recalls.[23]

The views of the classical economists underlie the rationale for the invisible hand that guides the free-enterprise system of competitive markets and private ownership of the means of production, propelled by workers, employers, and customers free to seek their own self-interest. In theory, at least, this system is more likely to arrive at optimal outcomes and bring greater satisfaction to a larger number of people than any other economic system.

Speculative capital markets, despite their occasional penchant for distorting values, probably come as close as markets anywhere to approaching this ideal set of conditions. But Samuelson, who is a skeptic about pure versions of the theory of rational expectations, argues that the manner in which speculative markets emulate the textbooks cannot be generalized into an accurate description of how markets in the rest of the economy behave.

Samuelson's own judgment about his analysis of speculative markets is mixed. Nearly twenty years after he developed the central idea that investors "in pursuit of avid and intelligent self-interest" would produce prices that fluctuate randomly, he commented that "the Theorem is so general that I must confess to having oscillated over the years in my own mind between regarding it as trivially obvious (and almost trivially vacuous) and regarding it as remarkably sweeping. Such perhaps is characteristic of basic results.'' Later he described his reaction to the notion that actual prices in the marketplace are the best estimate of shadow prices, or intrinsic values, as one of "initial shock—and then, upon reflection, that it is obvious [but] it was not a finding of fact. It is a purely deductive, theoretical piece."[24]

Still, Samuelson the pragmatist is eager to point out that his description of how speculative markets work may not "plausibly obtain" at all times and in all cases. He cites substantial evidence that prices are more readily predictable when there are no high-powered "analyst-whizzes" following a company, or only a few, than when there are many. These kinds of conditions were violated in the wild and woolly markets of the second half of the nineteenth century, when security analysis was an unknown art and when price manipulation was far easier than it is today. Even today, neglected stocks in the backwaters of the markets offer nineteeth-century-type opportunities, but surprises among big, actively traded stocks are so rare that they make headlines when they occur.[25]

To avoid sounding dogmatic, Samuelson makes another, more important point. Since the 1970s, he has distinguished between the difficulty of predicting the prices of individual securities and the difficulty of predicting the behavior of entire markets—stocks versus bonds, stocks in New York versus stocks in Tokyo, or junk bonds versus obligations of the U.S. government.

If investors were for some reason to place too high a value on Bristol Myers or IBM, Samuelson is convinced that the aberration would be extremely short-lived, because the professional analysts would sharpen their pencils and call it to the attention of their clients. But if *all* the 500 stocks in the Standard & Poor's Composite were to soar because investors become euphorically optimistic about the future, Samuelson believes that they would lose their shirts arguing with the tape. The Bachelier-type forces that make individual stock prices so difficult to predict do not necessarily operate on aggregate equity values. The history of the markets demonstrates that those kinds of bubbles—bloated and burst—are all too common.

Violations of Samuelson's proposition that speculative prices will fluctuate randomly but will best reflect intrinsic values are attracting lively interest among some of the most serious students of markets. Fischer Black, now of Goldman Sachs but formerly a colleague of Samuelson's at MIT and professor of finance at the University of Chicago, devoted his entire presidential address to the American Finance Association in 1986 to this topic. Titled "Noise," the paper is a lively description of how far real-world markets, even competitive markets, fall short of Samuelson's conditions.

Black contrasts noise with information. Noise arises as people buy and sell on what they *believe* is information but is really rumor, badly analyzed information, misinformation, or hunch. Confused by the noise, investors respond to their brokers' urgings to "Hurry, hurry!" Black suggests that many people trade on noise simply because they enjoy fooling around and trading on hunches. Others are not even aware that they are trading on noise—they believe they are trading on reliable information.

"Noise is what makes our observations imperfect," Black points out. Noise gets in the way of keeping observed prices in line with shadow prices or intrinsic values. Research leads to reliable and relevant conclusions only rarely, "because of the noise that creeps in at every step." Even people who have accurate information are uncertain about whether they are trading on information or on noise. The whizzes themselves seldom pass on recommendations to their clients without including qualifications and escape clauses.[26]

This state of affairs has two important consequences, one bad and one good.

First, noise obstructs rational decision-making: "Because there is so much noise in the world, people adopt rules of thumb. They share their rules of thumb with each other, and very few people have enough experience with interpreting noisy evidence to see that the rules are too simple."[27]

This tendency to oversimplify and to confuse cause and effect leads Black to doubt whether anyone can draw reliable conclusions from many of the studies that purport to be scientific. He could hardly have delighted his audience of academics at the American Finance Association when he declared:

No matter how many variables we include . . . there always seem to be potentially important variables that we have omitted, possibly because they too are unobservable. . . . In the end, a theory is accepted not because it is confirmed by conventional empirical tests, but because researchers persuade one another that the theory is correct and relevant.[28]

The good news is that noise trading is the primary motivation for market activity. When traders act on noise, they push prices away from intrinsic values. And when that happens, people with reliable information have an advantage. It may even pay them to spend money, time, and effort to seek out good information to guide them. Noise trading makes the market lively and liquid. People who need cash can raise it readily and those with cash to invest can put it to work promptly.

Were it not for the role of noise in creating lively markets, assets would be priced only rarely and with large discontinuities between transactions. The whole process of valuing real assets as well as financial ones, of arriving at rational investment decisions, of raising new capital, and of appraising the future would come to a stop. If the stock and bond markets were clones of the market for homes or office buildings, they could hardly function. Black sums it up: "Noise trading provides the missing ingredient."[29]

Black's analysis raises an interesting question about the impact on the market of people like Ivan Boesky, who are usually painted as villains because they trade on inside information. SEC regulations forbid anyone from trading on undisclosed information that would have a "material" effect on the price of a stock. The theory behind this rule is that everyone who buys or sells should have the same information, that the playing field should be level. Otherwise, when the inside information hits the markets later on, those who traded on it will enjoy a windfall at the expense of those who bought from them or sold to them.

But the case is more complicated. Suppose that the people with inside information religiously obey the rule, refraining from trading and from disclosing the information. Inside information is almost always good information. If people with inside information keep it to themselves and fail to act on it, they will not be driving market prices toward their shadow prices and there will be that much more noise in the market.

Thus does well-meaning regulation often lead to unexpected and undesirable consequences.

# Chapter
# 7

# The Search for High P.Q.

*215 egotistical orangutans with 20 straight winning flips.*

The man who went furthest to take Samuelson's ideas into richer territory was Eugene Fama, a third-generation Italian-American from Boston. Like Samuelson, Fama wanted to consolidate what was known about the behavior of stock prices into a comprehensive theory that would explain why prices appear to fluctuate randomly. Samuelson refers to Fama as a "remarkable fellow."[1]

Their lives and personalities contrast in many ways. Born in 1939, Fama is 24 years Samuelson's junior. Both men are thin and wiry, but Samuelson is blonde and blue-eyed, while Fama is dark with brown eyes. Samuelson grew up in an affluent background where intellectual achievement was expected; Fama was educated in a parochial school and was the first member of his family to go to college. Samuelson went to the University of Chicago, where "all the bright people" went, and his family paid his college expenses; Fama had to work while attending Tufts, a good Boston-based college but hardly a focal point for aspiring scholars.

Both men are irrepressible tennis enthusiasts. They played against each other on one occasion, but neither told me who won.

Unlike Samuelson, Fama never had the sense that economics was going to be his ultimate destiny. His great love at college was football and baseball, and his major was in French. He was elected three times to the Society of Scholars, which was made up of the two tops students in the sophomore, junior, and senior classes, and in his senior year he won the annual award as the school's outstanding student-athlete.

Then he got married, and earning power became more important. "I figured out that French wasn't going to make it," he told me. "Anyway, that was just working on other people's ideas instead of developing your own."[2]

Fama earned extra money at college by working with Harry Ernst, a professor who published a stock market letter that touted stocks on the basis of their price momentum. The notion that trends, once in place, would continue was precisely what Sidney Alexander was soon to prove valueless. Fama's job was to find workable buy-and-sell signals based on Ernst's system. Unlike Alexander, he had no computers to help him in this tiresome analysis; the only tools he used to prepare his graphs were a hand-cranked Monroe calculator and some sharp pencils.

Although Fama's efforts to develop profitable trading rules were by no means unsuccessful, the ones he found worked only on the old data, not on the new. He did not realize it at the time, but his frustrating experience was shared by many highly motivated investors seeking ways to beat the market. All too often, backtests give every promise of success but prove disappointing when investors try to apply them in real time. The environment shifts, market responses slow down or speed up, or too many people follow the same strategy and end up competing away one another's potential profits.

Like Alfred Cowles before him, Fama grew curious about why ideas that seem good on paper produce such disappointing results when real money is riding on them. Armed with the information on market prices he had acquired while working for Ernst, and now skillful in gathering and interpreting stock price data, Fama decided to go to business school to find out what was really going on.

His first thought was to go to Harvard. It was close by and its reputation was beyond question. Most of his Tufts professors were Harvard men, but, to his surprise, they urged him to go to the University of Chicago instead. He was, they told him, "more intellectual than the typical Harvard type."[3]

In 1964, after earning his doctorate at Chicago, Fama was invited to join the faculty as assistant professor of finance. Seeking a subject to teach, he went to his department chairman, Merton Miller, who had done pioneering work on the relationship between security market valuation and the capital structure of corporations. Miller's advice was: "Just teach what is not being taught."[4]

At the time, Chicago offered little on the theory of financial markets or portfolio composition. Fama also found that few of the professors even knew how to use a computer. Standard courses in accounting, corporate finance, and security valuation made up most of the finance curriculum. These courses offered no challenge to Fama, so he decided to teach the graduate school's first course on the theories of Harry Markowitz. Despite the innovative character of Markowitz's writings, and despite his association with Chicago, his work was virtually unknown when Fama first brought it to the attention of the finance department and its students.

Fama himself had taken none of the conventional finance courses, nor has he ever taken any basic courses in mathematics, having joined with two Chicago colleagues in teaching the material to one another. "I just read the books," he remarks.[5]

With a bull market that was now fifteen years old, the faculties of both the business school and the economics department were showing heightened interest in the behavior of the stock market. Fama found the atmosphere stimulating* and he co-authored several articles with Chicago colleagues during the 1960s.

Fama found one aspect of the Chicago environment especially congenial. Unlike the more theory-oriented atmosphere at MIT, where Paul Samuelson had developed his ideas about speculative prices, Chicago attracted scholars who were keenly interested in collecting facts—an activity that appealed to Fama. At the time, a huge data-gathering project was being conducted by two members of the Chicago faculty, James Lorie and Lawrence Fisher, who, in an early demonstration of what the computer could do, made the first comprehensive measurement of the performance of all common stocks listed on the New York Stock Exchange from January 30, 1926, to December 30, 1960. They analyzed total returns—dividends received as well as changes in capital as a result of price changes. This was a major advance over Cowles's data base, which had included only the movement of stock prices. Fisher and Lorie also considered the impact on returns of reinvesting dividends, brokerage fees, and capital gains taxes ("The

*The dean of the business school at the time was George Shultz, a member of Samuelson's first doctoral group at MIT in 1941 and a future holder of three cabinet posts, including Secretary of State under Ronald Reagan.

cumulative effect of the personal income tax on wealth is great").[6]

Aside from Cowles's data base, the Fisher-Lorie study had only one antecedent, which had been carried out forty years earlier. Edgar Lawrence Smith, a student of the stock market, had published a study in 1924 in which he reported a series of tests of returns from bonds, which he referred to as the "unassailably acceptable security,"[7] and contrasted those results with returns from common stocks, which most people believed were appropriate only for speculators. Smith's tests covered periods of at least 17 years and ranged from periods beginning in 1866 and in 1880 to the period from 1901 to 1922.*

Stocks beat bonds hands down, proving, according to Smith, that stocks should be the asset of choice for true long-term investors, no matter how conservative. Smith's analysis was so persuasive and attracted so much attention that it played an important role in the rising popularity of common stocks that fired the great bull market of the 1920s.

Lorie and Fisher did their work at the Center for Research in Security Prices, which was located at the University of Chicago and funded by Merrill Lynch—or Merrill Lynch, Pearce, Fenner & Smith, Inc., as the company was known at the time. The title of the Center was an awkward mouthful, and popular usage soon reduced it to the acronym CRSP, pronounced "crisp." Under a series of distinguished directors, CRSP has continued to play a central role in capital market research.

Lorie and Fisher's results appeared in the January 1964 issue of the prestigious University of Chicago publication, the *Journal of Business*. The *Journal* had been founded in 1920, the stone age of scholarly work in business and finance. By the mid-1960s, the *Journal* claimed to cover "new theory, new data, and advanced concepts over the broad range of business and business-related subjects." Irving Schweiger, the editor at the time, admitted that ". . . a fair number of articles are 'math-oriented' [but] the trend towards the greater use of mathematics is here to stay—it reflects a change in the business environment as well as in the academic community.†[8] The Fisher-Lorie study, which was not so much

---

*Smith's article won a favorable review from John Maynard Keynes in the *Nation and Athenaeum* of May 2, 1925.
†Mathematics was first introduced into economics in the nineteenth century, although it really took hold only after World War II. The earliest mathematical

mathematical as a mind-boggling accumulation of statistical calculations, certainly qualified as "new data, and advanced concepts."

The article was a bombshell. Academics and practitioners alike were astonished to find that an investor who had put $1,000 into the market in 1926, had reinvested all dividends received, had paid no taxes, and had held on until the end of 1960 would have seen the original $1,000 grow to nearly $30,000—a gain on the order of 9 percent a year. In an expansion of the article four years later, Fisher and Lorie confirmed and elaborated on their original research, with new data running from December 31, 1925, to December 31, 1965.

In light of the still vivid memories of the Great Crash, 9 percent a year was much greater than most people had believed likely. It far exceeded what an investor would have earned on bonds or mortgages or deposits in a savings bank during those years. Smith had got it right the first time!

Despite its pioneering character, the original Fisher-Lorie study looks primitive by comparison to later work on the history of financial markets. Return analysis has progressed from annual to monthly and ultimately to daily data, including dividend payments and adjustments for stock splits, stock dividends, and other capital adjustments. The scope of analysis now embraces small company stocks, a wide variety of bonds, real estate, and the financial markets of other nations.

Still, Fisher and Lorie's accomplishment makes an amusing contrast to something that happened at MIT's Sloan School of Management at about the same time. A retiring member of a stock exchange firm offered the school the actual New York Stock Exchange ticker tape, carrying every transaction from 1900 onward—about 100,000 hours of transactions. At first the MIT authorities were pleased, until they realized that the huge pile of spools would fill the room the faculty used for their daily coffee breaks. No thanks! When Paul Samuelson told me this story, he commented, "Finding any information on that tape would have been more difficult than writing the full text of the Encyclopedia Britannica."[9]

In referring to the coverage of their data, Fisher and Lorie point

economists were physicists who applied the terminology of that field to economic analysis. Expressions like "equilibrium," "function," and "vector" are common examples.

out that their rates of return are an average, assuming equal initial investments in each of the common stocks listed on the New York Stock Exchange. They add, "Of course, no one actually made such investments, and there may therefore be interest in the relationship between these rates and a feasible policy—say, random selection of stocks. . . . An investor who selected stocks at random would, on the average, have ended up with the same wealth as the investor who earned the rates [shown]."[10]

This assertion about the consequences of random stock selection was based on an analysis of the facts. But the theoretical pot was also beginning to boil. In 1964, Paul Cootner, a professor at MIT, published an influential 500-page book titled *The Random Character of Stock Prices,* which contained reprints of all the important work done up to that point, including some of his own analysis. Here the reader could find the writings of Kendall, Osborne, Working, Cowles, Alexander, and others. Cootner also reprinted the full text of Bachelier's 1900 thesis on the theory of speculation, now translated into English for the first time.

The final section of the book contained five articles on the statistical analysis of options prices, an area that was only just beginning to attract the attention of finance specialists; two of these articles were by Samuelson's protégé Richard Kruizenga. These five works formed the basis for the important and far-reaching research into this question that was to emerge at MIT around 1970 and that will occupy our attention later on.

Cootner's book also contained a short article by Fama, reprinted from the *Journal of Business* for October 1963, in which Fama expanded on an analysis of market behavior conducted by Benoit Mandelbrot, a French mathematician living in the United States whose work was published in the same issue of the journal. Mandelbrot proposed that stock prices fluctuate so irregularly because they are not sufficiently well behaved to submit to the kind of rigorous statistical analysis recommended by Bachelier and Samuelson.

Mandelbrot's research implied that stocks are riskier than had been assumed, that diversification might not work as well as Markowitz had indicated, that measures like variance could be highly unstable, and that major price movements would cluster more closely than anticipated. Mandelbrot's view of the stock market was the genesis of what is known today as Chaos Theory, of which Mandelbrot himself is an articulate proponent. The events

of October 1987 and less dramatic but qualitatively similar episodes lend some credence to Mandelbrot's warnings. Despite
those events, however, Mandelbrot remains on the periphery of
financial theory, both because of the inconvenience to analysts of
accepting his arguments and because of the natural human desire
to hope that fluctuations will remain within familiar bounds.

Soon after his foray into the feverish world described by Mandelbrot, Fama turned to full analysis of the random behavior of stock
prices. In January 1965, the *Journal of Business* published his article "The Behavior of Stock Market Prices." Seventy pages long,
it comprised his entire Ph.D. thesis—an extraordinary compliment from the editors of a leading journal to a young man who
was just beginning his career. Fama reviewed the available literature on stock market behavior, conducted his own tests of the
random movement of stock prices, proposed his own theories on
the matter, and joined those who had concluded that stock prices
are not predictable.

Nicholas Molodovsky, then editor of the *Financial Analysts
Journal,* considered this article so important that he invited Fama
to prepare an abridged and less technical version, so that his evidence and arguments could be brought to the attention of investment professionals. This simplified version, "Random Walks in
Stock Market Prices," appeared in the *Financial Analysts Journal*
nine months after the full version had appeared in the *Journal of
Business.* It made such a splash that it was reprinted in the English
analysts' journal in 1966.

Even more remarkable, *Institutional Investor,* reprinted the article in April 1968. This glossy, brash, informative, cocky
monthly had been launched just a year earlier by Gilbert Kaplan,
a 27-year-old economist at the American Stock Exchange. Its subscribers are professional investment managers, who were only
then, largely in response to the magazine's influence, beginning
to recognize their identity as a separate group with a community
of interests. One of their strongest common interests was the conviction they could outperform nonprofessional investors.

*Institutional Investor* held its first annual conference in the
early winter of 1968 and attracted 1,521 professional money
managers (and 17 people from the staff of the SEC) from 46 states
and 18 foreign nations, who were collectively responsible for
$213 billion in stocks and bonds. In his introductory remarks,

Kaplan referred to the theme of the conference—"The Revolution in Money Management"—to emphasize his conviction that "Today, the stature of both the security analyst and the portfolio manager are at the highest level we have ever known."[11]

Walter Heller, former chairman of President Kennedy's Council of Economic Advisers, was the opening speaker. When he saw the signs announcing the latest issue of the magazine—"Institutional Investor Is Out"—he peered out at the audience in the grand ballroom of the New York Hilton and remarked, "If you ask me, Institutional Investor is in!"

The members of a panel on investment performance moderated by "Adam Smith," the first editor of the magazine, apparently agreed with Kaplan. John Hartwell, one of the most successful money managers of the day, defined investment performance as "seeking to get better than average results over a fairly long period of time—consistently," and he expressed his confidence that the professional managers could achieve precisely that. "Most individuals make hash of their portfolios," he asserted.[12] Pierre Rinfret, a well-known economist with experience in investment management, debated the random walk and declared flatly: "The value of investment advice is substantial. . . . I will say to the random theorists, as was said to the aeronautical engineer whose airplane crashed, 'Go back to the drawing boards.' It's interesting, but highly inconclusive."[13]

Fama's effort to reach the investment profession was significant. As he points out in the simplified version of his article, most of the discussions of this important subject had appeared in technical journals in a form that most non-mathematicians would find incomprehensible. He expressed the hope that his article would encourage readers to turn to the "more rigorous and lengthy works" that he cites.

Fama first reviews the research on the random behavior of stock prices, including the work of Kendall and Alexander. He then throws down the gauntlet to the chartists and technical analysts who believe that the past pattern of stock prices makes future prices predictable:

The chartist must admit that the evidence in favor of the random walk model is both consistent and voluminous, whereas there is precious little published in discussion of rigorous empirical tests of the various technical theories. If the chartist rejects the evidence of the random walk model, his position is weak if his own theories have not been subjected to equally rigorous tests. This, I believe, is the challenge that the random walk theory makes.[14]

Now Fama moves to a deeper matter: the uses and value of information itself. This is a more serious issue than the accomplishments of the technical analysts, who eschew information and believe that market prices tell their own story of what is to come. It is also an intensely controversial issue.

Fama takes direct aim at the security analyst who pours over accounting data, interviews managements, scrutinizes industry trends, consults economists, probes into political forces, and worries over interest rates. He does not deny that the efforts of such an analyst bear fruit on occasion, but ". . . his choices should *consistently* outperform randomly selected securities of the same general riskiness . . . since, by the nature of uncertainty, for any given time period he has a 50% chance of doing better than random selection even if his powers of analysis are completely nonexistent."[15]

Fama is careful to avoid going all the way: *he never declares that security analysis is a waste of time.* Anticipating what Fischer Black would say more than twenty years later, Fama asserts that without security analysis the behavior of stock prices would be entirely different:

> If there are many analysts who are pretty good at this sort of thing . . . *they help narrow discrepancies between actual prices and intrinsic values* and cause actual prices, on the average, to adjust "instantaneously" to changes in intrinsic values. . . . Although the returns to these sophisticated analysts may be quite high, they establish a market in which fundamental analysis is a fairly useless procedure both for the average analyst and the average investor.[16](emphasis added)

Samuelson had summed it up as "No easy pickings." The market is so hard to outguess because so many smart people are out there doing the guessing.

That outcome is inevitable. In a market of dolts or a market of noise traders, many stocks would be mispriced, some way above their intrinsic value and others way below. Under those conditions, the smart people would make a killing; they would be truly rich. Not for long, however. Their sure pickings would attract other bright people into the game, and matters would end up precisely as Fama describes them.

The same thing would happen if everyone accepted Fama's views and decided that trying to beat the market was too onerous or too hopeless a task. Then investors would simply buy diversified portfolios and hold them for the long pull. That would mean easy pickings for the active traders who moved in to take advantage of the passive investors. As more active traders joined in the fun, once again matters would end up as Fama describes them. The story can have no other outcome so long as markets remain as competitive as they have been.

The implications of this line of reasoning are so disturbing that people tend to lose sight of the positive side. The idea that most investors are likely to do no better than average, even when armed with the best information (and are likely to do worse than average without the best information), seems like an insult to all those investors who think they know better. This grim prediction was what made the community of professional investors so antagonistic to the academic theories. They refused to recognize that the contention is a *compliment* to the avidity and intelligence and self-interest that motivate informed investors. If more investors were to become less zealous in pursuit of their fortunes, the keen and the swift would find the market a lot easier to beat.

In discussing one of Fama's later papers, William Sharpe explains what the dispute was all about. He points out that Fama's thesis that stock prices in a well-functioning and competitive market

> . . . will reflect predictions based on all relevant and available information . . . seems almost trivially self-evident to most professional economists—so much so, that testing seems rather silly. On the other hand, the idea seems truly revolutionary to the traditional security analyst. Only the most exhaustive testing could possibly convince some die-hard practitioners of the merits of the approach. Interestingly, professional economists seem to think more highly of professional investors than do other professional investors.[17]

Fama borrowed a phrase from Markowitz to sum up what he was saying. The market as he saw it is "efficient"—a market with minimal frictions between input and output. He coined the expressions efficient market and market efficiency, which soon became more familiar to theorists and practitioners than Markowitz's phrase "efficient portfolio."

Information is the key input to the market. In an effort to "beat the gun," as Keynes put it, investors rush to use new information as fast as they can, driving prices to the point where profitable opportunities to trade no longer exist. In an efficient market, prices immediately reflect all the available information. Consequently successive changes in stock prices in the same direction—that is, trends—are far less likely than random movements. Trends would indicate that investors were processing and acting on the information too slowly and that prices were not reflecting it immediately. Fama's own experience, together with Cowles's tests of Dow Theory and Alexander's studies, had already put that possibility to rest. None of them detected "imperfect knowledge of [the] facts," which to Alexander was the symptom of inefficiency.

An efficient market does not exclude the chance that some investors can do better than others. One widely followed weekly service, Value Line Investment Survey, employs a ranking system for stocks whose record over many years would make Alfred Cowles's eyes pop out. It was the bible in my own firm. In a famous article published in 1971, "Yes, Virginia, There Is Hope," Fischer Black, then at the University of Chicago, conducted a rigorous analysis of Value Line's track record and concluded: "It still appears that most investment management organizations would improve their performance if they fired all but one of their security analysts and then provided the remaining analyst with the Value Line service."[18] Value Line's performance has continued to earn high marks over the twenty years since Black's study.

Fama's point is that, *on the average,* information moves so fast that the market as a whole knows more than any individual investor can know. Value Line's performance, rather than contradicting Fama, confirms that point. The mutual funds Value Line manages according to its ranking system have a mediocre track record that is no match for the performance of the stocks recommended in its printed service. In order to avoid conflicts of interest, the mutual funds are forbidden to buy or sell until subscribers have received the service in the mail. By that time, the news is out.

*136*

The market defeats the portfolio managers' efforts to outperform it, even when the managers have excellent information.

An efficient market is not necessarily a rational market, nor is the information it reflects always accurate. Investors in their enthusiasm, or in their collective gloom, sometimes agree among themselves that certain stocks are somehow worth more or less than their intrinsic values. Although reality will ultimately assert itself, an efficient market is one in which no single investor has much chance, beyond luck, of consistently outguessing all the other participants.

The Fisher-Lorie study combined with Fama's exploration to fire up the enthusiasm of the finance group at Chicago. The diskdrives in the ponderous mainframe computers began to whir as professors and graduate students alike crunched the numbers to test their hypotheses against the facts. Fama himself led the way.

The American Finance Association invited Fama to come to its annual meeting in December 1969 to present a full review of the theory of efficient markets and the related empirical work. The conventional arrangements at these meetings include three papers at each session, and three discussants. On this occasion, Fama—who was only thirty years old and had been a full professor for just one year—presented the only paper. (This was the paper for which Sharpe was a discussant.) Fama's paper ran to almost forty pages when it appeared in the *Journal of Finance*. He told me he would never have undertaken it if the invitation had not been such an unusual one. One of the more notable features of the article was the pivotal role that Fama himself had played in the research, either as direct participant or as enthusiastic supporter.

Fama starts off by admitting that the statement that in an efficient market prices "fully reflect" available information is so general that it cannot be tested empirically. As an alternative, he suggests that an efficient market exists when trading systems based on available information fail to produce profits in excess of the market's overall rate of return.

Remembering his experience with Harry Ernst at Tufts, he asks, can we find any trading system for beating the market? Can we find some source or method for processing information that will unfailingly lead to superior results? Can we identify some group of stocks that consistently outperforms random selection? If the answer to these questions is no, we can assume that the market is efficient and that it does "fully reflect" all available information.

Fama then reports on three different sets of tests of market efficiency. The taxonomy he draws on had been developed earlier in a CRSP paper by his colleague Harry Roberts.

Fama groups the first set of tests into what he calls the "weak" form of market efficiency, which exists when past price behavior contains no information useful for future price behavior. His 1965 paper had already demolished the technical analysts, establishing the presence of the weak form of market efficiency under virtually all conditions.

The next level of tests examine what Fama defines as the "semi-strong" form of market efficiency, in which "the concern is the speed of price adjustments to obviously public available information (e.g. announcements of stock splits, annual reports, new security issues, etc.)."[19]

Finally, Fama looks into tests of the "strong" form of market efficiency. Here the question is whether some investors have been able to profit from "monopolistic information relevant for the formation of prices." Fama does not use the expression "monopolistic" to refer only to so-called inside information. In a broader sense, he means the ability of some investors to exploit, understand, or interpret information so that they have an advantage over other investors in recognizing a value when they see it. The strong-form tests are a fancy way of asking whether some investors really are smart enough to become rich. These are genuine tests of the value of information, whether it arrives in the form of explicit facts or of incisive analysis.

Reflecting the increasingly abrasive view among academics of the skills of professional managers, Fama asserts:

> . . . [W]e shall contend that there is no important evidence against the [efficient market] hypothesis in the weak and semi-strong form tests . . . and only limited evidence against the hypothesis in the strong form tests (i.e., monopolistic access to information about prices does not seem to be a prevalent phenomenon in the investment community).[20]

Fama's article cites a long list of studies that confirm the hypothesis of an efficient market. With almost monotonous unanimity, the evidence shows that stock prices move well in advance of the appearance of "identifiable information" such as earnings announcements, stock splits and associated dividend increases, changes in the Federal Reserve discount rate, offers to sell shares by major holders such as wealthy individuals or institutions, even changes in the interest rate on U.S. Treasury bills.

How could it be otherwise, when so many knowledgeable, eager investors are receiving all the hurry-up calls from their brokers, reading all the weighty analytical reports, heeding all the rumors about what the big investors are up to, watching all the jiggles in interest rates, and interpreting all the double-talk of the Federal Reserve Chairman? If it was impossible for professionals to beat the market with any consistency in Cowles's day, when Dow Jones was still sending out information by messenger boy, how could anyone expect the job to be easier at a time when the speed of communication, the sophistication of financial analysts, and the resources devoted to analysis had reached unprecedented levels? Only a weakening of the power of greed would make the job any easier. And who could believe that had happened?

Nathan Rothschild made millions when his carrier pigeons brought him the first news of Wellington's victory at Waterloo. Today, advanced communication technology moves information far more swiftly than pigeons can fly. On the morning after the first bombing of Iraq in January 1991, the Dow Jones Average opened 80 points above the previous day's close.

Practitioners were still incredulous in their gut reactions to Fama's notions. Agreed that the average little guy has no chance. Agreed that investors hear little of value from brokers. Agreed that everybody cannot do better than everybody else. Agreed that "the speed of price adjustments to other obviously public available information" is too great to provide consistently profitable trading opportunities.

But what about those investors who really do have "monopolistic information relevant for the formation of prices"? After all, information does not arrive everywhere simultaneously. And simple logic would suggest that professional investors who devote full time and substantial resources to the task must be adding something of value. As Rinfret had insisted at the *Institutional Investor* conference, what those investors were doing had to be worth more than just throwing darts at the *Wall Street Journal*— although the so-called "dart-board portfolio" soon became a sour joke and the random walk bogey to beat.

This was the selling pitch that we in the investment advisory business used with potential clients. "We may not know everything," we humbly admitted, "but there is every reason to believe that we will do better than you can do on your own or than you can do by randomly selecting securities. You spend your time doing other things; we spend full time at research, at listening to other experts, at drawing on years of knowledge and experience in the field." Few people could resist this compelling argument. Our business grew at an explosive rate during the 1960s as the market soared and as individual investors, pension funds, and endowment funds rushed in to join in the fun.

We fooled ourselves just as much as we fooled our prospective clients. We failed to recognize that the movement of increasing amounts of money into professional management, a process that was so rewarding to our own pocketbooks, would make it just that much more difficult for us to capture rewards for our clients' pocketbooks. With competition for information becoming ever more intense, professional managers were destined to have a hard time in trying to outperform one another. We could not beat the market because we were rapidly becoming the market.

Evidence of this disturbing trend was readily available. Although most investment counseling organizations in those days chose to keep their performance record private, the burgeoning mutual fund industry regularly published the returns it was producing for its stockholders. Managers of mutual funds have strong motivations for performance. Superior performance brings a rush of new assets, and a rush of new assets in turn boosts the income of the managers. So the returns being earned by these funds provided a first-class data base for research into the track record of professional managers.

Fama's paper cites several studies of mutual fund performance. He concentrates on an exhaustive analysis carried out by Michael Jensen, one of his graduate students at Chicago. Jensen's findings, which appeared in the *Journal of Business* for April 1969, covered the performance of 115 mutual funds over the ten years from 1955 to 1964.

Impressive as Cowles's investigation had been, it pales in comparison to Jensen's work. Cowles had analyzed rates of return as he found them, but Jensen studied the critical role of risk in determining investment returns. He derives his measure of risk from Sharpe's single-index model, which relates the volatility of an asset to the market in which it trades. Before calculating the performance of the mutual fund managers, Jensen adjusts the reported returns for the level of risk taken.

High returns are not necessarily a sign of skill. Investors who take big risks should win higher returns than timid investors. A man who wildcats for oil should earn a lot more than a man who puts his money in a savings account. An investor with a portfolio concentrated in two or three hot stocks should outperform an investor with a diversified portfolio of many stocks. Otherwise, risky strategies would make no sense at all. The basis for judging the results of the wildcatters and the plungers has to be different from the basis for judging the results of more conservative investors.

The high-risk investor may be deft in sensing where oil is hiding or which stocks will be the hottest. He may also be lucky. Distinguishing between luck and skill is tricky, but statistical tools can provide some guidance. Jensen drew on all the latest statistical techniques and the power of the computer to adjust the performance records for risk and to distinguish between results due to skill and results due to chance.

His findings were devastating. On average, investors who held mutual funds for ten years would have been worth 15 percent less than if they had merely bought and held a broadly diversified portfolio of common stocks with the same level of risk. According to Jensen's standards, only 26 of the 115 funds outperformed the market.

This dismal track record was partly the result of loading charges—that is, the commissions paid by customers to the brokers who sold the funds. As that money never reached the fund managers for investment, Jensen recalculated the performance of the funds by subtracting the loading charges. The result was only a little better. Now the loss of wealth was 8.9 percent and 43 of the 115 funds outperformed the market.

Jensen concludes that his results furnish striking evidence of the strong form of the efficient market, with broad implications for all investors, not just participants in mutual funds. After all, ". . . [O]ne must realize that these analysts are extremely well endowed. Moreover, they operate in the securities markets every day and have wide-ranging contacts and associations in both the business and the financial communities."[21] If they can't cut it, who could?

The answer seems to be, not many. Repeated studies of the performance of professional managers over the years confirm Jensen's findings. On the average, and after adjustment for risk, even "extremely well endowed" professionals appear unable to beat the market with any convincing degree of consistency.

But the matter is not quite that simple. An average, after all, is a mixture of good and bad. Every month, every quarter, every year, some managers *are* beating the average. A few have runs of success that keep them on top of the heap for several years running. Famous investors like the financier Bernard Baruch, the canny acquirer of companies Warren Buffet, and the investment theorist Benjamin Graham managed to accumulate immense wealth in the stock market without taking outlandish risks. Even an occasional mutual fund manager achieves spectacular results, such as John Neff with the Windsor Fund or Peter Lynch with the Magellan Fund. Fama himself cites a study of market-making specialists on the floor of the stock exchange who almost never fail to make money by buying low and selling high.

Although these achievements put a dent in the idea of the strong form of market efficiency, the dent is not very deep.

An average always includes some managers with above-average results, but their superior performance may easily be the result of luck. The difference between luck and skill is seldom apparent at first glance.

If Peter and Paul toss coins to see which of them can call "heads" or "tails" correctly the largest number of times, the results can play havoc with our intuition. Let them make 20,000 tosses and keep a cumulative tally of the results. Will each have been in the lead about half the time? Highly doubtful! An outcome in which either heads or tails will be in the lead after every one of the 20,000 tosses is 156 times more probable than one in which there is a 10,000 to 10,000 tie. What looks like skill and consistency is often nothing more than pure chance.

Consider this set of coin-tossing possibilities, proposed by Warren Buffet. Suppose 225 million Americans all join in a coin-tossing contest in which each player bets a dollar each day on whether the toss of a coin will turn up heads or tails. Each day, the losers turn their dollars over to the winners, who then stake their winnings on the next day's toss. The laws of chance tell us that, after ten flips on ten mornings, only 220,000 people will still be in the contest, and each will have won a little over $1,000. After that, the game heats up. Ten days later, only 215 people will still be playing, but each of them will be worth over $1,050,000.

Buffet suggests that this small group of winners will marvel at their own skills. Some of them will write books on "How I Turned a Dollar into a Million in Twenty Days Working Thirty Seconds a Morning." Or, they will tackle skeptical professors of finance with "If it can't be done, why are there 215 of us?" But, Buffet goes on to point out,". . . then some business school professor will probably be rude enough to bring up the fact that if 215 million orangutans had engaged in a similar exercise, the results would be much the same—215 egotistical orangutans with 20 straight winning flips."[22]

But what about the Buffets, Baruchs, Grahams, Neffs, and Lynches? Are they in the same class as the orangutans? Paul Samuelson admits that such market geniuses must exist, even in a totally efficient market: "It is not ordered in heaven, or by the second law of thermodynamics, that a small group of intelligent and informed investors cannot systematically achieve higher mean portfolio gains with lower average variabilities. People differ in their heights, pulchritude, and acidity. Why not in their P.Q. or performance quotient?"[23]

On another occasion, Samuelson commented that "what the speculator wants . . . is Irving Berlin's pup, 'the pup that gets the bugler up!' Such pups are hard to locate and expensive to rent."[24] The few with an extraordinary P.Q. are unlikely to rent out their talents "to the Ford Foundation or to the local bank trust department. They have too high an I.Q. for that."[25] They are more likely to invest their own money and keep their systems to themselves. Otherwise, others would copy them and spoil their advantage by making the market more efficient.

The implication of this suggestion is harsh, though substantially true. Baron Rothschild once observed that only three people in the world understood the meaning of money, and none of them had very much of it. On the average at least, Samuelson's law of the P.Q. means that the P.Q.s of the men and women who manage other people's money must be lower than the P.Q.s of the people who successfully manage their own! Why else would these managers be so kind as to make their talents available to others? On the basis of my long and broad acquaintance with professional managers, I am convinced that many of them have made their fortunes from the fees they earn from their clients rather than from investing their own money.

Even when the high P.Q. is for rent—John Neff and Peter Lynch have managed money for others—the ability to combine financial acumen with an acute sense of timing and assessment of risk seems to be non-transferable. Rarely has an investment firm continued to produce superior results after the departure of its star.

These considerations do not close the case in favor of the efficient market, however. The hypothesis has sustained a powerful attack from another angle.

Hindsight has revealed a number of anomalies in market behavior that early researchers missed and that reveal instances when stock prices were predictable. Even after adjusting for differences in risk, small company stocks have outperformed large company stocks over the long run, especially between the last week of December and the first week of January. Other seasonal variations appear in the behavior of stock prices, such as the tendency for prices to go up on Fridays and down on Mondays or to behave differently in the first half and the second half of the month. Stocks priced low relative to their earnings or their dividends also seem to be good long-run bets. Some researchers have identified what appear to be fads or overreactions in which good news drives stock prices way above intrinsic values and bad news drives them way below; these misvaluations may persist for so long that the investor is often better off riding the trend than trying to fight it.

Finally, a flaw in Jensen's approach to mutual fund performance has shown up. Recent research demonstrates that some mutual fund managers may have "hot hands" and others may have "icy hands." A fund that performs well one year is likely to perform well the following year, and the same is true of a fund that performs poorly. Once again, no easy pickings: The reason a pattern fails to last more than a year at a time may be that the newfound star is bid away by another organization, or that new money pours into the fund too rapidly to be invested at attractive prices, or that the management team loses its sense of urgency once its reputation has been established.

Fama himself in recent years has been in the forefront of an investigation that has identified waves in the movement of stock prices. Extended periods of sub-average returns appear to be followed by extended periods of above-average returns with some degree of regularity. Even Fama now suggests that under these conditions stock prices might be predictable.

Yet the pudding that Jensen and the early students of professional performance began to cook up in the 1960s continues to be eaten. Despite the anomalies, despite the identifiable price formation patterns, despite the power the computer brings to the task, beating the market with any degree of consistency remains as formidable a challenge as ever. Studies continue to demonstrate that the number of managers who outperform and underperform the market bears a remarkable resemblance to the number of heads that would turn up when each of 1,000 orangutans flips a coin ten times.

True, those are not orangutans out there. They are real human beings confronting an unknown future. No one, not even Warren Buffet and John Neff, knows for certain what the market is going to do. No one can avoid the tough choices demanded by the optimal allocation of their capital, or the capital of others. All must try to analyze the data in a mosaic of staggering complexity—a cardiogram of the heartbeat of the world economy—while taking risks that may wipe out the savings of decades or grossly misallocate scarce resources.

Now let us put more flesh and blood into our story. The sophisticated analyses of speculative markets that we have been exploring must be restated in terms of what investors actually do as they confront the battle for survival. How do they tackle the complexities of estimating expected returns and assessing investment risks? What happens in the marketplace when they act on their convictions about the future? And how does each individual investor's responses affect the fortunes of all other investors?

The answers to these questions change the flavor of the story. Academics will continue to dominate the scene, but now a few practitioners also begin to influence developments, and some of the characters move back and forth between both worlds. The path to joining gown and town is beginning to appear.

# What Are Stocks Worth?

# Chapter
# 8

# The Best at the Price

*It is people like you who are going to destroy this business.*

How's the market? Is that stock still a buy? When should I sell? These are the questions investors ask most often. They know that picking the right stocks at the right time makes a big difference. Even in the catastrophic market of 1929–1932, when the average stock fell by 90 percent, Scott Paper and Minnesota Mining rose in price.

Paul Samuelson and his cohorts consider questions like these a waste of time, because theory demonstrates that stocks will sell for what they are worth.* If deviations between price and value were large, more people would get rich from trading than from buy-and-hold. The efficient market hypothesis gives the benefit of the doubt to buy-and-hold.

Yet the case is not open and shut. Before we throw in the sponge and abandon the field to the Samuelson team, we should recognize that their basic assumption is vulnerable. Stocks will be priced at what they are worth *only* when a sizable number of investors, with big sums at play, know how to value stocks correctly. If that assumption fails to hold, the market is noise, a game of Snap, a casino.

Osborne's unrelieved bedlam and Kendall's Demon of Chance suggest that the market is not just noise. If it were, Cowles's knowledgeable investment advisors and Jensen's well-endowed mutual fund managers would have outperformed the market.

---

*Markowitz is as cavalier as Samuelson in assuming away the difficulties of valuing stocks correctly. He devotes only a footnote to the matter, recommending that reader "See, for example, *'Williams's Theory of Investment Value.'*"

Their failure to do so tells us that most of the time, stocks are priced close to what they are worth. So somebody, somewhere, is doing something right.

How do they go about it?

Wall Street does not lack for rules of thumb for deciding whether stock prices are high or low. Most of the rules relate the price of a stock to some attribute of the issuing company—its earnings, the dividend it pays, stockholders' equity in the company, or the company's sales volume. These ratios provide handy common denominators for comparing various stocks or for comparing a stock on one date with the same stock on a different date. But that is about as far as we can go with these rules of thumb.

The most rigorous, and also the most influential, method for determining intrinsic value was published in 1938 by John Burr Williams, the person who prompted Harry Markowitz's original insights into risk and diversification. Williams's solution to the riddle of intrinsic value continues to be applied to almost all valuation problems, not just in the stock market but throughout business and economics. It provides the only formal method for determining what a price/earnings ratio or a dividend yield should be. Comparing that ratio or yield with its actual level gives an indication of whether the asset is cheap or expensive. The wide acceptance of Williams's model probably explains why Markowitz felt no need to elaborate its role in portfolio selection and took its principles for granted.

Although the idea goes back at least to Irving Fisher's work, *The Theory of Interest,* published around 1900, no one before Williams had developed the concept so completely. A primer as well as a tour de force of financial sophistication, Williams describes the underlying theory and gives a variety of applications drawn from his experience as an investor.

Williams was wealthy and nearly ninety years old when he died in 1989, but he was already a highly successful investor when he began to study economics seriously in the early 1930s. As an undergraduate at Harvard, he had concentrated in mathematics and chemistry. After graduating in 1923, he went to the Harvard Business School, where he got his first taste of economic forecasting and security analysis. He then took a job as security analyst at the prestigious brokerage house of Hayden, Stone and subsequently at Lee, Higginson and Company. Here he experienced all the joys and horrors of the bull market of the 1920s and the Great Crash.

Many years later, in a memoir he wrote for the guidance of the younger generation, Williams recalled his experience with the stock of American & Foreign Power, which owned electric power plants throughout Latin America and was a darling of the bull market. At its peak, the stock sold for 199¼, or 100 times earnings per share. "How to estimate its fair value was a puzzle indeed," mused Williams, observing that the "savage bear market" subsequently drove the stock down to a low of 2. "The experience taught me a lesson. To be a good investment analyst, one needs to be an expert economist also. Hence, a few years later, I took time off to earn a Ph.D. in economics."[1]

At the age of thirty, in 1932, Williams enrolled in the Graduate School of Arts and Sciences at Harvard. He set out to find an economist who could explain to his satisfaction what had caused the recent debacle in the nation's economy, as Diogenes had set out with his lamp in search of one honest man. Williams got to know the greats of the Harvard economics faculty at the time—the quintessential Viennese Joseph Schumpeter, the plain midwestern American Alvin Hansen, and the irrepressible Wassily Leontief, newly arrived from the University of Kiel in Germany, to which he had fled after the Russian revolution. Much as Williams admired these figures, he confesses in his memoir that, like Diogenes, he never found the man he was seeking.

When it came time to write his doctoral dissertation, he conferred with Schumpeter about an appropriate topic. Schumpeter suggested that he choose the intrinsic value of a common stock, for which Williams's personal experience and background in economics would serve him in good stead. Williams notes that Schumpeter had a cynical, conspiratorial reason for suggesting this topic: "This choice would keep me from running afoul of the preconceptions of the other members of the Harvard faculty, none of whom . . . would want to challenge my own ideas on investments."[2]

Williams finished his thesis in 1937 and sent it to Macmillan for publication, even though he had not yet won faculty approval for his doctorate. Macmillan returned the manuscript with the complaint that it contained algebraic symbols. McGraw-Hill made the same complaint. Finally, Harvard University Press published *The Theory of Investment Value* in 1938, but only after Williams had promised to pay part of the printing cost.

Still busy as an investor, Williams waited until 1940 before taking the oral exam for his Ph.D. Schumpeter, Leontief, and Hansen were on the committee. Hansen was disturbed that Williams had published his thesis before it had been accepted by the committee; moreover, he resented Williams's skeptical view of Keynesian economics. After intense argument over the causes of the depression, during which Schumpeter showed "great delight"[3] at Williams's willingness to take on the great Hansen, the committee finally agreed to grant the degree.

Modesty was not Williams's long suit. In the preface to his book, he declares his objective: "To outline a new sub-science that shall be known as the Theory of Investment Value and that shall comprise a coherent body of principles like the Theory of Monopoly, the Theory of Money, and the Theory of International Trade, all branches of the larger science of Economics."[4]

He also makes a prescient observation at the outset about the algebraic symbols that had bothered the editors at Macmillan and McGraw-Hill. After reassuring nontechnical readers that he will explain everything carefully along the way, he declares that his use of mathematics is not to be taken as a drawback: "Quite the contrary! The truth is that the mathematical method is a new tool of great power, whose use promises to lead to notable advances in Investment Analysis."[5]

The words that set Markowitz on the path to a theory of portfolio selection thirteen years later appear at the very beginning of Chapter I: "No buyer considers all securities equally attractive at their present market prices whatever these prices happen to be; on the contrary, he seeks 'the best at the price.'"[6] In the rest of the book Williams explains how to find *the* best security at the price; he never stops to ask whether investors should occasionally settle for the second or third best security at the price, or, better yet, buy all three.

Markowitz was aware that flesh-and-blood investors are never certain they have found the one best value among all values. "The hypothesis (or maxim) that the investor does (or should) maximize discounted return must be rejected," he declares. "A rule of behavior which does not imply the superiority of diversification must be rejected both as a hypothesis and as a maxim."[7] But the only reference to diversification that Williams makes in his book is a passing comment about families who sell out large inherited positions in order to diversify their holdings.

Williams asks why a rational investor would buy a stock in the first place. The easy answer is that the investor expects the stock to rise in price, but that is only a hope. For the price to rise, other investors must change their mind about the value of the stock and bid up its price, and there is no guarantee that they will perceive the stock any differently from the investor who is still considering whether or not to buy it.

The investor must consider what return the stock might provide even if other investors never changed their mind about it. And that return can consist of nothing more than all the future cash flows paid by the company to its stockholders, out into the future as far as one can see. These payments will most often be dividends, though they may sometimes be liquidation payments or the proceeds of a takeover. This flow of cash back to the owner of the stock is quite literally a *return* of the money invested. No Wordsworth, Williams makes his point with these words:

In short, a stock is worth only *what you can get out of it*.
Even so spoke the old farmer to his son:

> A cow for her milk,
> A hen for her eggs,
> And a stock, by heck,
> For her dividends.[8]

An investor who buys 100 shares of General Electric stock at $40 a share may hope that someone else will be good enough to take it off his hands later on at $50, but who knows whether that kind soul will ever show up? The long-run flow of dividends from General Electric makes possible a far less speculative guess about the future. True, the investor's estimate of what GE will pay out to its stockholders over the next ten or fifteen years will inevitably have a large margin of error. But it will be more plausible than the prediction that some other investor will step up and pay more than $40 for the stock—especially when that other investor is looking at the same information and making the same kinds of calculations.

Williams admits that estimating future dividends is no easy task. He devotes a large part of his book to showing the best way to go about it, claiming that, "in so doing, this book seeks to make its most important contribution to Investment Analysis."[9]

Estimating cash flows is only the first step in determining value. Williams's next step is more complicated.

Money expected in the future is never worth as much as money on hand today. There is always uncertainty about whether the money will be there when the time comes. Even when the investor has every reason to expect that it will be, money to be received tomorrow cannot be invested to produce a return until tomorrow; only money on hand today can be invested today. Therefore, as economists express it, the present value of future cash flows is always less than the face value of those payments.

The process of giving future payments a haircut to allow for uncertainty and the passage of time is known as discounting, and investors call this valuation technique the Dividend Discount Model. The model is applicable to any kind of investment that is designed to produce cash flows to its owner in the future.

Few investors perform the elaborate calculations required by the model. In a market that is always sensitive to the latest item on the broad tape, estimating cash flows out into infinity sounds like a silly and unproductive task. One would do better just to predict earnings for a year or so, or, perhaps, listen to a friendly broker's latest story about the company.

That was the view of Gerald Tsai, a money manager who was described by Gilbert Kaplan in 1968—when Tsai was at his zenith—as "a man who bears the same relationship to performance funds that Joe Namath does to the American Football League, the man who broke the price ceiling on talent."[10] In discussing his strategy at the first *Institutional Investor* conference in January 1968, Tsai observed, "Since the cycle of appreciation of investments has accelerated, so, too has the cycle of anticipating earnings been stretched out. And several stocks in Manhattan's portfolio are now based on 1969 earnings, not 1968."[11]

Even after investors have projected the long-run flow of dividends, they must still decide what discount rate to apply. In choosing the appropriate rate, the available return on alternative and less risky assets like Treasury bills or high-grade bonds must be taken into account, as well as the uncertainty inherent in the long-run estimate of future dividend payments. After considering all these factors, investors will find the seat-of-the-pants application of familiar ratios of price to earnings or dividends a convenient short-cut around Williams's elaborate procedure.

Yet no other formula for determining intrinsic value makes sense. By specifying the discounted value of future cash flows, Williams's Dividend Discount Model reveals the only tangible return an investor can expect. The games investors play in trying to predict what the price of a stock is going to do are purely speculative. Samuelson was on target when he compared this approach to what goes on at Las Vegas and Churchill Downs.

It may sound strange that one must forecast cash flows into infinity, but that is precisely what investors do even when they make shorter-term projections. Suppose they decide to limit their forecasts to only five years into the future and then try to predict what the price of the stock will be at that point. They will not have escaped the demands of the model, for the price of the stock five years from now will still reflect estimates of dividend payments another five years into the future and so on.

A novel view of the problems investors encounter with the Dividend Discount Model appeared in an article titled "Growth Stocks and the Petersburg Paradox," written by David Durand, an MIT professor of economics, and published in the *Journal of Finance* in September 1957. Durand discusses a puzzle posed by the famous French mathematician Daniel Bernoulli in a paper he delivered in 1738 before the Imperial Academy of Sciences in St. Petersburg, a paper that *Econometrica* had considered important enough to reprint in 1954. Bernoulli posed the following problem:

> Peter tosses a coin and continues to do so until it should land "heads" when it comes to the ground. He agrees to give Paul one ducat if he gets "heads" on the very first throw, two ducats if he gets it on the second, four if on the third, eight if on the fourth, and so on, so that with each additional throw the number of ducats he must pay is doubled. Suppose we seek to determine the value of Paul's expectation.[12]

Durand points out that Paul should not necessarily rely on the mathematical expectation of his winning, which is infinitely large. He reviews what several famous scholars had to say about the problem of what Paul should realistically pay to enter the game.

Some of them questioned whether the basic assumption of the game was itself realistic. Such a game cannot continue indefinitely, because the players are mortal: "After a misspent youth, a dissipated middle age, and a dissolute dotage, one of them will die . . . heads or no heads." And how can a fortune be infinitely large? With an initial stake of a dollar, Durand calculates that "Peter's liability after only 35 tails exceeds the gold reserve in Fort Knox. . . . After three more, it . . . approximately equals the national debt." Some of the scholars wondered how much infinite amounts of money in the future would be worth to a player today. By the time you have won the value of all the gold in Fort Knox, how much further effort should you spend on the chance that you might win three of four more Fort Knoxes, or even more?[13]

Durand uses this story to generalize about how much investors should pay for growth stocks—stocks whose earnings and dividend streams, like Peter's liability, are expected to rise continuously into the future. He observes that all future cash flows are uncertain and that far-distant cash flows, even big ones, have little present value. He concludes with some sound advice:

> [G]rowth stocks . . . seem to represent the ultimate in
> difficulty of evaluation. The very fact that the Petersburg
> Problem has not yielded a unique and generally acceptable
> solution to more than 200 years of attack by some of the
> world's greatest intellects suggests, indeed, that the growth-
> stock problem offers no great hope of a satisfactory
> solution.[14]

The publication of Durand's article in 1957 came at an appropriate time, but the managers on Wall Street paid no heed to his warnings. Their love affair with growth fired up the Favorite Fifty boom of the 1960s. Managers who thought they were being prudent pushed these stocks ever higher by valuing them on the basis of naive extrapolations of recent earnings growth into the indefinite future. That simple-minded practice cost investors like my charitable foundation billions of dollars when reality finally set in.

Many investors find the theoretical and the practical difficulties of the Dividend Discount Model insurmountable. A less rigorous methodology developed by Benjamin Graham in the early 1930s has long been the most popular approach to security analysis.

Graham was a successful investor, a respected market scholar, and a prolific writer, lecturer, and teacher. His textbook, *Security Analysis,* written with Professor David Dodd of Columbia, became the bible of the profession as soon as it appeared in 1934 and has sold well over 100,000 copies since. Graham's more popular version of that book, *The Intelligent Investor,* which appeared in 1949, has scored a comparable success among serious non-professionals trying to manage their own affairs or acting as fiduciaries for others.

Graham was born in London in 1894, but his parents emigrated to New York City when he was only a year old. He went to public school and then took night courses at Columbia. He worked full-time during the days to help support his widowed mother, part of whose savings had disappeared when her small margin account was wiped out in the panic of 1907. That was Graham's first exposure to the vagaries of the stock market.

Graham graduated second in his class in 1914 and was offered teaching appointments by the English, math, and philosophy departments at Columbia. Unable to decide which to accept, he consulted the dean, whose predilection was to send bright students like Graham into business. Graham took the dean's surprising advice and started as an assistant in a Wall Street house at $12 a week. There he not only analyzed credits but helped write the stock quotations on the blackboard, operated the switchboard, and even delivered securities. He was so good at analyzing bonds that in 1914 his boss promoted him, with a 50 percent increase in salary, to "statistician," as security analysts were known in those days.

By 1920, Graham had become a partner. By 1923, he was managing a substantial pool of money for a group of the firm's customers. By 1928, he was managing a full-fledged investment fund and advising Bernard Baruch on his investments. At about that time Graham had an amusing, and revealing, experience in his search for security values.

Consolidated Edison was a hot stock just then because most people believed, on the basis of the truncated and incomplete reporting permitted by regulators in those days, that the dividends being paid by the company represented only a small portion of the actual earnings of its operating subsidiaries. Graham decided to find out whether Con Ed was in fact accumulating a tremendous stream of invisible earnings. He took the time and trouble of going to City Hall, where the records of utility companies were stored, and found that the earnings of Con Ed's subsidiaries were negligible. In an effort to hold up its stock price, Con Ed was playing out to its shareholders just about every penny it earned. When Graham published his findings, one of the stockbrokers he was working with took him aside and said, "Young man, it is people like you who are going to destroy this business."[15]

It was not the likes of Graham but the likes of that broker who ultimately did destroy the business. There was not much place to hide when the Great Crash came. Graham shared in the disaster, though he was sufficiently quick-witted to keep from losing everything.

The textbook itself was motivated by his conviction in the early 1930s that the stock market was placing a ridiculously low value on American business. He wrote three articles in successive issues of *Forbes* in June 1932 that carried the suggestive title, "Is American Business Worth More Dead Than Alive?"

Graham was interested in more than wealth. He read Greek, Latin, Spanish, and German, thought with astonishing rapidity, and never lost his passion for mathematics. While pursuing an active career as an investor, he taught security analysis at Columbia for 28 years and won an enthusiastic following among his students. His most famous student, and perhaps his most devoted acolyte, is Warren Buffett of the conglomerate Berkshire-Hathaway. Buffet has used Graham's fundamental philosophy to build a fortune of more than a billion dollars.

Although Graham believed that investors should base their decisions on the intrinsic value of a security, he admitted that intrinsic value is not necessarily a hard fact. In their textbook, Graham and Dodd had described intrinsic value as "an elusive concept" and suggested that an approximate measure would suffice. They pointed out that "inspection [can reveal] whether a woman is old enough to vote without knowing her age, or that a man is heavier than he should be without knowing his exact weight." They defined intrinsic value as simply "that value justified by the facts, e.g. the assets, earnings, dividends, definite prospects."[16]

The generality of this statement from their textbook is significant. Graham and Dodd believed that Williams's emphasis on earning power was mistaken: "The concept of 'earning power,' expressed as a definite figure . . . cannot be safely accepted as a *general premise* of security analysis." They also rejected Samuelson's argument that market value is identical to intrinsic value in a market propelled by investors in pursuit of self-interest: "It is a great mistake to imagine that intrinsic value is as definite and as determinable as market price."[17]

Graham himself prescribed diligent analysis of balance sheets and income statements. Recognizing that "security analysis does not seek to determine exactly what is the intrinsic value of a given security," he devised a complex set of rules that would permit him to buy only when stock prices were low beyond a doubt, both absolutely and historically, compared to a company's earnings, working capital, and stockholders' equity. He considered impeccable balance sheets essential to survival in the event of another depression—a view that has gone in and out of fashion with the passage of time. Even when all Graham's criteria were satisfied, he would not buy a stock if interest rates were high enough to make high-grade bonds an attractive alternative.

Graham considered risk a secondary consideration, because it was already encapsulated in the divergences between his careful calculations of true value and market prices. As early as 1919 he had remarked, "If a common stock is a good investment, it is also an attractive speculation."[18]

Graham's emphasis on balance-sheet data rather than on income flows created trouble for investors who were using his approach during the 1950s. As investors grew more optimistic about the future and less concerned about a return of the Great Depression, their expectations of corporate America's long-run earning power rose and their concerns about the business cycle diminished. *Time* magazine's issue of December 31, 1958, exulted: "In the new economy, many of the old classical rules of economics no longer apply; over the years the U.S. has made and learned new rules all its own."

At the end of 1958, stock prices averaged eighteen times current earnings per share, a huge jump from thirteen times in the autumn of 1957. That increase in valuation was startling. Now a dollar invested in the stock market would produce less in current dividend payments than the interest income of a dollar invested in the high-grade bond market. Interest payments on bonds are contractually fixed at a constant amount for the life of the bond, while dividends on stocks are paid at the whim of boards of directors and tend to vary with fluctuations in corporate earnings. Apparently investors had decided that rising streams of future income on stocks, even if uncertain, were worth more in a dynamic and sometimes inflationary world than fixed streams of future income on bonds.

My older partners, hard-bitten veterans of the Great Depression with memories that reached back even further, could not believe what was happening. Stocks are riskier than bonds; so stocks should be valued more cheaply than bonds. They assured me that matters would soon come right and that we should stay as far away from the stock market as we could.

The spread between bond and stock valuations has never returned to the traditional relationship. The only world my partners had ever known, the world that had prevailed in the capital markets for more than a hundred years, had come to an end.

Growth had replaced solvency in market valuation. Although the Dividend Discount Model could capture this shift in expectations in the form of an increase in anticipated cash flows and a lower rate of discount applied to them, Graham, like my partners, had not conceived of anything like that. Graham's preference was for discovering companies that were worth more dead than alive. As more and more stocks floated away from his strict rules, Graham and Dodd revised their textbook to reflect the realities of the new world of investing. Eventually they brought in a younger author, Sidney Cottle, to ensure that they would stay in tune with the times.

Graham believed that just about everybody else in the market was a noise trader or was engaged in playing musical chairs. He delighted in the opportunities that these less scrupulous investors provide for cool-headed, objective, sophisticated analysts to make profits. "Wall Street people . . . learn nothing . . . and forget everything," he declared in a 1976 interview just a few days before he died at his home in Aix-en-Provence. He never thought the old classical rules would go out of fashion, and he stuck by the warning he and Dodd had issued in the first edition of *Security Analysis* against ". . . overemphasis on the superficial or the temporary. Twenty years of varied experience in Wall Street have taught the senior author that this overemphasis is at once the delusion and the nemesis of the world of finance."[19]

How did Graham feel about the efficient market hypothesis? "I am sure they are all very hardworking and serious," he answered, referring to the academic proponents of the efficient market and random walk. But, he added, "I don't see how you can say that the prices made in Wall Street are the right prices in any intelligent definition of what right prices would be."[20]

That was a curious statement. As far back as the 1962 edition of *Security Analysis,* Graham and Dodd had argued that the investment results analysts can hope to achieve depend less on their skill than on competition: "The more skillful analysts there are, the harder it will be for the average practitioner to 'beat the market.'" In fact, Graham and Dodd had anticipated the key ideas of market efficiency:

> The real accomplishment of the many thousand analysts now studying not so many thousand companies is the establishment of proper relative prices in today's market for most of the leading issues and a great many secondary ones. . . . [I]nsofar as stock prices are relatively "right" on the basis of known and foreseeable facts, the opportunities for consistently above-average results must necessarily diminish. . . . [R]elative market prices already reflect pretty well those facts and expectations on which nearly all analysts would agree.[21]

This view differs little from Fama's admonition that "fundamental analysis is a fairly useless procedure both for the average analyst and the average investor," or from Samuelson's comment about investors hurrying "in pursuit of avid and intelligent self-interest."

This issue is central to what this book is all about. If everyone is a noise trader, the market will be chaotic. No theory about a market like that is possible. The presence of avid and intelligent investors is a necessary condition for a market that lends itself to systematic analysis and understanding. The unhappy part of the story is that the more avid and intelligent those investors are, the more difficult they make life for one another. We are all blessed that there is just enough opportunity for one or another of them to win just often enough that the game takes on its zest. A little inefficiency goes a long way in making the game worth playing.

Graham's system is a set of rules rather than a theory of value. Each of us can honor the system and still have a different set of rules to satisfy our own beliefs about what is important. The Dividend Discount Model *is* a theory of value; it rests on the propositions that an asset is worth only what its owner can get out of it and that its future cash flows diminish in present value as we move further out in time. Whereas Graham uses existing accounting data as inputs, the Dividend Discount Model uses expectations about the future.

Despite these differences, the two approaches end up recommending the same kinds of stocks for purchase and for sale. The stocks that meet Graham's criteria for buying tend to be depressed, unwanted, unloved. The stocks that meet his criteria for selling tend to be in great demand by other investors. But the expected stream of cash payments calculated from the Dividend Discount Model will also be more attractive when you can buy a stock at a low price than at a high price, which means that investors who use the Dividend Discount Model also end up looking for stocks that are unloved and selling the ones in great demand.

Investors who play musical chairs buy what is rising and sell what is falling. They chase prices, while value-based investors wait for prices to come to them. They buy as price falls and sell as price rises. Neither strategy is right all the time. Price chasers set up golden opportunities for the value-based investors, but meanwhile they can dominate stock prices for long periods of time before the misvaluations become too obvious to ignore.

Value-based strategies require great patience and fortitude as well as skill in interpreting accounting statements and projecting cash flows. Stocks seldom fall to new lows or rise to new highs for no reason at all. Recognizing that today's rise or fall is likely to be temporary is difficult at best, in part because it is not always true. Acting on that perception is even more difficult. One of my friends, a skilled investor who swears by the Dividend Discount Model, insists that the strategy works only when he and his colleagues all have bellyaches; if they feel fine, they have picked the wrong stocks.

We now turn to three variations on the theory of value. The first looks at it from a fresh angle—from the viewpoint of the issuer rather than the buyer of securities. The second describes another of Sharpe's innovations, a systematic method for determining the discount rate to be applied to future cash flows; this achievement turned out to be far more significant and far-reaching than his simplification of the Markowitz approach. The third opens up an entirely new vista, not only to valuation, but to the endless possibilities revealed by the theories of portfolio selection and market behavior.

# Chapter
# 9

# The Bombshell
# Assertions

*Franco has the mind of an arbitrager, an Italian currency speculator.*

At about the time James Tobin was revising Keynes and upsetting the interior decorators of the investment profession, two macroeconomists were putting a novel twist on the question of what stocks are worth. The valuation problem had nothing to do with what they had set out to find, but their approach to it turned out to be a radical break with conventional wisdom.

The influence of their work has spread far beyond the valuation of securities. Some people hold them responsible for the debt explosion of the 1980s; others, more moderate, blame them for the takeover craze that led to the disappearance of revered corporate names and the loss of jobs in formerly stable communities. Still others find their conclusions so foreign to common sense that they could not possibly influence any one beyond a few impressionable students. Yet both of them are Nobel laureates.

Franco Modigliani and Merton Miller were an odd couple when their collaboration began in 1956. Modigliani, who won his prize in 1985, was the senior partner, with nearly twenty years of teaching experience. Born in Italy, he barely managed to escape the anti-Semitic persecution there in the years before World War II. He and his bride landed in New York on August 28, 1939, just three days before war broke out.

Miller, five years younger, had had only five years of teaching experience when they started working together. Boston-born, his

*163*

accent still suggests his origins even though he left the Boston area nearly fifty years ago. He won his Nobel Prize in 1990 while he was at the University of Chicago.

Miller speaks of one of the contrasts between them: "I am . . . not noticeably more ebullient. On an ebullience scale of 1 to 10, most economists would rate Franco as at least a 9 and a half, and possibly even higher in his younger days. I think they would rate me no better than a 6."[1] He significantly underrates himself.

After graduating from Harvard in 1943, Miller spent the next few years in Washington, first at the Treasury and then at the Federal Reserve. But he found life at the Fed too constraining and decided to leave. He was also disillusioned by the kind of economics he had learned at Harvard, where classical theories about the functioning of competitive markets received short shrift. So he entered Johns Hopkins, where he received his Ph.D. in 1952, and then taught U.S. economic history for a year at the London School of Economics. In 1953, he joined Carnegie Tech to teach economic history and public finance.

In 1956, his dean, George Leland Bach, asked him if he would like to fill a vacancy in corporate finance at the Business School. Miller recalls that economists in those days were "kind of snobbish about that," and he told Bach he was not interested.

Bach replied that perhaps he had not made himself clear. "The Business School salaries are up here," he said, pointing to the ceiling. "The economics scale is down there," pointing to the floor. He suggested that Miller choose between snobbishness at an economist's wage and "an opportunity to help out in our flagship program. . . ." Bach had struck the right key: Miller and his wife had just had their second child. "We should talk about this a little further," Miller said.[2]

By 1958 Modigliani was already widely known and respected in the economics profession for his work in macroeconomics and monetary theory. He had earned his doctorate at the New School for Social Research in New York in 1941, supporting himself by selling Italian books for his father-in-law, who had been a distributor of books and newspapers in prewar Italy and was now living in the United States. Modigliani spent his days selling books, his evenings taking courses at the New School, and his nights studying.

Modigliani speaks enthusiastically about the education he received at the New School. The New School had been founded in

1919 by the economists Thorstein Veblen and Wesley Mitchell and the historians Charles Beard and James Harvey Robinson as a free-form institution of higher learning for adults; over the years it had attracted many outstanding and controversial teachers.

In 1933, shortly after Hitler seized power, Alvin Johnson, then president of the New School, saw a unique opportunity to bring some of Europe's most distinguished scholars to the school. Rapidly gathering the money needed for the purpose, he launched the University in Exile, a graduate school with a long list of illustrious scholars, not all of them Jewish, who in turn attracted brilliant students like Franco Modigliani.

Modigliani soon became close friends with Jacob Marschak, who left the New School in 1943 to join the Chicago faculty and to become Director of Research at the Cowles Commission—and who was later to be Markowitz's mentor. "I even called Jascha by his first name," Modigliani recalls.[3] The friendship with Marschak was important, because Modigliani was eager to learn quantitative methods. This approach was still unknown to most economists in Europe, but it was under intense development by European economists in the United States. Marschak was a leader in this area.

Modigliani also became friendly with the Dutch economist Tjalling Koopmans. Koopmans was then working in New York for a Dutch shipping company, where he was applying his new technique of linear programming to the company's scheduling problems.

Modigliani then launched forth on a varied teaching career. He began at the New Jersey College for Women. In 1942, he moved to Bard College, a small institution on the Hudson River with an economics department that consisted of only two people when he arrived. He then went on to stints at the New School, at Chicago (at Milton Friedman's recommendation), and at the University of Illinois.

While Modigliani was teaching at the New School, some Harvard friends tried to lure him to Cambridge. He went up for an interview with Harold Burbank, then head of the department. Modigliani describes Burbank as "a famous anti-foreigner and anti-semite."[7] Samuelson is even harsher: "Burbank stood for everything in scholarly life for which I had utter contempt and abhorrence."[5] The interview did not go well. Burbank reviewed the list of all the famous people on the Harvard faculty, expressed

*165*

his doubts that Modigliani could match their skills, and suggested that the young man go home.*

Though he had decided that Harvard was clearly not for him, Modigliani did have lunch with Joseph Schumpeter and Gottfried Haberler while he was in Cambridge. Haberler was another senior and foreign-born member of the Harvard department. "They gave me hell," Modigliani recalls, when he told them he had decided to return to the New School.[6] They insisted that Burbank had overstepped his authority and had no business rejecting the choice of the economics faculty. Unpersuaded, Modigliani took the train back to New York City that afternoon.

In 1952, Modigliani moved to Pittsburgh to join Carnegie Tech, now Carnegie Mellon University, where he stayed for eight profitable years. He enjoyed his colleagues and wrote some of his major papers there, not the least of which was the paper written in collaboration with Merton Miller.

When Miller at last accepted Dean Bach's invitation to move up in the world, he knew almost nothing about corporate finance beyond what he had picked up while working in the Division of Tax Research at the Treasury. At Bach's suggestion, he took the courses in corporate finance that were being offered that fall of 1956 and started to teach the subject the following spring. Bach assigned two senior faculty people to keep "an avuncular eye" on his progress. One of them was Modigliani, whose office right next door placed them, as Miller describes it, "cheek by jowl in the same bay."[7]

As Miller looked more deeply into corporate finance, he stumbled onto a question that was the mirror image of the question that had concerned Markowitz and Tobin. They had asked how investors should select securities to buy for the optimal portfolio. Miller turned that question around by asking how a corporation should select securities to *sell* to arrive at an optimal balance between debt and equity—the claims of creditors versus the claims of stockholders.

---

*I had an identical experience with Burbank. While I was teaching at Williams College in 1946, I was toying with the idea of working for a doctorate, and, as my undergraduate degree was from Harvard, I drove over to Cambridge to get the lay of the land. Burbank did everything possible to discourage me by listing all the brilliant people of my vintage who had already signed up for graduate study at Harvard. He succeeded!

One of the jobs of a corporate finance officer is to raise money for the company on the most favorable terms. The higher the price of the company's securities in the market, the less interest the company will have to pay on its outstanding debt and the smaller the share of the company it will have to sell to raise a given amount of capital. The lower the "hurdle rate," the easier it is for the company to grow. In the lingo of corporate finance, maximizing the value of the corporation in the market contributes to the well-being of the stockholders and reduces cost of the corporation's capital.

Miller observed that, although some companies borrowed a lot more than others, the business community seemed to be running on a set of unorganized rules-of-thumb. He could find no systematic guidelines that would tell a corporate financial officer how deeply to go into debt—whether going into debt would matter at all. He reasoned that there had to be some method for converting corporate finance from a mixture of seat-of-the-pants decisions made by accountants and Wall Street bankers into a structured theory that would produce a better outcome.

His immediate goal was to find the combination of debt and stockholders' equity that would persuade investors to pay the highest possible price for the corporation's securities—not just its stocks, not just its bonds, but both together. He began by analyzing the relevant facts.

The research agenda that Miller laid out for his graduate students involved a series of statistical industry studies to seek evidence of the fabled "optimal" capital structure. To their astonishment, the target of their search simply did not show up. The weighted average costs of capital that the market demanded from the corporations seemed to bear no relation to the ratio of debt to equity in their capital structures. How much the corporations borrowed seemed to have no effect on whether a corporation's cost of capital was high or low. The data were little more than mish-mash.

Modigliani was moving along a different road. He was teaching macroeconomics and doing research on the forces that determine periodic fluctuations in business activity. In exploring the strategic role of business spending on plant and equipment, he turned to the impact of the corporation's capital costs on these investment decisions.

In 1952, at a conference sponsored by the National Bureau of

Economic Research, Modigliani presented a paper on the effect of the availability of funds on business investment. One of the other speakers at the conference was David Durand, the MIT professor who wrote "Growth Stocks and the Petersburg Paradox."

Durand gave a paper in which he proposed the notion that the value of the firm as a whole is independent of the relationship between borrowed money and stockholders' money in the firm's capital structure. If the value of the firm is independent of its capital structure, then its capital structure does not matter! More debt, less debt, more stock, less stock—the result is the same either way. Durand dubbed this hypothesis Entity Theory, "entity" referring to the corporation as a whole, distinct from its parts.

Having made this challenging proposal, Durand turned around and proceeded to reject his Entity Theory. He argued that it did not conform to the the real world, and that equity investors do not value the parts of the capital structure in relation to the whole. Rather, they value stocks separately, without regard to the value of the firm's debt obligations. Important institutional investors like life insurance companies, and, in the early 1950s, most fiduciary investors like personal trusts and endowment funds, were pretty much excluded from buying common stocks. They were limited to investing most of their assets in bonds, a limitation that led them to lend money at lower rates of interest than they would demand in a completely free-market situation. He concluded that a corporation that borrows money is likely to pay less for its total capital than a firm that issues only common stock. He recommended an increase in the ratio of debt to equity to reduce the cost of capital.

Modigliani had a hunch that Durand's original idea of Entity Theory was right. He fussed with the subject whenever he had the chance. Every time, he convinced himself all over again that the value of the firm is indeed independent of its capital structure.

During the spring semester of 1956, Modigliani presented his ideas, with mathematical proof, to a class in macroeconomics that Miller happened to be attending. Immediately, Miller recognized that here was the solution to the cost-of-capital problem that had been bothering him. "My mind was already prepared for it," Miller told me, "and when I told him [Modigliani] of my empirical results . . . he began to regard the possibility of no optimum [in the debt/equity mix] as more than just a theoretical curiosity."[8]

The two decided to work together to develop their ideas. Although Modigliani had broader knowledge of the macroeconomic implications of the matter, he was grateful to be able to link his views to Miller's competence in corporate finance and familiarity with the empirical evidence.

The subject matter held commanding importance. In the very first paragraph of their paper, "The Cost of Capital, Corporation Finance, and the Theory of Investment," Modigliani and Miller point out that the cost of capital and the value of the corporation are critical issues for corporate finance officers and for executives who budget the funds the company spends on new assets—its prime source of growth. The cost of capital motivates capital spending, which means that it influences the pace of overall business activity and the nation's rate of economic growth. It also has significance for investors—the buyers of securities—and for the issuers of securities, because what makes the Modigliani-Miller solution "work" is the behavior of investors in a Fama-type, efficient-market environment.

Modigliani and Miller's central point is simple. They pick up on Durand's 1952 paper on Entity Theory and declare that "the market value of any firm is independent of its capital structure."[9] Whether a corporation borrows a lot or borrows a little, its cost of capital will remain the same.

Modigliani and Miller acknowledge the work of a number of other authors who had offered close equivalents of this proposition, but they give Durand the recognition he deserves. One of their references is to John Burr Williams, who, twenty years earlier in *The Theory of Investment Value,* had declared that the value of a company "in no wise depends on what the company's capitalization is." Williams gave this idea the imposing title of the Law of the Conservation of Investment Value and compared it to "the indestructibility of matter or energy":

> Clearly, if a single individual or a single institutional investor owned all the bonds, stocks, and warrants issued by a corporation, it would not matter to this investor what the company's capitalization was. . . . To such an individual it would be perfectly obvious that *total* interest- and dividend-paying power was in no wise dependent on the kind of securities issued to the company's owner.[10] (emphasis added)

Modigliani and Miller distinguish their approach from other approaches by giving uncertainty a pivotal role in their analytical structure. If the return to the corporation from new investment projects is uncertain—which is the way life happens to be—certain traditional assumptions fall apart. For example, the assumption that corporate managers can maximize the company's profits is a matter of faith among most corporate managers. Yet, if profits are an uncertain stream of income, how can anyone find ways to maximize them? The assumption holds only when the return from capital spending is certain.

Corporate executives have a more feasible alternative. They can try to maximize the value that investors in the market put on the company's stock and bonds. To achieve that goal, they must subject every investment project to the following test: "Will the project, as financed, raise the market value of the company's shares? If so, it is worth undertaking." The expectation is that the market value of the company's stock will rise if the anticipated earnings from the project exceed the cost of financing for the corporation *as a whole,* not just if they exceed the direct cost of the particular project.

In plain English, let the market decide. Investors are continually making judgments about the streams of income they expect corporations to produce over time for their owners and creditors, judgments about the uncertainty surrounding those future income streams, and judgments about the relative riskiness and relative earning power of each corporation relative to other corporations.

Although the owners of a company that borrows money are in a riskier position than the owners of a debt-free company, the value of the company's bonds and stock, *taken as a totality,* will still depend on the company's overall expected earning power and the basic risks the company faces. That is the essence of Williams's law of the Conservation of Investment Value. Under these conditions, and ignoring just for the moment transactions costs, taxes, and the possible lack of sufficient information, the market will place the same valuation on all companies with equal earning power and equal risk. No other outcome is possible when the market is functioning as Samuelson theorized that it should and as research into the efficiency of capital markets has demonstrated that it does.

As people in Wall Street like to say, it sounds good in theory but does it work in practice? To prove that the outcome they describe is the only possible outcome, Modigliani and Miller make what is probably their most ingenious contribution to the theory of finance. They seize on a common feature of competitive markets and elevate it to the level of a driving force. In so doing they make a significant advance over both Williams and Durand.

That feature is known as arbitrage, or, among economic theorists, as the Law of One Price. Two assets with identical attributes should sell for the same price, and so should an identical asset trading in two different markets. If the prices of such an asset differ, a profitable opportunity will arise to sell the asset where it is overpriced and to buy it back where it is underpriced. The arbitrager will then lock in a sure profit, otherwise known as a free lunch. The familiar aphorism that "There is no such thing as a free lunch" applies only to perfect markets; imperfect markets provide a playground for the "arbs," as they are known in Wall Street slang.

Arbs have acquired a certain notoriety, because they seem to be operating in some price-manipulative fashion. This is a misperception. Actually, they keep the markets honest. They bring perfection to imperfect markets as their hunger for free lunches prompts them to bid away the discrepancies that attract them to the lunch counter. In the process, they make certain that prices for the same assets in different markets will be identical.

Recalling their discussions about this line of argument, Miller smiled and said, "Franco has the mind of an arbitrager, an Italian currency speculator. He always thinks in those terms."[11] Modigliani, in an understatement, observed that this approach was what made their 1958 paper "quite novel, even beyond the radical character of the core topic."[12]

Even tourists ignorant of the theory of finance can turn into arbitragers. The Law of One Price was violated in the early 1980s when the foreign exchange rate for the dollar was so high that everything abroad seemed extraordinarily cheap to Americans. A *Wall Street Journal* reporter demonstrated that an American who flew to London, enjoyed fancy meals and hotel accommodations for a few days, and loaded up on items like sweaters, whiskey, and china, could save enough money, compared to the cost of the same items in New York City, to cover the cost of the round-trip airfare. As time passed, prices in England rose and altered the exchange rate between English pounds and dollars until the discrepancy no longer existed. At that point, it no longer paid to buy cashmere sweaters at Harrod's; one could do just as well at Saks Fifth Avenue.

Arbitrage will also tend to equalize the market values of companies with equivalent earning power and riskiness *regardless of how they are financed.* Consider two companies that we shall call General Motors and General Electric, both of which, for the sake of argument, earn $10 million a year. Assume that investors believe that both companies will be able to sustain or increase that earning power at the same rate over time.

The companies have been financed differently. General Motors was financed with an issue of common stock equal to $100 million. General Electric took a different path and used what is known as leverage: It issued only $60 million in common stock and borrowed $40 million by issuing bonds paying 5 percent a year interest.

With only common stock outstanding, General Motor's total earnings of $10 million accrue to the owners of its shares. General Electric, however, must first pay interest of $2 million on its bonds, leaving $8 million for its stockholders.

What happens if the Law of One Price is violated? Suppose General Motors stock is selling for its issue value of $100 million, while General Electric stock is selling for $70 million, or $10 million more than its issue value of $60 million. Together with its $40 million in bonds, General Electric as a totality is valued in the market place at $110 million, more than the market value of General Motors. Despite the different market valuations, the two companies still have identical earning power and riskiness.

Now Mr. Arbitrager smells a free lunch. He owns 1 percent of General Electric's stock, which makes him worth $700,000 and earns him an income of $80,000 a year. He sells his shares in General Electric and simultaneously buys a 1 percent position in General Motors stock. Problem: A 1 percent position in General Motors will cost $1,000,000 but the proceeds of his sale of the General Electric shares will buy him only 0.7 percent of General Motors; he is $300,000 short. Solution: Borrow $300,000 at 5 percent.

Now Mr. Arbitrager owns 1 percent of General Motors, which brings him an income of $100,000. He cannot pocket the whole amount, because he owes $300,000 on which he has to pay $15,000 in interest. But he is still ahead of the game: After paying the interest on his loan, he still has $85,000 in his pocket. That is

$5,000 more than he had been earning on his 1 percent position in General Electic stock, and the risk is no greater than it was before. This is a free lunch par excellence: He has made a profit without taking on additional risk.

Modigliani and Miller use the expression "home-made leverage" to describe Mr. Arbitrager's borrowing on his own to buy the General Motors stock. General Motors had financed itself without leverage; Mr. Arbitrager used home-made leverage to turn the trick. But the opportunity is too good to last. Now a crowd of arbitragers will follow his lead, selling General Electric stock and buying General Motors. They will drive up the price of GM and push down the price of GE until the total market values of the two companies are once again equal.

It sounds almost too good to be true. Yet, when Modigliani and Miller set the whole process in the active, competitive, information-flooded capital markets of the real world, they gave their argument a ring of veracity and inevitability that was lacking in the work of others. The use of arbitrage and home-made leverage avoids the institutional peculiarities that stand in the way of Durand's Entity Theory, peculiarities that Modigliani and Miller characterize as "large and *systematic* imperfections in the market which permanently bias the outcome."[13]

Miller declares that the arbitrage proof makes their conclusion unassailable:

> This arbitrage proof was the decisive distinction between our approach and those of our predecessors, David Durand and John Burr Williams. They thought it might or might not hold; we showed it *had to* hold in the kind of perfect capital markets that economists had long made central to their analysis. . . . [I]f it did not hold, the capital markets would be grossly and consistently violating one of the most venerable tenets of economics, to wit, the Law of One Price.[14]

The analysis is elegant, but it still seems hard to accept. Corporations can almost always save money and increase earnings for their stockholders by borrowing instead of issuing stock, even aside from tax considerations. Thanks to leverage, General Electric in our example earned $8 million on its $60 million issuance of common stock, or 13 percent, while General Motors, with no debt, earned only 10 percent on its common stock. Why should General Electric not be worth more than General Motors?

Markowitz supplies the answer: risk. The earnings on General Electric common stock will be more volatile, because the fixed charges for interest have a prior claim on the company's earning power. General Electric stock may earn more per dollar invested than General Motors stock, but that does not mean that it is worth more than General Motors. It will be worth more *only* if General Electric has good prospects of earning more than $10 million before interest or it has good prospects of going into less risky lines of business with no loss of earning power.

Modigliani and Miller use a colorful analogy to drive this point home:

> Under perfect markets, a dairy farmer cannot in general earn more for the milk he produces by skimming some of the butter fat and selling it separately, even though butter fat per unit of weight sells for more than whole milk. The advantage from skimming the milk rather than selling whole milk would be purely illusory; for what would be gained from selling the high-priced butter fat would be lost in selling the low-priced residue of thinned milk.[15]

In the early stages of their work together, Modigliani was more skeptical than Miller about the validity of the theory. But Miller, a passionate believer in the power of free markets to forge optimal and predictable outcomes, stood his ground: "I *believed* it! I felt from the very beginning that this is right," he told me with a broad smile.[16] With Modigliani's help and inspiration, Miller proceeded to construct a full-fledged theoretical edifice, complete with carefully articulated assumptions and a broad-ranging exploration of its meaning for the economy as a whole.

The resulting body of theory has come to be known as "MM." You have only to mention these letters to finance people, and they know what you mean.

By the time Modigliani and Miller had finished their work, they had produced a long, intricate paper. They gave it its first public airing at a meeting of the American Econometric Society in December 1957. In June 1958, "The Cost of Capital, Corporation Finance, and the Theory of Investment" appeared in the official publication of the American Economic Association, the *American Economic Review,* familiarly known as the *AER.*

Modigliani and Miller's unorthodox ideas were to stir heated controversy in the profession, but their article caused problems even before it saw the light of day. It was one of the first articles to appear under joint authorship in the *AER,* though that is now a common practice in most academic journals. It was also much too long. The editor, Bernard Haley, threw out a lengthy appendix that dealt with the macroeconomic implications of the theory, retaining only the parts that related directly to the corporation.

Modigliani and Miller gave Haley another headache. In mathematical notation, the conventional symbol for the average, or mean value, of a group of numbers is $\bar{x}$. So few articles with a mathematical orientation had appeared in the *AER* up to that time that the typesetter had no automatic way to place the bar over the x, and Haley wanted to charge Modigliani and Miller for setting this unusual symbol. Today, the *AER* routinely carries Greek formulations that are far more intricate than Modigliani and Miller's little bar.

In September 1959, the *AER* published a hostile review of MM theory by David Durand, who was not easily persuaded to give up his own view of the matter. By coincidence, Durand would soon write another unfriendly review, this one of Harry Markowitz's book, aiming, as Miller described it, "to consign Markowitz to oblivion." Miller laughs when he recalls Durand's reviews: "He was wrong on both—just colossally wrong!"[17] Miller is grateful to Durand, however, because he believes it was Durand's 25-page attack and the opportunity for Modigliani and Miller to publish a 15-page response in the same issue that really put their theory on the map. The *AER* subsequently published four more critiques of MM theory, of the many that were submitted.

Two years later, Miller moved on to a tenured position at the University of Chicago, where he has remained ever since. He now holds the title of Robert R. McCormick Distinguished Service Professor in the Graduate School of Business. Modigliani left Carnegie Tech in 1960 to go to MIT, where he has remained.

Their creative collaboration survived that separation. In October 1961 they published an important paper on the relevance of MM theory to corporate dividend policy, which appeared in the Chicago University's *Journal of Business.* And in June 1966 the *American Economic Review* published their full-scale empirical investigation of the cost of capital for the public utility industry. Miller, alone or in collaboration, has continued to study, publish, and proselytize the MM theorems.

*175*

Modigliani and Miller's ideas have aroused both criticism and admiration ever since they appeared. A paper published in 1989 by Professor Myron Gordon of the University of Toronto cites 48 articles and books on the subject over a period of some twenty years, almost all of which take issue in one way or another with their 1958 paper and subsequent research.

Criticisms of the theory have not been directed to its internal logic, which, given the assumptions, is impregnable. The most frequent complaint is that MM is not "realistic."

If changes in capital structure have no impact on the overall valuation of a corporation, then why was there so much fuss about all that so-called "funny money" and "Chinese paper" that the conglomerates issued to buy up companies in the early 1970s? If the ratio of debt to equity is irrelevant, why was there all the shouting about the junk bonds and concern about debt/equity ratios in the 1980s? If dividends do not matter, why do corporations bother to issue them at all? If the only thing that matters is the fundamental earning power of the corporations's underlying assets, why are all those corporate finance officers and their investment bankers spending so much time fine-tuning and modulating the firm's financial structure?

MM theory was admittedly an abstraction when it was originally presented. Like all economists, Modigliani and Miller tried to run their experiments with clean test tubes. In their antiseptic world there are no taxes, no transaction costs, information is freely available to everyone, growth is treated in simplified fashion, and corporations make investment decisions first and then worry about how to finance them.

No one—least of all Modigliani and Miller—would claim that the real world looks like this. But by starting with immaculate laboratory equipment, they can test their hypotheses, analyze the consequences of their assumptions, and determine how closely their theory accords with the real world. Their simplifications help clarify how, and if, investors make the flat assertions of the theory operational through arbitrage and home-made leverage in a way that keeps the value of the corporation independent of its capital structure. If it turns out that financing policy in the real world does influence the company's cost of capital, MM theory at least defines the necessary conditions under which that will happen.

Followed to its ultimate conclusion, the theory leads to what is perhaps its most controversial feature: The value of the corporation will be the same whether the corporation pays a big dividend, a small dividend, or no dividend at all. Miller has written about how he and Modigliani failed to realize what a blockbuster they had with that one. He says that they had been led "to dismiss the whole dividend question as 'a mere detail'—not the last time, alas, that we may have overworked that innocent word 'mere'"[18]

The real issue, they argue, is how dividend payments affect the way the corporation finds the money to finance its growth, which they assume is independent of dividend policy. A company's investments in its future competes with the demand of stockholders for dividends; attending to one will either constrain the other or force the company into the capital markets to raise funds. Stockholders like to receive cash dividends. But dividends paid today shrink the assets of the company and reduce its future earning power. The cash must be replaced either by borrowing money or by issuing new shares of stock. Paying dividends will influence how the company finances its growth, but it will have no lasting effect on the company's value in the marketplace; that will still depend on its growth potential and its riskiness.

What happens to MM theory when we move into the real-world environment in which taxes must be paid, in which stock prices go up when dividends are raised, and in which financing decisions dominate and even motivate corporate growth strategies? MM theory is robust enough to weather these fundamental alterations in its assumptions. When its predictions fail to hold up, that very failure reveals what is happening and what the corporation must do to maximize its value.

Although the original theory assumed a world without taxes, it still provides valuable insight into the role taxes play in determining the cost of capital and in guiding the responses of the capital markets. Taxation encourages borrowing, because the interest paid on borrowed money is a deductible expense. Less paid in taxes means more on the bottom line—and more for stockholders. With more earning power after taxes, debt finance should raise the value of the corporation. Capital structure *does* matter.

Although Modigliani and Miller had suggested this possibility in their original paper, they clarified the issue in a paper published in 1963. In a memoir published in 1988, Miller recalled:

This [proposition] carried not very flattering implications for the top managements of companies with low levels of debt. It suggested that the high bond ratings of such companies, in which the management took so much pride, may actually have been a sign of their incompetence; that the managers were leaving too much of their stockholders' money on the table in the form of unnecessary corporate income tax payments . . . [of] many billions of dollars.[19]

The sleepy managers of earlier decades had indeed been missing an opportunity to benefit their stockholders. The highly charged financial environment of the 1980s woke them up. In recent years many leveraged buyout deals have involved debt that is nine or ten times as large as the stockholders' equity—"far beyond anything we had ever dared use in our numerical illustrations of how leverage could be used to reduce taxes," says Miller. But these deals also "redirect attention to the assumption . . . crucial to the MM dividend irrelevance proposition, that the firm's financial decisions can be taken as independent of its real operating and investment decisions."[20]

What Modigliani and Miller call "the leverage proposition" will probably continue to provoke heated debate. Miller returned to it in his Nobel Prize address in Stockholm in December 1990 when he admitted that his positive view of the leveraged buyouts of the 1980s is still "far from universally accepted among the wider public."[21] But he remains unrepentant. He argues that losses on junk bonds were no proof that over-leveraging had occurred and that increased leveraging by corporations does not imply increased risk for the economy as a whole.

He points out that the buyers of junk bonds knew they were taking outsize risks. Why else would they have demanded such high interest rates? "For all save the hopelessly gullible," these investors were fully aware that some of the junk bonds would end up in default. Their expectation, consistent with orthodox finance theory, was simply that the return they would earn from taking these risks, after defaults, would be larger than if they had bought riskless bonds instead.

What about the accusation that the corporate debt explosion has made the whole economy more brittle? Leverage "serves merely to partition the risk [or the company's earnings stream] among the firm's security holders."[22] When a company borrows money to buy in its own stock in a leveraged buyout, or LBO, the creditors have a larger claim and the stockholders have a smaller claim on the company's assets, but the company's basic earning power remains the same.

The bondholders also are in a riskier position, because the protection they receive from a cushion of stockholders' money has been reduced. Even so, the company's total risk has not changed: more of the company's capital is now in the form of bonds that have a prior claim on the company's assets and are therefore inherently less risky than stocks. Both classes of securities, considered separately, are riskier than they were, but the *total* risk has not risen because some of the riskier security, stock, has been replaced by a less risky security, bonds.

Despite Miller's forceful arguments, certain complications and contradictions persist. Interest payments that are deductible for the borrower become taxable to the lender who receives them. Consequently corporate debt issuance to save taxes is less of a blessing than it appears to be. Taxes also influence dividend policy. Under conditions where the tax rate on dividends is higher than the tax rate on capital gains, the less the company pays out and the more it reinvests—or uses to repurchase outstanding shares—the better off the taxable shareholders should be. Once taxes come into the picture, even borrowing money to repurchase shares can have positive consequences for corporate valuation.

The tax issue is not the only issue Modigliani and Miller have had to confront. The appropriate model for the valuation of corporate earning power remains an unsettled question. Leverage carried too far leads to risk of bankruptcy, an issue Miller believes is exaggerated. Still, leverage does put limits on borrowing, so that capital structure is not always irrelevant. Advances in financial theory have suggested that dividends may be irrelevant in the MM sense, but in a world in which all information is not freely available to everyone dividends send important signals to stockholders about management's expectations for long-run corporate earning power. Miller himself wrote in 1987 that dividends clearly matter for individual investors:

> . . . [Common stocks] are usually more than just the abstract "bundles of returns" of our economic models. Behind each holding may be a story of family business, family quarrels,

legacies received, divorce settlements, and a host of other considerations almost totally irrelevant to our theories of portfolio selection. That we abstract from all of these stories is not because the stories are uninteresting, but because they may be too interesting and thereby distract us from the pervasive market forces that should be our principal concern.[23]

The final test of any theory is how accurately it portrays the real world, blemishes and all. The academic literature carries numerous discussions of what the optimal corporate capital structure should be, but, as Modigliani and Miller predicted, a coherent theory is still elusive. If Miller's graduate students were to undertake a project today similar to the one they undertook some forty years ago, they would come up with similar results: Corporations with approximately the same earning power and the same degree of riskiness continue to have significantly different capital structures. That is perhaps the most eloquent testimony that capital structure does not matter.

In a world as jumbled as this, Modigliani and Miller's original insight—that the market value of the firm is independent of its capital structure—looks remarkably sturdy. In 1990, James Vertin, author of the lead article in the first issue of *The Journal of Portfolio Management,* was still able to refer to their work as "bombshell assertions."[24] The bombshells are still exploding, and the world is still reverberating to them.

# Chapter
# 10

## Risky Business

*Knack, feel, whim, and intuition are . . . useless relics.*

Markowitz, Tobin, and Sharpe all describe rational investors as masters of their fate. The theories of portfolio selection show investors choosing this asset over that, carefully balancing risk against expected return, and arranging their choices into optimal combinations called efficient portfolios.

Samuelson and Fama describe a different world. In their theories of market behavior, investors are no longer masters of their fate; they are at the mercy of unrelieved bedlam and the Demon of Chance. Even if investors happen to look smart occasionally, Jensen, Cowles, and Osborne are quick to remind us that they are nothing but egotistical orangutans. After all, didn't Bachelier, decades ago, prove that the expected return in a speculative market is zero?

In the Modigliani and Miller model, conscientious investors make judgments about the riskiness of each corporation and then meticulously apply John Burr Williams's rules to their expectations of the corporation's future earnings stream. Most players are not so painstaking, but the essential principle is valid. Noise traders who take their tips from stories told at cocktail parties, chase only what is hot, and dump their stocks in a panic lose out in the long run, no matter how smart they may seem in the short run. They end up selling too cheaply to better-informed, more patient investors, or else they pay too dearly for stocks that more systematic investors are kind enough to sell them. Modigliani and Miller understood this pattern of behavior. They conclude their 1961 article on the relevance of dividends with the comment, "Investors, no matter how naive they may be when they enter the mar-

ket, do sometimes learn from experience." They add, "[P]erhaps
. . . even from reading articles such as this."[1]

MM theory demonstrates that it is the market—that is, all the
investors buying and selling at any given moment—that fixes the
value of the corporation. Granted, the board of directors, the chief
executive officer, and the chief financial officer deploy the corporation's assets for future growth and decide how to finance the
corporation. But their decisions do no more than influence investor perceptions. An entire profession of investor relations consultants has sprung up to sway those perceptions, and annual reports
often carry as much hype as information. Still, research reveals
that investors have a sharp nose for smelling out the truth for
themselves.

Thus, Modigliani and Miller put investors back in the catbird
seat, with corporate managers at their mercy. Through arbitrage,
profit-seeking investors can eliminate discrepancies in the perceived risk/return trade-offs of one security relative to another to
the point where no one has any incentive to buy or sell. Trades
take place only when investors disagree about the future of a company or when new information surfaces. Modigliani and Miller's
market is a market in equilibrium.

And yet equilibrium is only a rough approximation of reality,
because information pours into the marketplace constantly, in
every shape and form. Most investors are restless, and even those
who are more relaxed are beset by brokers hurrying to tell them
what stocks are hot. Fischer Black suggests that most investors
are noise traders at least part of the time, whether they think so
or not. Nevertheless, persistent forces are constantly driving the
market *toward* MM equilibrium. That is what the massive evidence in support of market efficiency tells us. Modigliani and
Miller helped us understand how and why.

But there was more to come.

Benjamin Graham had devised a method for determining
whether a stock is cheap or expensive. That method has stood
many if not all the tests of time, but it is still not a theory. Graham
told the investor what to do but said little about why his prescriptions would work.

Williams came closer to building a theoretical structure and
provided the underpinnings for the theories of Markowitz, Modigliani, and Miller. But even Williams stopped short. The Dividend
Discount Model asks investors to make a forecast of a company's

long-run earning power and then tells them to trim their forecast to allow for uncertainty. Although all valuation procedures boil down to those two steps, Williams failed to suggest a rigorous method for dealing with the uncertainty side of his method. How can investors determine how much to trim their forecast of Ford's future earning power or IBM's or a young start-up company's?

Jack Treynor, who was editor of the *Financial Analysts Journal* from 1969 to 1981, believes that a security analyst can learn more about a company's earning power by looking at what the market thinks the company is worth than by studying the numbers that accountants so meticulously prepare—important as the accounting numbers may be. This view is in the spirit of Modigliani and Miller, but it is the opposite of how most analysts go about their work. Analysts *do* study accounting data in arriving at their estimate of what a company is worth, but, in a 1972 editorial in the *Journal* titled "The Trouble With Earnings," Treynor points out that accountants make "arbitrary mechanical estimates" of value when they prepare statements of earnings. But to make estimates of value one must *start* with earnings data. Skeptical of such circular reasoning, Treynor remarks, "Unless he thinks that 'garbage in-garbage out!' applies only to computers . . . the thinking security analyst is not going to be happy with this answer."[2]

Treynor is something of an oddball. He is also one of the more important figures mentioned in this book. He is neither an academic nor a practitioner in any conventional sense. Although he took some graduate courses, he never earned a Ph.D. He has written many articles, but he has written no book on the theory of finance. His most important paper was never published; it is occasionally cited in the academic literature, always as an "unpublished manuscript." His name does not even appear on my mimeographed copy of that manuscript.

Treynor is tall, lean, intense, and introverted. When he talks to you, he spends more time looking at the ceiling than looking you in the eye. He has sported a crew cut most of his life, even when less inner directed men were capitulating to longer hair. When I asked him on one occasion how he was spending his time, he answered, "I think." With little time in his thinking for matters of ego, he is shy and unduly modest about his accomplishments.

On one occasion, when he was preparing to address a CRSP seminar, Treynor spent the evening before covering the blackboard with mind-boggling equations. He started his talk the next morning by remarking that one simple equation would summarize his entire paper. He searched the blackboard but discovered that he had omitted that one equation.

Treynor was born in 1930, the son of a successful doctor. He went to college at Haverford, where he had planned to major in physics but ended up majoring in math because he believed the physics department was weak. Now he wonders why he chose math. He feels he was never very good at math and really preferred physics.

After serving in the Army during the Korean War, he entered Harvard Business School, where he decided to concentrate in corporate finance and accounting. He found the program hard to take: "Nothing in my family culture of doctors prepared me for business school," he recalls. He was impressed—"Highly!," he adds—with the professors' skill in "seeing connections between seemingly unrelated ideas," but he was critical of their lack of analytical strength.[3]

He told me that he left Harvard Business School in 1955 "with an enormous impression that finance needed help—a terrible mistake that shaped my whole professional career." He took a job at the consulting firm of Arthur D. Little in Boston, drifted from one area to another there, and learned computer programming ("I wasn't good at it, because I'm not very logical"). Finally ADL, as the firm is known to its employees and clients, assigned him to work on Yale University's endowment fund.[4]

Treynor characterizes this stint "as a truly formative experience." He visited money management organizations all over the country to see what they were doing, how they were doing it, and why they were doing it. He was astonished at the diversity he discovered: "No two were doing it alike, but every one of them thought they were doing it the right way. This was very perplexing."[5]

In the summer of 1959, Treynor went to Colorado on a vacation with his parents. This was the year in which Castro came to power in Cuba, the United States went crazy over hoolahoops, and Alaska and Hawaii became states. But Treynor paid little attention to the headlines. He describes his stay in the Rocky Mountains as "three weeks of unremitting meditation."[6] He was searching for a systematic answer to the question of how rational investors take risk into consideration when they are deciding whether an asset is cheap or expensive. He hoped to develop a model that would specify the discount rate that Williams requires in calculating the present value of a future earnings stream. No one to Treynor's knowledge had ever asked this question or had tried to deal with it in theoretical terms.

Still struggling with the question, he returned to Boston with forty-four pages of notes and equations. But he continued to struggle. Friends with connections at the University of Chicago persuaded him to show a rough draft of his work to Merton Miller, who was sufficiently impressed to send it to Modigliani at MIT. After reading the paper, Modigliani called Treynor on the phone and said "Let's have lunch and talk."[7] Modigliani subsequently arranged for Treynor to present his paper, in two separate sessions, to the finance faculty at MIT.

Modigliani recalls that Treynor was "economically unsophisticated,"[8] but he suggested that Treynor come to MIT and work on a study program that Modigliani would lay out for him. Treynor followed Modigliani's advice and took a year's leave from ADL. Modigliani told me that "I made a mistake with Treynor. He was trying to bite so big a bullet that I did not give sufficient stress to the one part that was right."[9]

Modigliani suggested that Treynor break his paper into two parts. The first part would deal with how investors made their selections within a single time period—a minute, a day, or a year. The second part would explore what happens over several time periods—a sequence of minutes, days, or years. When Treynor set to work, he ran into a problem: The mathematics required for the second part was so intricate that, with only a BS degree in math, he had to give up on it. Modigliani was also uneasy about it and advised him that the problem was "basically impossible" to solve.[10]

The math required to expand the analysis of investor responses to risk from one time period to a sequence of periods turned out to be something known as Ito's lemma. It had been developed by Kiyoshi Ito, a Japanese mathematician, who first described it in 1951 in a publication of the American Mathematical Society.

Robert C. Merton, a mathematician and economist at MIT, would shortly introduce Ito's lemma into the theory of portfolio management. Merton invoked Ito's lemma to unlock the secrets that Treynor had been seeking to discover. These are obscure secrets indeed for non-mathematicians.

A lemma is a proposition introduced to prove another proposition. Merton describes Ito's lemma as providing "the differentiation rule for the generalized stochastic calculus."[11] In plain English, it provided the key for describing how randomly fluctuating security prices change from one short period to the next short period, or, in Merton's terminology, in "continuous time."

Modigliani came up with the title for Treynor's paper, finally completed in 1961: "Toward a Theory of Market Value of Risky Assets." Treynor liked the wording, because he regarded his work as an approach "toward a theory" rather than a statement of ultimate truth.

His goal, Treynor states at the outset, is to "lay a groundwork for a theory of market value which incorporates risk."[12] His purpose was also to join forces with Modigliani and Miller in determining the cost of capital to a corporation. The paper had important implications for portfolio management as well.

Treynor goes at theorizing with zest. He chooses to start at the highest level of abstraction:

> The human mind loves small, concrete, beautiful, elegant relationships, so it's very hard to see the big, fuzzy, stubborn, confusing, resistant relationships. Emerson said that 'Every idea is a prison.' At low levels, you start in prison and can't get out. Grief comes to small solutions that fail to consider this.[13]

Like Markowitz's seminal piece, "Toward a Theory . . ." sketches out the big picture, with little attention to refinements and details. The paper runs to only eighteen double-spaced typewritten pages. Half are straight text and the rest are taken up by equations.

Treynor allies himself at once with the "portfolio theorists"—Markowitz, Tobin, and Sharpe. He acknowledges Tobin as his most direct theoretical ancestor. As the expression "Separation Theorem" had not yet been introduced to describe Tobin's concept, Treynor uses the term "dominance" for the one combination of risky assets that is dominant, because, quoting Tobin, "it gives the investor the highest possible expectation of return available to him at that level of risk." Optimal portfolios will always include that dominant combination of risky assets, and "an investor's attitude toward risk will be reflected in the fraction of his portfolio held in cash, rather than in the . . . composition of the non-cash [risky] assets."[14]

This option to hold assets in cash, or, to be more precise, in a liquid asset like Treasury bills that provides a return known with certainty in advance, is critically important. With the choice of a risk-free asset always available to them, investors will buy risky assets only if they can expect a return greater than the risk-free return. Treynor refers to this anticipated spread between risky and risk-free returns as the "risk premium."[15]

Treynor's contribution to the theory of finance was to devise a method for predicting the risk premium and to demonstrate its overarching importance in the behavior of capital markets as well as in portfolio selection. Markowitz, Tobin, Sharpe, and Modigliani and Miller had all recognized that investors will hold risky assets only if they can expect to earn a premium return for doing so, but none of them had come up with any systematic method for predicting what that risk premium would be. Williams and Graham had been equally silent.

Treynor notes that, although stocks tend to move up and down together, they do not all behave in the same fashion. Some are more volatile than others and swing up and down over a wider range than the average, while others are less sensitive than the market. The emerging growth stocks favored by the aggressive executive suit his taste because they are so volatile, even though he may be taking on more risk than their returns justify. The stodgy stocks of electric utilities, which fluctuate over a narrow range, suit the taste of the widow, even though she may be putting too many eggs in that one basket.

More rational investors, seeking high returns while trying to minimize risks, see no particular advantage in buying stocks that merely keep pace with the stocks they already own. Such stocks offer nothing in the way of diversification or in reducing the basic risks an investor assumes when accumulating a portfolio. Investors will hold them only if they offer a higher expected return than the securities already in the portfolio. In Treynor's idealized market, "the risk premium per share . . . is proportional to the covariance of the investment with the total value of all investments in the market."[16]

As he was working his way through these questions at MIT, Treynor was unaware that William Sharpe was at the time wrestling with almost identical questions—and arriving at similar solutions. By that time, Sharpe was teaching computer courses and investments at the University of Washington, where he had gone after receiving his doctorate at UCLA. He had also published a few papers based on the work he had done while simplifying Markowitz's methods for portfolio selection.

Sharpe enjoyed his seven years at Washington, though he missed the highly charged atmosphere he had known at the University of California. His colleagues in finance at Washington were essentially accountants with no sense of how capital markets behave or how rational investors should manage their portfolios. No one there, he recalls, had ever done any genuine research into the theory of finance. And the faculty in the economics department wanted nothing to do with finance.

Sharpe set out to discover how risk would influence the valuation of *all* the assets that make up the market at any given moment. That goal was more ambitious than Treynor's, but Sharpe's paper on the subject followed much the same path. Treynor comments on the resemblance:

> We use the same premises to reach the same conclusions. I see no difference in objectives.
>
> Sharpe appeals in his paper to the language and concepts of economists, making the argument far more accessible—at least to economists. Actually, Sharpe's paper is probably more accessible even to non-economists, because he spells out many of the implications in words.[17]

Like Treynor, Sharpe speaks of the "absence of a theory that can give any real meaning to the relationship between the price of a single asset and its risk. . . . Unfortunately, little has been said concerning the particular risk component which is relevant."[18]

Sharpe takes off from the propositions that underlie both Markowitz's position and the Single Index Model: The returns of securities are related "only through common relationships with some basic underlying factor."[10] In diversified portfolios, the riskiness of any single asset is submerged by the behavior of the portfolio as a whole. This insight leads Sharpe to the same conclusion that Treynor and Markowitz had reached: *The only thing investors should worry about is how much any asset contributes to the risk of the portfolio as a whole.*

Sharpe uses the term "systematic risk"[20] to define this kind of dominating common relationship risk. In his basic equation he identifies systematic risk with the letter "b," and until at least

1970 most scholars referred to it that way. Later on, Wall Street began to use the Greek letter "beta," and beta it has been ever since, even in Sharpe's writings.

The calculation that produces beta is a simple operation. Beta measures how much any given asset fluctuates in sympathy with the dominant "combination," as Sharpe calls it. That combination could well be the stock market itself. Sharpe declares at the end of his paper that "only the responsiveness of an asset's rate of return to the level of economic activity is relevant in assessing its risk."[21]

Yet both Sharpe and Treynor emphasize that identifying the dominant factor is beyond the limits of what they set out to demonstrate. Their more modest objective is to show that the covariance of any asset with existing holdings is what determines its risk premium—that is, the extra return an investor demands over the risk-free rate.

When the beta concept came to the attention of professional portfolio managers, they reacted with confusion, then disgust, then annoyance, and finally total skepticism. Trading risk for higher reward seemed more complicated, more subtle, and more intuitive than just judging the volatility of the asset relative to the market.

As late as September 1971, in an article titled "The Beta Revolution: Learning to Live with Risk," *Institutional Investor* magazine reported that most practitioners regarded beta as a mystery, a threat, or some kind of ploy. The article states that the chief barrier to beta's acceptance was "the vast educational gulf between the cognoscenti and the hoi polloi."[22]

A frustrated MBA at an insurance company who tried to introduce his superiors to the use of beta in measuring risk finally confessed that "you can't exactly expect them to embrace you as the new Messiah." Beta was clearly a threat to conventional forms of portfolio management: "Knack, feel, whim, and intuition are considered to be . . . useless relics of a more innocent past."[23]

The manager of the best-performing mutual fund in the first half of 1971 admitted he had never heard of beta. The vice president for common stocks at Prudential Life Insurance barked, "My definition of risk is that which keeps the investor awake at night."[24] A senior economist at the management consulting firm Booz, Allen & Hamilton declared: "These people with math and computer backgrounds . . . who think they can assign precise degrees of risk to five or six decimal places are nothing but charlatans. . . . Beta is nothing but a fad, a gimmick. . . . These knaves must be driven from the temple!"[25]

Sharpe's ideas shook up orthodox methodologies even more profoundly than that. Sharpe pointed out that the market never explains 100 percent—and often no more than 30 percent-of a stock's performance. A stock reflects the unique characteristics of the company that issues it and the industry to which the company belongs as well as the size of the company, the liquidity of the market in which the stock trades, and whether the stock is owned primarily by institutions or by individuals. Sharpe uses the expression "unsystematic risk" to define that part of an asset's variability that is independent of what happens in the market. *

This was easy enough to understand. But a difficulty arose when Sharpe insisted that *unsystematic risk has little or no impact on the value of a stock.* Investors who bet on unsystematic risks are taking two risks: the risk of trading in the market in the first place and the risk that differentiates one stock from another. The first risk is unavoidable for anyone who ventures beyond just holding something like Treasury bills; the second is a matter of choice. There is little to be gained from buying US Steel simply because it is a steel stock or IBM simply because it is a computer stock. Investors demand higher returns for stocks with risks that cannot be diversified away—stocks that move up and down in sympathy with the portfolio—but they do not expect to earn a premium for stocks with risks that *can* be diversified away. Holding stocks with risks like that turns out to be a zero-sum game, with some investors winning what others lose.

If that is what the world is like, then security analysts trained in the tradition of Graham and Dodd will soon be obsolete. If beta is all that matters in determining expected returns, and if beta can be estimated with a hand-held calculator, who needs security analysis?

That question overstates the case. Betting against the market is not doomed to be a losing proposition, but an investor's appetite for unsystematic risk should reflect the quality of the information that leads to the decision. Treynor and Fischer Black later co-authored an ingenious guide for security analysts in this new

---

*Treynor's nomenclature comes close, but implies the critical role of diversification in reducing risk: He uses the expression "uninsurable risk" for systematic risk and "insurable" for unsystematic risk.

world of systematic and unsystematic risks: "How to Use Security Analysis to Improve Portfolio Selection" appeared in the *Journal of Business* in January 1973, at a moment when an appreciation of the importance of risk was about to separate the men from the boys among professional investors. Richard Brealey and his colleagues at London Business School also used Sharpe's ideas to develop innovative techniques for making money out of unsystematic risks.

At this point Sharpe steps out ahead of Treynor. Treynor was in search of a theory that would explain the systematic impact of risk on asset valuation. Sharpe has the broader aim of constructing "a market equilibrium theory of asset prices under conditions of risk."[26] What would happen, he asks, if everybody calculated the trade-off between risk and return in the logical and rational manner that he (and Treynor) suggested?

Then stocks with low betas would appear to be the most desirable to investors. They would be more highly valued than riskier stocks with high betas, and everyone would want to hold them. But then the expected returns on the low-beta stocks would be lower. Risk-averse investors might still be content to hold them, but they would have to be content with the lower expected returns.

What would happen to the high-beta stocks that nobody wanted? If a company has publicly traded stock and those shares exist, someone, somewhere, must own them; they cannot exist in limbo. Investors cannot limit their holdings to the stocks that seem most attractive at any given moment. So the high-beta stocks would be traded, but at prices low enough to provide the risk premium that would persuade investors to own them.

As this process worked itself out, the market would settle into a state of equilibrium. All shares would be owned by someone. Less risky stocks would have lower expected returns than riskier stocks, which is what theory predicts. This line of reasoning leads to the surprising conclusion that all stocks have identical expected returns once their prices have been adjusted for systematic risk.

The primary role of the Capital Asset Pricing Model (CAPM) is to predict expected returns, or to place a valuation on risky assets. The expected returns come in three parts. First, a stock should be expected to earn at least as much as the risk-free rate of interest available on Treasury bills or a government-guaranteed savings account. Second, as stocks are a risky asset, the market as a whole should actually earn a premium over the risk-free rate. Third, an individual stock's beta—its volatility relative to the portfolio's volatility—will then determine how much higher or lower the expected returns of that stock will be relative to what investors expect from the market as a whole.

The theory is almost defiantly simple. It is also a far cry from the traditional analytic paradigm of Benjamin Graham and his balance sheets and income statements. Yet it is strictly logical. Merton Miller greeted it with enthusiasm; the 1971 *Institutional Investor* article quotes him as saying, "It was really kind of a miracle to get this tremendously complicated problem reduced down to a point that a nontrivial fraction of the variation can be explained in terms of a single factor."[27] Despite its explanatory power, however, CAPM falls short of reality, because it is exquisitely dependent on its underlying assumptions of a frictionless and competitive market.

It ties together into one neat package the market behavior theories of Samuelson and Fama and the portfolio selection theories of Markowitz and Tobin. But it would be a useless tool for investors in the market Keynes described; in Keynes's world, everyone is a noise trader. The model would also be misleading in markets where obstacles like high taxes or brokerage fees stand in the way of the trading necessary to compose optimal portfolios, and where some investors have a monopoly on information. Sharpe himself, in his Nobel Prize address, reveals the model's limitations when investors are either unable or unwilling to sell short—to sell securities they do not own in the hope of purchasing them later at a lower price.

The implications of the model's links to efficient market theory are especially important. At an equilibrium such as Sharpe describes, all stocks are appropriately priced. Each promises a reward in accordance with its riskiness; no stock is relatively more attractive than any other. This means that a rational investor will want to own all stocks; anything less would be less than optimal. Thus the market as a whole—or the market portfolio, as it has come to be known—is Tobin's super-efficient portfolio that dominates all others, and the super-efficient portfolio of Sharpe's single-index model as well.

This concept of the market portfolio as the super-efficient portfolio has been applied in various ways, none of them congenial to conventional methods of portfolio managements. For example, the California Public Employees Retirement System invests some $20 billion in stocks with one manager and two part-time traders. The traders sit in a room no bigger than a kitchen, surrounded by ten computer terminals with brightly colored screens alive with jumping numbers.

Part of this extraordinary arrangement is possible only because of Sharpe's beloved computers, but the underlying philosophy stems directly from his theoretical brainchild. The army of security analysts researching individual stocks has disappeared, because the System holds a convenient replica of the market portfolio. The outside managers earning handsome fees have lost the System as a client, because their decisions would be redundant. The brokerage community no longer wins fat commissions, because the System's traders feel no urgency to buy or sell any particular stock, preferring to let the market come to them. The System frequently trades electronically with other large investors, bypassing Wall Street altogether.

But we are ahead of our story. This history of the Capital Asset Pricing Model and the later careers of those who developed it make a strange tale.

Sharpe set his ideas down in 1961 and chose the wordy but descriptive title "Capital Asset Prices: A Theory of Market Equilibrium Under Conditions of Risk." Markowitz and Hirshleifer were helpful, along with a few colleagues at Washington, but it was pretty much a solo performance: "The rest of the world was just out there somewhere," he told me.[28]

That is a bit of an exaggeration. In the fall of 1961, Sharpe was invited to present his ideas at the Quadrangle Club in Chicago, where the "old guys" gathered periodically to talk about research. Those "old guys" included Merton Miller from Carnegie Tech and James Lorie from Chicago. Eugene Fama, a young recruit, was also there that day. Even now, Sharpe wonders, "God knows how they heard of me."[29]

He made a sufficient impression on the group to receive an offer to teach at Chicago. When he visited there in early 1962, he went through the customary procedure of spending fifteen minutes with each faculty member and then presenting a paper to the group—once again, his ideas on the Capital Asset Pricing Model. Then it was time to get down to business:

> The final negotiation involved Allen Wallis, then Dean of the department, offering me a salary of $1500 more than whatever I was making, on the grounds that Lake Michigan required more than Lake Washington. I eventually responded that I thought Lake Washington was worth more than $1500 over Lake Michigan and we agreed to drop the negotiations. When I had talked to Harry Markowitz about it, he told me "Go with your gut."[30]

Academic scuttlebutt being what it is, word of Sharpe's paper on the Capital Asset Pricing Model reached Modigliani at MIT, who arranged for Sharpe and Treynor to exchange manuscripts some time in late 1962 or early 1963. Sharpe refers to the coincidence of their joint interest in the theory in a footnote to his paper in the *Journal of Finance:* "After preparing this paper, the author learned that Mr. Jack L. Treynor, of Arthur D. Little, Inc., had independently developed a model similar in many respects to the one described here. Unfortunately, Mr. Treynor's excellent work on this subject is, at present, unpublished."[31]

Treynor was not the only scholar digging in this fertile territory, however. John Lintner at Harvard was also tackling the same set of problems and coming up with a similar set of answers; Lintner held chairs in both the economics department and the Business School.

The exact source of Lintner's inspiration is obscure. As he is dead, it must remain a mystery. Nevertheless, Treynor relates that in 1959 or 1960, before he met Modigliani, he had shown a rough draft of his paper to Lintner, whom he knew from his days at the Harvard Business School. He was hoping for some encouragement from Lintner but got none. Laconically, Treynor remarked to me, "Perhaps if I had been a student of Lintner's he would have felt more responsibility toward me."[32]

In 1963, Sharpe put CAPM into final form and sent his paper off to the *Journal of Finance.* This paper—which has since been cited more than 2,000 times by other writers—was quickly rejected by the editor of the *Journal,* Dudley Luckett of Iowa State University, acting on the advice of a referee.

Luckett told Sharpe that his assumption that all investors made the same predictions was so "preposterous" as to make his conclusions "uninteresting."[33] Yet that assumption is the logical consequence of a market in which information is freely available to all and in which all investors are rational, risk-averse diversifiers. Treynor recently remarked: "Assuming, as Sharpe and I did, that all investors had the same expectations was merely an analytical convenience, like Newton assuming away air resistance in theorizing about falling bodies. One tackles the world's complexities one at a time."[34]

Sharpe dutifully revised the paper and it shuttled back and forth between his office in Seattle and the *Journal*; meanwhile the editorship of the *Journal* changed hands. The paper, Sharpe's seventh to appear in print, finally won acceptance and was published in the September 1964 issue of the *Journal*. The Beatles movie, "A Hard Day's Night," which had just opened, would have provided an equally appropriate title for the story of Sharpe's long struggle.

In the meantime, Jack Treynor had gone back to his old job at Arthur D. Little in Boston. His boss promptly asked him whether the "unpublished manuscript" over which he had labored so long and so hard had any practical value. Treynor thought it did.

His system of analyzing the correlation between the behavior of a portfolio and the behavior of the market as a whole, he insisted, would reveal a lot about how portfolio managers were doing their job. It would provide a measure of how much risk they were taking with their clients' money and would reveal whether their results were consistent with that risk. The track record of some managers who looked like winners at first glance might turn out to be just the consequence of their concentrating in risky stocks in a bull market. Managers who looked a bit sleepy from their raw performance figures might be doing much better than other conservative managers were doing.

Treynor proceeded to apply his system to a sample of mutual funds and the *Harvard Business Review* published his results in the issue of January-February 1965. As Treynor was an unknown quantity at that stage of his career, it is a credit to the editors of the *Review* that they recognized the importance and originality of what he had to say.

Although Treynor's analysis covered the returns for only twenty funds, the article still stands as the classic statement on performance measurement. Its main rival is a related piece by Sharpe that appeared in the *Journal of Business* in 1966. Jensen's more comprehensive and elaborate analysis of 115 funds published in the *Journal of Business* in 1969, drew explicitly on Treynor's methodology. Every authoritative study of performance measurement since that time has followed either Treynor or Sharpe, or both, by relating the returns earned to the volatility of the portfolio.

When I asked Treynor why he had selected the *Harvard Business Review,* a publication outside the mainstream of academia, he said that he hoped it would generate consulting business for Arthur D. Little. An article in the *Harvard Business Review* would be good marketing. "You can imagine," he added, "what would have happened if I had sent it to the *Journal of Finance!*"[35]

But the ADL job was about to come to an end. After a six-month courtship, he went to work at Merrill Lynch as assistant to Donald Regan. Regan, who was then the strong-willed chief executive of Merrill Lynch, subsequently served as an equally strong-willed Secretary of the Treasury and then as chief of the White House staff under Ronald Reagan. History produces coincidences: the strongly conservative Regan was Jack Kennedy's classmate at Harvard, and mine, too!

Treynor refers to his time at Merrill Lynch as a "peculiar experience," a case of Catch-22.[36] Regan kept him out of the top-level meetings until he knew more about what was going on, but the only way he could find out what was going on was to attend the meetings.

Treynor was still puzzling his way through the intricacies of risk and return. He has always believed that the market is less than totally efficient and that patient investors who are willing to look beyond the obvious can beat it. In particular, careful analysis of unsystematic risks should provide reliable guides for composing optimal portfolios that differ from the market portfolio.

In 1968, Treynor collaborated with Fischer Black, who at the time was a colleague at Arthur D. Little, on a preliminary version of their 1973 article in the *Journal of Business.* In it they presented what Treynor refers to as "quick and dirty ways for portfolio managers to translate risk measurements for stocks into risk measurements for portfolios—short and simple—somebody had to say it."[37] The preliminary version appeared in the *Financial Analysts Journal* and led to Treynor's first meeting with its editor, Nicholas Molodovsky.

I remember Molodovsky as an elegant, urbane, continental, and gracious gentleman, with a charming Russian accent. After he died in 1969, one of his admirers had it just right when he said that Molodovsky "never offended anyone; his erudition simply spilled out by accident."[38]

Molodovsky was born in St. Petersburg in 1898 to a family of high-ranking civil servants who lived in Grand Duke Michael's palace. He attended a military academy and from 1917 to 1920 fought with the White Armies against the Reds. In 1920, he fled to Novorossisk on the Black Sea, where he joined his family on the last boat to sail. He made his way to Paris, where he worked, studied law, became a crack stenographer, and won a scholarship to the Harvard Law School. Soon after his arrival, he transferred to the graduate school in economics.

Molodovsky returned to Paris in 1928, earned a Ph.D., wrote several plays, and joined White, Weld, a major New York brokerage firm. He was a highly successful broker even while pursuing scholarly studies of the stock market. With the outbreak of war in 1939, he returned to the United States, where he continued as broker and scholar.

In 1964, Molodovsky became editor of the *Financial Analysts Journal*.* There he made a major contribution to the profession by bringing to the *Journal* many articles on the new theories of investment and finance. He also made significant theoretical and practical advances on his own by incorporating the concept of growth into Williams's Dividend Discount Model for valuing stocks.

When Molodovsky died suddenly of a heart attack—otherwise known as overwork—the Financial Analysts Federation invited Treynor to take over as editor of the *Journal*. At first Treynor demurred: "I had never even edited a high school year book!" But then he accepted: "If I had stayed at Merrill, they would have made me into a narrow quant."[39] A zealous editor, Treynor encouraged the publication of papers on the new theories, wrote a series of challenging short editorials, and contributed articles himself under the pseudonym Walter Bagehot.

His role was not to be an easy one. Concepts like random walks, efficient markets, complicated versions of risk/return tradeoffs, and betas, with their complex mathematical formulations, scan-

---

*The physical appearance of the *Journal* has never been especially appealing, though the current editor, Charles D'Ambrosio of the University of Washington, has managed to brighten it up.

dalized the more traditional members of the *Journal*'s advisory board. James Vertin, then at Wells Fargo in San Francisco and an ally of Treynor's on the board, recalls, "They were going to close it down because it had all this dumb stuff in it that nobody could understand!"[40]

The board pressured Treynor to ease up. Some time in the middle 1970s, the members asked him to count up the number of articles he had published along these lines. Even he was impressed. "I was staggered," he told me, "it really was quite a bunch."[41]

About the time that Treynor took over as editor of the *Financial Analysts Journal,* Sharpe's Capital Asset Pricing Model appeared in the *Journal of Finance.* By this time, as I have mentioned, Sharpe had heard of Treynor, whose article in the *Harvard Business Review* was about to be published.

Sharpe also heard that Lintner had been working along lines parallel to his own. He understood that Lintner was "pretty much ready to go."[42] Lintner was no minor figure. He held full professorships at the Harvard Business School and in the economics department of Harvard's School of Arts and Sciences. But Sharpe had the jump on him. Lintner's paper, with the even windier title "The Valuation of Risk Assets and the Selection of Risky Investments in Stock Portfolios and Capital Budgets," appeared in Harvard's *Review of Economics and Statistics* in February 1965.

In a further coincidence, another article that came to virtually the same conclusions appeared in *Econometrica* in October 1966. Its author was Jan Mossin, a Norwegian economist who had studied at Carnegie Tech but had spent most of his career in Bergen, where he died twenty years later. Sharpe remembers Mossin as "a quiet, gentle, and extremely pleasant person."[43]

Shortly after Sharpe's article appeared in September 1964, Lintner called him to suggest that they meet during the professional meetings that December. Sharpe had only recently been promoted from assistant to associate professor, and he was intimidated by his meeting with this senior full professor. Merton Miller has described Lintner as "the only person I knew who could actually talk in italics."[44] Sharpe laments that this was "the only time in my life when somebody talked me into the idea that I was wrong."[45]

Sharpe is still convinced that there were no important differences between his version of the model and Lintner's. "John's was a very pretty piece," he maintains, and regrets that they never got together—despite his efforts—on a joint article that would have resolved any differences that did exist.[46]

Lintner carried on a substantial consulting business in addition to his academic duties. He once told Sharpe that he had never discussed the capital asset pricing theory in his consulting work— or even in class—and had made no effort to develop practical applications of it. "It's just theory," he declared.[47]

Sharpe returned to Seattle, in a mood of elation mixed with depression: "I knew that article was going to be the best thing I would ever do. The phone would start ringing any moment. After one year, still total silence. Nobody cared. It took quite a while."[48]

But the long wait was worth it. In 1989, on the occasion of the 25th anniversary of the publication of Sharpe's article, Wells Fargo Investment Advisors celebrated "a worthy man . . . honored in his own time." Noting that "CAPM has given us all a fertile intellectual garden to grow in," they reported that they had run an electronic tabulation of citations of the article but had "stopped after two thousand citations and references, because our budget ran out." They pointed out that Sharpe's model, in addition to serving portfolio managers as a means of predicting both risk and expected returns, had spawned valuable measures of portfolio performance, index funds, applications in corporate finance and corporate investment, and procedures for setting utility rates, as well as major theoretical innovations in the study of market behavior and asset valuation.[49]

In 1968, Sharpe left Seattle for the University of California at Irvine. Two years later, he was appointed Professor at Stanford, where he enjoyed a distinguished teaching career. In 1989 he chose to become Professor Emeritus at the young age of 55.

Over the years, he has consulted extensively with practitioners to work out practical applications of his theories. He has written six books, including one on computers, and more than a hundred articles on theory and practice. In 1970, Merrill Lynch retained him to put them into the business of publishing estimates of the betas of more than a thousand stocks. For many years he was a driving force in Wells Fargo's pioneering efforts to develop practical applications of all aspects of portfolio and capital market theory. Now with his own consulting service, he advises large pension funds on how to allocate their portfolios among large and small company stocks, international stocks, domestic and international bonds, and risk-free securities.

Treynor also moved on. He left the *Financial Analysts Journal* in 1981 to join a small investment management firm, to think and develop ideas rather than manage portfolios. The firm was headed by Harold Arbit, a leading innovator in the practical applications of portfolio theory and, during his years at the American National Bank in Chicago, one of the first to put the theory to real-time use. One of Treynor's most enthusiastic admirers, Arbit was eager to try out some of his ideas on how to bet on unsystematic risks. Treynor describes his stint with Arbit as "four absolutely fascinating years," but, at Arbit's suggestion, they parted ways. After scrupulously observing a four-year noncompete agreement with Arbit, Treynor now runs what he describes as "a little money management firm" of his own.[50]

Despite the undeniable importance of the Treynor-Sharpe-Lintner-Mossin Capital Asset Pricing Model, I do not mean to suggest that it opened up the surest route map to the road to riches. Investors are not always rational beings. Taxes and transaction costs often prevent them from trading freely enough to price all assets precisely as they should be priced. Information is not always freely available, nor does everyone understand it in the same way and act on it as soon as it appears.

That is not all. In a world where the future purchasing power of money is uncertain, how does one determine a risk-free rate of interest? Is the capital market the only "basic underlying factor" that influences the value of the assets traded there? What about inflation and the distribution of wealth, to name just two possible factors that might come into play as well? And how do we define and measure "the market" when capital assets exist all over the world and include everything from cash, stocks, bonds, and real estate to art, gold, venture capital, and even intellectual capital like education and acquired skills?

Time plays a critical role in all aspects of investing, yet CAPM, as originally conceived, described how investors act only at a given moment rather than over continuous time. It provided no guide to what will happen when underlying economic conditions change—in other words, its beta measurements may be unreliable in an ever-changing world. The conversion of this single-period model into a more realistic model that worked across time periods was precisely what had stymied Treynor before the relevance of Ito's lemma became apparent.

So it should come as no surprise that empirical tests of the model have revealed many flaws. Other theorists have attempted to overcome some of those flaws and have improved the usefulness of the model. For example, Merton's intertemporal model overcomes the problem of a single time period, and multi-factor models have introduced driving forces in addition to the market alone. More sophisticated and complex methods have helped to stabilize the beta concept, making its predictions more reliable.

The most interesting extension of CAPM is a concept known as Arbitrage Pricing Theory, which was developed in 1976 by Stephen Ross, a Harvard Ph.D. who was then a young professor at the University of Pennsylvania and is now Sterling Professor of Finance at Yale. Although some tests of its applicability have been inconclusive, Ross and an associate from UCLA, Richard Roll—a protégé of Eugene Fama at Chicago and a distinguished theorist in his own right—are using it with success to manage several billion dollars of clients' money.

APT differs from CAPM in important ways. CAPM specifies where asset prices will settle, given investor preferences for trading off risk for expected returns, but it is silent about what produces the returns that investors expect. It also identifies only one factor as the dominant influence on stock returns. APT fills those gaps by providing a method to measure how stock prices will respond to changes in the multitude of economic factors that influence them, such as inflation, interest rate patterns, changing perceptions of risk, and economic growth. Through the use of arbitrage, APT also provides investors with strategies for betting on their forecasts of the factors that shape stock returns. Finally, the construction of APT enables it to avoid the rigid and often unrealistic assumptions required by CAPM.

And yet CAPM combines so many strands of theoretical innovation that it remains the keystone in investment theory, theories of market behavior, and the allocation of capital in both private and public enterprises. Moreover, its theoretical significance is equaled if not surpassed by its widespread use in business and finance. Wells Fargo has declared that CAPM "would be only one more model in a long line of models, if it had not impacted commercial practice so dramatically."[51]

Though that impact has been dramatic, it was far from immediate. Sharpe himself commented on the eerie silence of his phone in Seattle. But the use of the word "revolution" in the title of the 1971 *Institutional Investor* article cited above was justified by some of the other quotes. A pension fund consultant explains: "All the hip investment managers like to show how they've got risk reduced down to a nice simple computer model. . . . I mean . . . it's getting to be that if you don't know all about beta these days, you've had it."[52]

A San Francisco investment manager asks: "A lot of people are simply going to be put out of business. I mean, what are they really doing? . . . What passes for security analysis today, in my opinion is 150,000 percent bullshit. . . . But whether it's accepted or not, the truth is the truth."[53] Even the lawyers agreed: The author of an article in *Harvard Law Review* was inspired to disparage traditional concepts of risk that failed to incorporate the benefits of high return, intoning that "True risk is uncertainty risk."[54]

CAPM also inspired the last theoretical innovation that I shall describe in this book. The similarities between its genesis and the CAPM story are remarkable. Like Sharpe and Treynor, and like most other innovators, the authors of this breakthrough were early in their careers and relatively unknown. One of them was working at Arthur D. Little and was a kind of intellectual hanger-on at MIT. They were in a race to see who would be first to discover the answers. Their intellectual progenitors were Samuelson and Fama and Markowitz and Tobin as well as Modigliani and Miller. They unleashed a stream of new ideas with novel applications that no one had dreamed of before.

There was one important difference. The impact of this last innovation was almost instantaneous upon its publication in 1973. That was a tribute to its extraordinary originality, but it was also a sign that the world had come a long way between 1964 and 1973 toward accepting a theory of finance and investments.

# Chapter
## 11

# The Universal
# Financial Device

*We did not make money but we did learn some more
truth.*

In Book I of *Politics,* Aristotle conducts a lengthy analysis of the
accumulation of wealth. He takes a dim view of the whole
thing. Although he considers such matters "not unworthy of philosophy," he adds that "to be engaged in them practically is illib-
eral and irksome." He refers in particular to earnings from interest—the Greek word for which, "tokos," literally means
"offspring." He then observes: " . . . interest, which means the
birth of money from money, is applied to the breeding of money
because the offspring resembles the parent. Wherefore, of all
modes of getting wealth this is the most unnatural."

Aristotle goes on to tell the story of the philosopher Thales the
Milesian, who developed a "financial device which involves a
principle of universal application." People had chided Thales because he was a poor man, taking his poverty as proof that philosophy is of no practical use. Thales knew what he was about, however, and set out to demonstrate the foolishness of this reproach.

Thales had exceptional skill in reading the stars. One winter he
foresaw that the autumn olive harvest would be much larger than
normal. He took the little money he had saved up and paid quiet
visits to all the owners of olive presses in the area, placing small
deposits with each of them to guarantee him first claim on the
use of their presses when fall arrived. He was able to negotiate
low prices, for the harvest was still nine months off, and, anyway,

*203*

who could know whether the harvest would be large or small. The story ends as you may have guessed: "When the harvest-time came, and many [presses] were wanted all at once and of a sudden, he let them out at any rate he pleased, and made a quantity of money. Thus he showed the world that philosophers can easily be rich if they like, but that their ambition is of another sort."

Aristotle's anecdote about Thales and his financial device is the first recorded mention of the instrument that has come to be known as an option. An option is essentially a contract that gives the owner the right to take a stipulated action under conditions specified and agreed to in advance.

Option contracts do not oblige the owner to act unless he wishes to do so. If the olive crop had turned out to be disappointing, Thales would have let his options lapse; he would have exercised them only if the crop had turned out to be great enough to overwhelm the olive-pressing capacity of the community.

A 1688 treatise on the workings of the Amsterdam stock exchange by Joseph de la Vega reveals that options and similar types of securities in common use today were already dominating trading activities at the time. This is significant, as Amsterdam was the most sophisticated and important financial center of the seventeenth century, even more important than London. And we have seen that Louis Bachelier, in the course of writing his thesis in Paris in 1900, was attracted to the problem of valuing options.

Options are everywhere around us. The father who tells his little boy to stop watching television and go to bed "or else" is giving his son an interesting option. The boy has no obligation to turn off the TV and go to bed, but his father has given him the right to take up the option of keeping the set on and accepting his punishment. A direct command to abandon the living room for the bedroom would not have been an option.

Thales won out on his options because, as it turned out, he had a better idea than the press owners of how big the harvest was going to be. Still, his arrangement would have made sense even if he had been less prescient. The owner of an olive grove might simply have wanted to hedge against the risk that, come harvest time, no presses would be available for his crop. He could buy an option on the use of the presses, taking it up if the crop turned out to be large, letting it lapse if the crop was small. It would cost him something, but, as with any hedging scheme, it would protect him against catastrophe.

Options perform an almost endless variety of functions. Some people seek a high return; others hope to hedge their risks. Each group accommodates the other. People like Thales, who believe they know what the future holds, use options to speculate on the future; they are willing to run the risk of losing a small amount in return for the hope of making a much larger gain. People like the olive growers, who have no knowledge of the future, will pay a small amount to hedge against risks and to limit losses that might otherwise ruin them; those options will also provide some revenue for the owners of the presses that will come in handy if the crop turns out to be poor.

The primary function of options is to give investors some control over how changes in the market will affect their portfolios. For a cost, buyers of options can limit losses without placing any limits on their profits. They can also use options to give them time to see how the market moves before committing their full capital. Sellers of options who expect little change in market prices can pocket an extra premium. In short, options satisfy the needs of both hedgers and speculators.

In the world of business and finance, there are markets in options on thousands of individual stocks and on the major indexes of the stock market as a whole, both in the United States and in foreign financial centers as well. There are options on bonds, commodities, foreign currencies, and on so-called futures and forward contracts that obligate the holder to deliver these assets to another party before a specified date.

There are also less visible options that are even more pervasive. Bonds that the holder can convert into common stock at will and bonds whose issuer has the right to prepay them are known as implicit options.

Anyone who has ever taken out a home mortgage with a prepayment privilege has purchased an option from the bank. The cost of that option is included in the interest rate on the mortgage, which will be higher than it would be without the prepayment privilege.

When you insure your car against collision, you are buying an option from the insurance company. That option will be worthless if you never have an accident—you pay the premium and collect nothing. But if your car is totaled, you have the right to leave what remains of it with the insurance company and collect a check for the insured amount.

An option that gives the holder the right to acquire an asset is known as a call option. Thales bought a call option on the olive presses. A homeowner with a prepayment privilege on the family mortgage also has a call option, because the family has the right to repurchase the mortgage from the bank if interest rates decline. An option that gives the holder the right to require another party to buy an asset at the will of its owner is known as a put option. You buy a put option when you insure your car against collision. Put options cover situations in which asset values are likely to fall; call options cover situations in which asset values are likely to appreciate.

My investment counseling firm began using options markets in the mid-1960s when we set up a small speculative mutual fund for our clients. In those days, nobody thought very much about how to value options in any systematic manner. Rules of thumb sufficed.

Options on a small number of big stocks traded over-the-counter at that time, with prices set largely by seat-of-the-pants negotiations. We sold calls on the stocks owned by our fund—that is, we gave others the right to buy those stocks from us at prices specified ahead of time—because the belief among professionals was that the speculators who bought calls were characteristically overoptimistic and tended to pay too much for them. In selling calls, we were betting that the greed of the buyers would give us a built-in advantage.

As we were winging it in the over-the-counter options market, we had little theoretical basis for the prices at which we made our transactions. The only considerations we explicitly factored in were time and the rate of interest. The longer the owner of the call enjoyed the right to buy a stock from us, the higher the price we charged. Because the call could be exercised at any moment during that time, we had to be ready to provide the shares to the option-owner when the call came. This tied up our money and cost us interest income, while the option-owner kept earning interest on his money right up to the moment he decided to exercise the option. The premium we received had to compensate us for that lost interest.

One other matter seemed too obvious to require much attention. The call options stipulated a price—called the exercise price—at which the owner could buy the stocks from us during the life of the option. At an exercise price of $50, the option would be worth more when the stock was selling at $60 than when it was selling at $40. At $60, the option was worth at least $10, and more on the chance that the stock might go even higher (unless the option was about to expire). In such a situation the option is said to be in-the-money. The option would be out-of-the-money when the stock was selling below the exercise price; the option would have no intrinsic value under those conditions. The world of out-of-the-money options was murky, and the bargaining between us and the buyer was less systematic.

We were happy skimming a nice return from speculators who were as unsophisticated but hungrier than we. What we did not know was that a theory to establish the scientific principles for valuing options was just then becoming a hot topic among the finance and economics faculty at MIT. This was heady business for mathematically inclined economists, because it called for a harmonized response, on the one hand, to the uncertainty of how the price of the stock would move and, on the other hand, to the factors we were already taking into account:—time, interest rates, the current price of the stock, and the exercise price specified in the option contract.

I saw Paul Samuelson once in a while on social occasions, but I was unaware that he, as usual, had started another ball rolling with a paper published in 1965, "Rational Theory of Warrant Pricing." Warrants are essentially the same as options. They give the owner the right to buy a specified number of shares of stock at a specified price during a specified period of time; as with options, the owner is under no obligation to exercise that right. There are two minor differences. Warrants are issued by corporations and sold by them to investors, while investors create and sell options to one another. And warrants typically run a much longer time than options before they expire.

Samuelson's paper was the culmination of some ten years of work, inspired in part by his first looking into Bachelier and in part by the simple desire to make some money for himself—the desire that had led him originally to subscribe to the "RHM Warrant and Low-Price Stock Survey." Kruizenga, the student who had been sent back to the drawing boards in 1956 by the discovery of Bachelier's work, was writing his doctoral thesis on this very subject at Samuelson's suggestion.

Samuelson's paper almost succeeded in solving the valuation problem, but—uncharacteristically—he did not quite get there on this particular occasion. Although his solution was on the mark, it was not sufficiently generalized to be applicable in all instances. Samuelson himself has noted that "the results of the paper were not obvious. . . . [I] was not sure how they would come out until the work was done." Although his younger colleagues would build on his work later on, Samuelson's frustration at his inability to develop a formula for all seasons once led him to complain that "Too little is written about the 'near misses' in science."[1]

Samuelson was not alone in his search. In addition to the two papers by Kruizenga in the late 1950s, Paul Cootner's book, *The Random Character of Stock Market Prices,* included a paper on warrant prices by Case Sprenkle dated 1960, based on a Ph.D. thesis at Yale and acknowledging an intellectual debt to James Tobin. Cootner's book also contained papers on the subject by A. James Boness and Herbert Ayres, both of whom had done the underlying work while studying at MIT. MIT must have been a hotbed of curiosity about options and warrants.

The prime movers in bringing the theory of option pricing to fruition were Fischer Black, a young mathematician in Boston who would end up on the MIT faculty, and Myron Scholes, a fledgling member of the MIT faculty.

At the time Black began his study of options, he had little awareness of Samuelson or his work, had not yet arrived at MIT, had never taken a course in either economics or finance, and had no idea that he would ever be associated with Samuelson or MIT. Black had graduated from Harvard in 1959 with a degree in physics and with considerable exposure to mathematics and psychology. He received his Ph.D. at Harvard in 1964 in applied mathematics, with an emphasis on operations research, logic, computer design, and artificial intelligence. His main interests were in applying these subjects to methods for processing information.

A year after receiving his doctorate, Black decided his studies had been too abstract. Seeking a spot in the world of business, he took a job at Arthur D. Little. There he met Jack Treynor and the two became fast friends. Treynor, who was still deep in ruminations about the Capital Asset Pricing Model, found Black a stimulating intellectual companion. Black became so fascinated by CAPM that he gradually gave up his work with computers and information processing and shifted to finance.

Black's decision to switch career paths is another example of how the study of financial markets seems to pull scientists into its orbit. Bachelier was lured from mathematics, Sharpe from medicine, Osborne from astronomy, Working and Kendall from statistical theory, and Treynor from physics and math.

Black decided that the Capital Asset Pricing Model was right up his alley—"the notion of equilibrium in the market for risky assets had great beauty for me. . . . I worked on the Capital Asset Pricing Model because I wanted to discover the truth."[2] He was especially attracted by what he calls the "cruel truth" of the model: "To get higher expected gain, you must take more risk. If you wish to climb a tall mountain, you must be prepared to suffer some pain."[3]

The linkage between gain and pain is what propels the market toward the equilibrium that Modigliani and Miller had described and in which Black believes passionately. Although Black recognizes that "noise traders" frequently drive asset prices away from their intrinsic values, he rejects the notion that chaos plays any role in the financial marketplace: "When people are seeking profits, equilibrium will prevail."[4]

By happenstance, Black learned how to fit this concept into the structure of financial theory by serving as intermediary in a debate on the issues between Treynor at ADL and John Lintner at Harvard Business School. Each would tell Black, "This is the way it is in finance." Treynor refers to this exchange as a "strange dialogue," but, in view of Black's subsequent career, his education as intermediary must have been very good.[5]

A short time after Treynor left Arthur D. Little and Boston to work for Donald Regan at Merrill Lynch in New York, Black inherited some of the work that Treynor had been doing at ADL in analyzing and designing portfolio management systems. Inspired by what Treynor had done, Black set out to apply the Capital Asset Pricing Model to assets other than stocks. He experimented with it on bonds, corporate decisions on direct investments in plant and equipment, and the pricing of warrants.

Black chose to work on warrants rather than options because the pricing of options in the over-the-counter market at that time—the market in which my firm was dabbling—was less efficient than the pricing of warrants, which traded on the active markets at the New York and American stock exchanges.

When he applied the Capital Asset Pricing Model to the valuation of warrants, Black assumed that both the warrant and the associated stock would obey the model at every moment and at every possible price of the stock. In other words, each would have an expected gain "proportional to the part of its risk that can't be diversified away"—proportional, that is, to its beta, or its relative volatility.[6]

That assumption can be expressed by means of calculus, which is a method for comparing rates of change among different variables. That comparison, in turn, coupled with the assumption that both the stock and the warrant are priced according to the Capital Asset Pricing Model, leads to an equation known as a differential equation. Black expected that solving this equation would give him a formula for finding the value of the warrant at any given price of the associated stock.

Deriving the differential equation was the easiest part of the task, because, as Black admits, he did not know the standard methods for solving such equations. Converting the differential equation into a formula that would give the value of the warrant turned out to be far more difficult than deriving it in the first place.

But for Black persistence is the name of the game. A poster in his office shows a man running down a long country road, with the caption "The race is not always to the swift but to those who keep running." Black recalls the frustration he felt:

> I applied the Capital Asset Pricing Model to every moment in a warrant's life, for every possible stock price and warrant value. . . . I stared at the differential equation for many, many months. I made hundreds of silly mistakes that led me down blind alleys. Nothing worked. . . .
>
> [The calculations revealed that] the warrant value did not depend on the stock's expected return, or on any other asset's expected return. That fascinated me.
>
> He adds: "Then Myron Scholes and I started working together."[7]

That was in 1968. Scholes, who had graduated from McMaster University in Hamilton, Ontario, in 1962, had recently received his doctorate in finance from the Graduate School of Business at the University of Chicago, at which point he had two job offers: The University of Texas at Austin offered him a teaching job at $17,000 but held out the temptation of juicy fees from consulting work with the local millionaires. MIT offered him an $11,500 teaching job, with no hint of side benefits. Scholes chose the MIT offer.

Black and Scholes were an even odder couple than Modigliani and Miller. Black is fair, blue-eyed, cool, soft-spoken, tall, and courtly. His words are few and usually monosyllabic, his sentences mostly declarative (though he asks questions too). His presidential address to the American Finance Association in 1985, with the simple title "Noise," took him less than fifteen minutes to deliver; such speeches usually run at least three-quarters of an hour. That paper has turned out to be one of the most frequently cited papers in the literature. The paper on option pricing that he wrote with Scholes, though extremely complicated, begins: "The simplest kind of option is one that gives the right to buy a single share of common stock."[8]

Scholes is dark, voluble, and temperamental. Always ready for an argument, he would have made an unbeatable litigator. When Merton Miller, no shrinking violet, sent me a photograph of himself walking with Scholes on the University of Chicago campus, he remarked, "Guess who's doing the talking!"[9] Yet Scholes is often disarmingly gracious, and his friends are deeply attached to him.

I first met Scholes when he was the discussant for a paper I gave in December 1972 at the annual meeting of the American Finance Association. The subject was "What Rate of Return Can You Expect?" I concluded that the stock market was so high that, even under the best of circumstances, the rate of return I could foresee was too small to justify the risk of staying in. Scholes, immersed in the philosophy of the efficient market, argued that my kind of forecast was impossible.* If the expected rate of return was as poor as I found it to be, investors would refuse to buy stocks and stock prices would already have fallen. He had no confidence in the ability of any one individual to know more about the future than all the informed individuals whose buying and selling set the prices of stocks and bonds each day. He declared that he expected a much higher return than what I was predicting and that he would continue to be fully invested in a diversified portfolio of common stocks.

---

*This assertion is comparable to the apocryphal story about the Chicago University professor whose student spotted a $100 bill on the sidewalk. "The bill is not there," expostulated the professor. "If it were, the market is so efficient that someone would already have picked it up." But how many $100 bills do we find lying on the sidewalk?

Luck was with me on this occasion, though I would still defend my analysis. The stock market did not return to the levels of late 1972 for another ten years. Scholes recently asked me, "Are you still keeping score?"[10]

Like many of the other actors in this story, Scholes did not start off with his eye on finance. He had originally planned to go to law school after college, but his family wanted him to join them in their book publishing business. "Naturally rebellious," as he describes himself, he decided he was not ready to go into business and enrolled at Chicago Business School. He loved it: "I will never get over the joy and excitement those professors had about their work."[11]

Scholes turned down his family's invitation to spend his summer vacation working in the family business and took a job at the University that he hoped would help him to learn about computers. He was low man at the computer programming center, but no one showed up to help him out. So he taught himself. He got so good at programming that he became the favorite programmer among the school's professors, who were still, in Fama's phrase, "computer illiterates." One of those professors was Merton Miller, who introduced Scholes to financial theory and encouraged him to enter the Ph.D. program at Chicago.

Scholes's doctoral dissertation was an original and powerful piece of theoretical and empirical research that supported the efficient market hypothesis. He took as his subject the impact on the market of large sales of stock by major holders.

Scholes argued that investors are more interested in portfolios than in individual holdings, which means that all securities are potential candidates for inclusion in investor portfolios. If each security is only a small percentage of the assets held in a portfolio, many securities are readily substitutable for one another. "The efficient market will price assets such that the expected returns of assets of similar risk are equal," he concluded.[12] Under these conditions, the price of a stock should not decline just because some larger seller wants to get rid of it—unless, that is, the fact that that particular investor wants to sell the stock constitutes new information.

Scholes's painstakingly thorough empirical analysis demonstrated that prices do tend to move when the seller is likely to have adverse information not available to the public, such as information available only to the corporation itself or to its officers

"The industrial market is destined to be the great speculative market in the United States," declared Charles Dow in 1882, at a time when less than a dozen industrial stocks were listed on the New York Stock Exchange. Dow was also convinced that stock prices were predictable — an assertion that would fire controversy for decades to come; it met its first powerful theoretical challenge twenty years later from Louis Bachelier. Dow started his Wall Street career in 1879 writing news bulletins carried to subscribers by messenger boys and was the first editor of the *Wall Street Journal. (Courtesy Dow Jones & Company, Inc.)*

An enthusiastic amateur statistician and scion of a Chicago Tribune fortune, Alfred Cowles was inspired by the Great Crash of 1929 to launch the first investigation into whether the experts can predict stock prices. Foreshadowing the work of future scholars, his pioneering statistical analysis arrived at the blunt conclusion, "It is doubtful." He founded the Cowles Commission in Economic Research, bankrolled the Econometric Society, and his work formed the basis for what is now known as Standard & Poor's stock indexes. *(Photo by Moffett Studio)*

"Nothing ventured, nothing gained" and "Don't put all your eggs in one basket" are the immutable principles for selecting securities for an investment portfolio. In 1952, Harry Markowitz *(above left),* a graduate student in economics at the University of Chicago, took only one afternoon to convert these homespun notions into a set of rules involving the use of diversification and optimization of the tradeoff between risk and return. Markowitz's ideas became the building blocks for all future advances in financial theory and practice, and he won the Nobel Prize in economic sciences in 1990. Just four months after Markowitz's article on portfolio selection appeared in 1952, Cambridge University professor and former artillery officer Andrew Roy *(above right)* published an article on the same topic that followed an almost identical line of argument. Yet Roy and Markowitz had never heard of each other. The resemblance between the two articles was all the more remarkable because no one had ever before tried to develop a theory of portfolio selection.

Investors taking a traditional approach to portfolio management would be shocked at the suggestion that an elderly widow with modest capital should hold the identical set of common stocks to a successful young business executive. One reason that James Tobin of Yale *(left)* won the Nobel Prize in 1981 was his 1958 paper that turned the traditional theory of portfolio management on its head. Tobin's analysis demonstrated that the appropriate equity portfolio for any investor should be independent of the investor's attitude toward risk. *(Photo by T. Charles Erickson, Yale University Office of Public Information)*

In 1961, William Sharpe *(left),* who was studying under Harry Markowitz at the time, took a footnote in Markowitz's Ph.D. dissertation and combined it with Tobin's work to explain how the behavior of the market as a whole determines the performance of individual portfolios. Sharpe subsequently used these ideas to build asset-pricing theories. In 1990, he shared the Nobel Prize with his mentor, Markowitz. *(Courtesy of News and Publication Service, Stanford University)*

"It is not easy to get rich in Las Vegas, at Churchill Downs, or at the local Merrill Lynch office," proclaimed Paul Samuelson of MIT *(right)* in a paper in the early 1960s that was to form the basis for the development of the random-walk concept and the efficient-market hypothesis. Samuelson was among the first economists to resurrect Louis Bachelier's argument of 1900 that stock picking is a zero-sum game. Shown here in the 1950s, Samuelson was the first American to win the Nobel Prize in economic sciences.

Eugene Fama *(left)* deserted the study of French civilization to find out why his after-school job trying to develop profitable investment strategies produced such impressive results on paper and such disappointing results in practice. His efforts led to proofs supporting the hypothesis that even the smartest analysts cannot beat the market, primarily because there are so many smart analysts trying to do just that.

Nobel Laureate Franco Modigliani of MIT was described by his younger colleague Merton Miller, with whom he worked "cheek by jowl" at Carnegie Tech in the late 1950s, as having "the mind of an Italian arbitrageur." This was not altogether in jest:Modigliani and Miller made arbitrage the central feature of their argument that the value of the corporation is independent of its capital structure. In doing so, they took the crude rules of thumb that had dominated corporate financial decisions and replaced them with rigorous theoretical analysis.

Merton Miller, who shared his Nobel Prize in 1990 with Harry Markowitz and William Sharpe, is the other "M" of the "MM" propositions. Miller excels in the art of the controversial. He has employed his knowledge of taxation and finance to defend the leveraging of corporations in the 1980s and to play down widespread alarm at these developments. He played a critical role in shaping the careers of such younger scholars as Fischer Black, Eugene Fama, Myron Scholes, William Sharpe, and Jack Treynor.

In the mid-1950s, the investment course at Harvard Business School was so boring students dubbed it "Darkness at Noon." Jack Treynor left HBS at that time "with an enormous impression that finance needed help." Three weeks of "unremitting meditation" resulted in his most important paper—never published—a theory of how investors incorporate risk into the pricing of stocks; his approach was almost identical to Sharpe's and was developed at just about the same moment. *(Photo by Fabian Bachrach)*

After a notable professional career at Chicago and MIT, Fischer Black led the parade from gown to town by joining Goldman Sachs in 1984. He originally started out in science and mathematics and never had a course in economics or finance. In 1965 while working at Arthur D. Little in Boston, he met Jack Treynor and was captivated by his theories. Although not yet an academic, Black collaborated with Myron Scholes and Robert Merton in the early 1970s to develop the most widely used formula for pricing options.

Fischer Black had been stuck on the options problem for "many, many months" when he started working with Myron Scholes. Scholes collaborated with Black to unlock the puzzles of option pricing. Their article on the subject was rejected at first as excessively specialized, but thanks to Merton Miller's intervention it finally appeared just as the Chicago Board Options Exchange opened for business in 1973. The Black–Scholes formula was soon in general use there and has subsequently formed the basis for many investment, trading, and corporate finance strategies. *(©1990 photography by Andy Feldman)*

In 1968, MIT was the only graduate school that would accept Robert Merton, now of Harvard Business School, when he decided to abandon math for economics. Paul Samuelson immediately selected Merton as an assistant and collaborator and stimulated his interest in option pricing. Merton was also an active participant with Black and Scholes in working out their formula for pricing options. His development of the concept of continuous-time finance has dramatically extended the power of finance theory and enhanced the practical applications of asset pricing and option pricing theories. *(Photo by Bradford F. Herzog)*

"Can you really run money with this stuff?" asked the chairman of Wells Fargo Bank in 1963 when John McQuown offered to provide the bank with real-time investment applications of theories of Markowitz, Sharpe, and Fama. McQuown leaned heavily on the academics to help him pull Wells Fargo — and Wall Street — into the space age.

When John McQuown arrived at Wells Fargo in 1963, James Vertin *(above left)* was in charge of trust investments and "could just see the fin of the shark cutting through the water." At first worried about "guys in white smocks with computers whirring," Vertin was soon converted to the new ideas and became an evangelist for the cause. After attending MIT "for retrofitting," he transformed his department into an organization that spearheaded the development of the index fund. In 1969, convinced that professional portfolio management sorely lacked discipline, William Fouse *(above right)* proposed the establishment of an index fund to his boss at Mellon Bank's trust department, and was "figuratively thrown out of the policy meeting" for his efforts. He left after this confrontation to work for McQuown and Vertin at Wells Fargo. There he led them in developing applications of the new thinking, including the dividend discount model, asset allocation, and indexing.

While living on a tugboat and teaching at Berkeley, Barr Rosenberg *(left)* launched a consulting practice in 1969 that played a dominant role in introducing portfolio managers to applications of the theories of Sharpe, Markowitz, and Fama. He left consulting in 1985 to start his own portfolio management group, which now has some $10 billion under management.

When Berkeley economist Hayne Leland *(above left)* found his personal finances deteriorating in 1976, he decided that "lifestyles were in danger, and it was time for invention." The invention was portfolio insurance, the most controversial portfolio strategy of the 1980s. "I'm surprised I never thought of that myself," declared Hayne Leland's Berkeley colleague Mark Rubinstein *(above right)* when Leland described the broad outlines of his scheme for portfolio insurance. Rubinstein was a distinguished options theorist, and he and Leland immediately formed a consulting firm that by 1987 was supervising over $60 billion of assets under insurance programs and still innovating new applications of their basic theoretical ideas.

and directors. Most other sellers, no matter how large their positions, have little or no apparent impact on the price of the stock when they offer their shares for sale.

When I told Scholes that I had found his paper especially interesting because it was both counter-intuitive and persuasive, he laughed. "That was just one idea," he said, "there are so many ideas."[13]

At the time he first met Black, Scholes was himself already deep into the option pricing puzzle and had considered how the Capital Asset Pricing Model could be used to solve it. When they realized they were both wrestling with the same problem, they joined forces. Their association soon produced major progress toward a solution.

They found to their surprise that neither risk nor expected return, the two integral elements of CAPM, belonged in the equation after all. Risk and expected return disappeared from the equation because they canceled each other out. Consider two stocks, one much riskier than the other, but each selling for $20 a share. To simplify matters, assume that neither pays a dividend. The market believes that the less risky stock will be selling for $32 five years from now, or within a range of, say, $30 to $34, for an average expected return of 10 percent a year. The market believes that the riskier stock will be selling for $40, within a much wider range of $32 to $48, for an average expected return of 15 percent a year.

But the two stocks are selling at the same price of $20 today because investors have taken into consideration the differences in risk, even though the expected future prices of the stocks differ widely. The higher risk cancels out the higher expected return and leads to the same price today for the risky stock as for the less risky stock.

With differences in risk canceling out differences in expected gain for all securities, Black and Scholes concluded that the expected gain on a stock, option, or warrant is irrelevant in calculating what the current price of an option or warrant should be. This insight allowed them to solve the option equation and derive their formula for setting a value on the option. But they arrived at this original derivation by building their structure on the foundations of the Capital Asset Pricing Model.

At this point, enter Robert C. Merton, a round-faced, curly-haired, friendly colleague on the MIT finance faculty. Merton was younger than Black and Scholes and had not yet earned his Ph.D. He had studied engineering mathematics at Columbia and then at California Institute of Technology but his first published paper, "The 'Motionless' Motion of Swift's Flying Island," was about *Gulliver's Travels.* It appeared in the *Journal of the History of Ideas* in 1966, the year he earned his B.S. degree at Columbia.

Friends in the Cal Tech economics department had attracted Merton to their circle. His appetite for economics and finance had already been whetted by his experiences in trading convertible bonds and warrants with his own money. So Merton decided to switch to economics. When he canvassed the graduate schools, he found that his lack of formal training in economics was an obstacle, but MIT accepted him and gave him a fellowship to boot.

Good luck set him to work in 1968 as a research assistant to Samuelson, who was still exploring the theory of warrant pricing. Merton's performance in that role led Samuelson to suggest that they write a paper together. "I thought that was very nice," Merton recalls. Then Samuelson suggested that they present the paper to the inaugural session of the Harvard-MIT mathematical economics seminar. "That was terrific." Then Samuelson proposed that Merton present the paper by himself. "That was more terrific." Merton confessed to me that he has never worked on anything as hard as he worked on that maiden presentation. "After that, nothing fazed me about giving papers."[14]

Samuelson has long been an enthusiastic admirer of Merton's. Recently, in the introduction to a collection of Merton's essays, he wrote:

> Among connoisseurs, Robert C. Merton is known as an expert among experts, a giant who stands on the shoulders of such giants as Louis Bachelier. . . . I am proud to have figured in the Mertonian march to fame. . . . One of the great pleasures of academic life is . . . the rare sight of the companion at arms who forges ahead of you as you were able to do at the inflection point of your own career.[15]

Merton's work on warrant pricing soon led him to portfolio theory, which was still an unknown subject for most economists in the late 1960s. No courses on the subject were available at MIT at that time. Even with Samuelson, Sidney Alexander, and Franco

Modigliani on the premises, the work done by Markowitz, Tobin, and Sharpe was rarely mentioned.

Merton immediately set about developing a dynamic version of portfolio theory and came up with the "intertemporal capital asset pricing model." Until then, CAPM had described only how the market values assets at a given moment. Recognizing that financial markets around the world are open for trading virtually around the clock, Merton used a concept known as "continuous time analysis" to transform CAPM into a description of what happens over a sequence of time periods during which conditions are changing rather than standing still. Rather than diluting the importance of the earlier work, his dynamic analysis reinforced the static models that preceded it.

It was this shift from static to dynamic modeling that had led Modigliani to discourage Treynor from pursuing his explorations into asset pricing any further, given Treynor's limitations in mathematics. Merton had no such limitations. In the spring of 1969, he decided to incorporate Ito's lemma "and all that stuff," as he puts it, into his intertemporal model of portfolio selection.[16]

Merton first applied this concept to the valuation of warrants and options. When he applied it to the Capital Asset Pricing Model, he was able to write out the dynamics of the whole process. Unfortunately, nobody in economics had even heard of Ito's lemma. According to Merton, Samuelson himself "could not tell whether the mathematics was right or wrong."[17]

Markowitz has made some interesting comments about Merton's achievement. In a letter to Samuelson in October 1985, he wrote: "Ito's lemma turned out to be a cornucopia of interesting results, and Bob's work has become central to much of the modern theory of finance. The one thing that bothers me about continuous portfolio selection is that I don't really understand it."*[18]

Despite the mathematical complexity of his work, Merton had made a giant leap. As he himself has described it: "The mathematics of the continuous-time model contains some of the most beau-

---

*In a note written shortly after receiving the Nobel Prize in October 1990, Markowitz told me that "after much intense study, I am almost mediocre in the mathematics of continuous time models." Merton doubts that Markowitz is expressing false modesty: "Harry probably imposes such exacting standards on himself that, should the rest of us do the same, we would be *well below* mediocre." Yet, Ito's lemma is now standard operating procedure in the finance courses at many of the leading business schools.

tiful applications of probability and optimization theory. But, of course, not all that is beautiful in science need also be practical. And surely, not all that is practical in science is beautiful. Here we have both."[19]

Although it bears an unmistakable resemblance to the Capital Asset Pricing Model, Merton's theory has philosophical roots in the work of Kenneth Arrow and Gerard Debreu, both Nobel Prize winners. Arrow and Debreu describe a world in which everything is tradable, from the value of an education to the housewife's ironing of the family sheets, and under an infinite variety of conditions, or "states of nature." The continuous-time model provides a framework for converting such "pure" securities into a form that will permit them to be traded. Merton also pays his respects to Bachelier's "magnificent dissertation on the theory of speculation."[20] On the more practical side, Merton incorporates into his theoretical structure the institutional functions and risk-taking activities of financial intermediaries such as banks and mutual funds.

When Merton went looking for a job in late 1969, he did not have to look far. At Modigliani's suggestion, he stayed on at MIT and joined the faculty at the Sloan School of Management. Scholes had arrived on the scene about a year before, and he and Merton soon became good friends.

In the spring of 1970, Scholes told Merton what he and Black were trying to accomplish and how far they had progressed. Their challenging problem was just the kind of thing that Merton enjoyed sinking his teeth into, especially as his interest in Samuelson's work on warrant pricing was still running strong.

Black and Scholes had advanced to a point where they were linking options to the underlying assets in a wide variety of combinations. They were particularly interested in what happened when they combined stocks with different quantities of options in such a way that, at any given moment, the values of the options and the values of their underlying stocks would move in opposite directions by *precisely* the same amount. They found that, whether the stock rose or fell in price, the value of the combination would be independent of what the market was doing. As the option-holder gained on one side what he was losing on the other, he could predict precisely where he would stand at any given moment in the future.

How can two securities, each of which is risky in its own right, be combined to mimic the behavior of an asset that has no risk at all? Suppose an investor buys a stock and, at the same moment, also buys a put. The put gives him the right to sell the stock at a predetermined price within a stated period of time. No matter how low the stock might fall, the investor's loss will be limited, because he will be able to sell the stock at that predetermined price. The put will become more valuable when the stock is falling, but it will be less valuable when the stock climbs away from the exercise price of the option.

An investor who buys a stock and a put option at the same time can easily turn into a manic-depressive. If the stock rises in price, that is good news. But as the stock moves further away from the exercise price, the put will lose value. That is bad news. Now look at it the other way. If the price of the stock falls, the investor will be sorry he owns it, but, at the same time, he will be glad he was prescient enough to buy the protective put.

Merton was not convinced that Black and Scholes had unlocked the secret of the puzzle by basing their solution on the Capital Asset Pricing Model. Black and Scholes were convinced that they had. Intense discussions followed. Scholes recalls those days with nostalgia: "Bob Merton is a great colleague—he pushes you all the way."[21]

One Saturday afternoon, Merton called Scholes on the phone and exclaimed, "You're right!"[22] They were right, however, for a reason that they themselves had failed to recognize. Merton was able to offer them a more elegant derivation of the option pricing formula.

He pointed out that investors will seek out combinations of stocks and options in which the good news will outweigh the bad. If the prices of the stock and the put option are out of line with each other, the stock might rise in price by more than the value of the put falls. The news, in other words, would be net good, with more gained from the rising stock price than lost from the shrinking value of the put. Such strokes of luck are to be taken advantage of.

Modigliani and Miller had emphasized that active capital markets are crowded with investors looking for free lunches. As arbitragers rush to take advantage of such opportunities by buying the stock and selling the put, the stock will become more expensive while the put gets cheaper. The free lunch will disappear, and the symmetry between the two assets will return as they move back into proper alignment.

If the gain on one side of the combination is precisely offset by a loss on the other, the investor will be holding a riskless position that is the equivalent of holding a Treasury bill or some other liquid asset with a certain return known in advance. If the combination of stock and option offered more than this risk-free rate, investors would compete for the opportunity to own it and would bid the opportunity away. If it offered less, investors would shun it and its value would fall to a point where it once again offered the riskless rate of return.

Only one small step remained. The option-pricing formula had to calculate the price of the option that would give the stock-option combination that risk-free result. In an efficient market, there is no other price that the option could command.

In our unsophisticated fashion, my firm had had the correct intuition. The prevailing rate of interest on risk-free assets like short-term Treasury bills is an essential input to the option-pricing formula. As we had also recognized, the inputs must include the price of the underlying stock, the price at which the option is selling, and the time remaining until the option expires.

But there was one more item to be plugged into the formula. No investor will buy or sell an option on a stock without some expectation about what the future action of the stock will be. Will the stock be volatile, like Apple Computer, or sleepy, like Consolidated Edison? In valuing options, volatility matters a lot. The option-holder has a claim on which he can lose relatively little: Thales made only small deposits on the olive presses. But the option-holder can gain a great deal: Thales made a killing when the olive crop turned out to be unexpectedly large. This means that options are more interesting to their owners in cases where something big is likely to happen than when nothing is likely to happen. If conditions promise to be stable, why spend money for an opportunity that will be profitable only when conditions change?

More is involved here than just beta—that is, a stock's volatility relative to the market as a whole. Expectations about whether the stock is going to move *at all* dominate expectations about whether the stock is going to move up or move down. To owners of call options, who have the right to buy at a specified price, big downward movements in the stock price do not matter, because the risk of loss is limited to the premium paid; big upward movements are what matter. So long as the other four inputs are the same, an option on Apple is going to be a lot more interesting than an option on Con Ed.

The sellers of options have the opposite requirement. They like stocks that stand still. They simply pocket the premiums they collect on the sale without having to take any further action. They are like a company that sells insurance: they collect the insurance premiums while hoping that nothing will happen to the policy-owner—no houses burning down, no premature deaths, no burglaries, no catastrophic illness.

Investors who use options to hedge their risks will also be more eager to hedge big risks than small ones. If the olive harvest is about the same every year, there is little risk that press capacity and olive production will be badly matched. If the harvest is unexpectedly large, the olive grower will want to hedge against the possibility that he will have no access to the presses when his crop comes in.

In light of all these considerations, how does an investor determine whether an option is cheap, expensive, or priced about right? The answer is to use the Black-Scholes formula. The investor knows the current prices of the stock and the option, the price at which the option can be exercised, the time to expiration, and the going rate of interest. With this information, the model will provide an estimate of the stock's volatility that is implied in the price of the option. Then it is up to the investor to judge whether the market's expectations about volatility look too low, too high, or about right.

This game is fun as well as essential for option-traders. Take the option on the Standard & Poor's Composite Index of 500 stocks, which trades on the Chicago Board Options Exchange. On September 23, 1990, the S&P 500 closed at 311.32. An investor could buy a one-month call on the index, carrying the right to buy at 310, for a cost of $9.38. That option would be slightly in-the-money: the actual price of 311.32 was just above the exercise price of 310. At the same moment, the interest rate on Treasury bills was 7.50 percent.

When this information is put into a computer, the pricing model reveals that the market was expecting the monthly volatility of the S&P 500 to be 7.4 percent. In other words, people were expecting the index during the month ahead to move generally within a range of plus or minus 7.4 percent, or 23 points, on either side of 311.32.

With concerns about the crisis in Kuwait and impending recession running high, this volatility estimate in September 1990 turned out to be considerably above the long-run volatility of the index, which was 5.9 percent a month, and even further above the 4.4 percent average of the preceding twelve months. A volatility estimate this far above past experience was unusual: most of the time, people expect the near future to look pretty much the way the recent past has looked.

The same experiment revealed that the implied volatility of individual stocks reflected the differences in their fundamental characteristics. American Telephone and Telegraph's implied monthly volatility was only 10.8 percent, compared to 19.3 percent for Chrysler, a company that was in deep trouble at that moment. The implied volatility for UAL was way up at 22.8 percent, reflecting the uncertainty about the airline's takeover prospects.

Note that each of these stocks had an implied volatility above the 7.4 percent of the S&P 500. That should come as no surprise. The index is a widely diversified portfolio; an individual stock, no matter how stable, is still a totally undiversified portfolio. Eggs in one basket are a lot riskier than eggs distributed among many baskets.

After Black and Scholes had committed their ideas to paper, they started off on a frustrating adventure. Their first draft, titled "A Theoretical Valuation Formula for Options, Warrants, and Other Securities," was dated October 1970. Black sent it to the *Journal of Political Economy,* a Chicago University publication. It was promptly rejected. The *JPE* said the paper was excessively specialized, because it had too much to do with finance and not enough to do with economics—the same problem Harry Markowitz had had with his thesis on portfolio selection. Then Black tried Harvard's *Review of Economics and Statistics.* Another prompt rejection. Neither journal even sent the paper out for review. Although both authors were surprised by the rejections, Black suspects that part of the problem was his nonacademic return address. Scholes adds, "Who knew me?"[23] In any case, they decided to rewrite the paper with more attention to its broader economic implications.

The title of their new draft, dated January 1971, reflected their effort to beam their ideas to economists. They titled the paper "Capital Market Equilibrium and the Pricing of Corporate Liabilities." At this point they received help from another quarter. Eugene Fama and Merton Miller had been aware of their work, had given them extensive comments on it, and were following their publishing ordeal. Now these two Chicago professors put in a good word for them at the *Journal of Political Economy*. That did the trick.

Throughout this story, Merton Miller has played the role of power-broker. He had encouraged Eugene Fama, still a novice, to teach entirely new material. He had guided Scholes into finance. He had introduced Treynor to Modigliani. He had immediately recognized Sharpe's talent. And finally he was instrumental in providing Black and Scholes with the notice that their work surely deserved.

The final draft, carrying the simpler title, "The Pricing of Options and Corporate Liabilities," was dated May 1972, but it was not published in the *Journal of Political Economy* until the issue of May/June 1973. In one of those odd twists of academic journalism, the *Journal of Finance* of May 1972 had carried a paper by Black and Scholes that reported their successful empirical results with their formula, but the theoretical paper on the formula did not appear for another full year.

That delay created a problem for Robert Merton. Following up on his collaboration with Samuelson, he had continued to work on options valuation and its broader applications to the valuation of the corporation as a whole. He had drafted a major paper on the subject titled "The Theory of Rational Option Pricing."

While Merton was considering where to send his paper for publication, a colleague at the Sloan School, Paul McAvoy, had recently become editor of a new journal to be published by the Bell Laboratories, the research arm of the American Telephone Company. McAvoy expressed interest in Merton's work, even though Merton warned him that it was "pretty thick" and would probably run to about forty pages in print. McAvoy, eager to get his new journal off the ground, said, "We'll publish any size paper. We'll also pay you $500 for the manuscript." This was irresistible bait for a young assistant professor still earning a starting salary of $11,500.[24]

Merton was reluctant to have his article appear ahead of Black and Scholes's main paper, because his paper drew on and commented on theirs. So he asked McAvoy to hold up publication until the Black-Scholes paper had appeared. But, as Merton recalls, Black and Scholes were "having this dance with the JPE. I heard only the entrails of it from Myron."[25] As a result, even though the last version of Merton's paper is dated August 1972, it appeared in the *Bell Journal* issue of Spring 1973, almost simultaneously with the appearance of Black-Scholes.

The friendly rivalry among these three men has another twist. Separately, but early on, Black, Scholes, and Merton had recognized the significance of options theory for valuing the corporation as a whole. As Modigliani and Miller had demonstrated, the total value of the corporation is determined by its earning power, and the claims against the corporation—the value of its outstanding debts and shares of stock—must equal that total value. If one claim rises in value, another must fall. They are all in the same boat. Once this is recognized, the corporation turns out to be a complex maze of options.

Are the stockholders the true owners of a company? Not really. The creditors—the people who have lent the company money—have the first claim on the company's assets. The stockholders are entitled only to what is left after the creditors have taken what they are entitled to. The stockholders are the true owners of the company only when they do not owe a single cent to anyone other than themselves.

Although the stockholders do not own the company, they have a call option on its assets. They can exercise that option by paying off the company's debts. The exercise price of the option is the principal amount borrowed. And its expiration date is the due date on which the debts are payable.

When the company's debts come due, the stockholders have the right to let their call option on the assets lapse, leaving the bondholders in possession of the company's assets—or holding the bag, as Wall Street puts it. This is exactly what happens when the owners refuse to pay their debts and let a company go into bankruptcy. Most of the time, the stockholders exercise the option and redeem their debts—until they borrow fresh money and activate a brand-new option.

The price the stockholders pay for the option of walking away from their obligations is reflected in the interest rate on the company's debts. The cost of that option is determined just like any other. The interest rate will be low when the company's assets are large relative to its liabilities—if, in technical terms, the option is deep in-the-money. The interest rate will be low when the debts come due sooner rather than later, and if the company's business is stable and predictable rather than volatile. The interest rate will be high when the company is deeply in debt, when the maturity of the debts is far off, and when its business is exceptionally volatile. American Telephone and Telegraph pays a lower rate of interest on its bonds than Chrysler or Citicorp.

This use of options to value corporate liabilities has come to be known as Contingent Claims Analysis. Merton, who was one of the pioneers in the development of this concept, has commented that the nomenclature "sounds like an insurance adjuster,"[26] but it has become the richest vein in the gold mine of options theory.

Meanwhile, Scholes, who enjoyed "teaching the Young Turks who would become the mavens of the quant world,"[27] had been actively involved in a major consulting arrangement with Wells Fargo Bank in San Francisco. In July 1970, he arranged for Wells Fargo to sponsor a conference at the Sloan School at MIT, where he and Black gave an early version of their options pricing paper. Merton was also planning to give a paper at this conference. Black and Scholes included in their presentation their ideas on the applicability of the option-pricing process to the valuation of corporate liabilities, and the 1971 draft of their paper makes specific reference to this in its title. Merton inconveniently overslept that morning and missed their paper. It was only later that he discovered that they were all working the same side of the street.

Despite the competition for ideas, there was nothing among these men that smacked of the abrasive relationship that had developed between Sharpe and Lintner. Nearly twenty years after Merton's alarm clock failed him, Black had this to say on the occasion of Merton's leaving MIT to cross the Charles River and join Harvard Business School: "A key part of the option paper I wrote with Myron Scholes was the arbitrage argument for deriving the formula. Bob gave us that argument. It should probably be called the Black-Merton-Scholes paper."[28]

The friendly rivalry that Black, Scholes, and Merton enjoyed reflected the unique atmosphere in which they were working. At the time, the finance department at the Sloan School consisted of only four assistant professors, Merton, Scholes, Gerald Pogue (now at the City University of New York, Markowitz's home base), and Stewart Myers, who is still at Sloan. None of the four had tenure, and none was the designated leader. Though Black was an eager participant in their activities, he was still in the consulting business. Modigliani had a joint appointment at the Sloan School and the economics department and provided some intellectual leadership, but he did not take part in the day-to-day master's degree program or administrative activities in the area. Samuelson was barely acquainted with any of the four other than Merton.

Merton describes the little group during this short period of the early 1970s, with the whole world open to them, like "kids in a candy store, with more to do than we had time to do. Research results were flowing so rapidly that we sometimes didn't even bother to write them all down."[29] As the efficient-market theory, the CRSP data tapes, and Sharpe's CAPM had stirred the research pot at the University of Chicago to the boiling point in the last half of the 1960s, so option pricing, corporate liability valuation theories, and intertemporal portfolio selection provided a research monopoly at the Sloan School in the early 1970s.* The whole environment had moved far away from the traditional finance setting, where accounting and the elements of corporate finance were the daily fare.

It was not all teaching and research. Black recalls that, "though the search for the formula was an academic search for truth, we did try to use it to make money." They started with warrants. First, they estimated the volatility of the stocks of companies with warrants outstanding. Then, when their own estimates differed from the volatility implied in the prices of the warrants, they bought the warrants that seemed very low in price and waited for them to go up. "As it turned out, we did not make money," says Black, "but we did learn some more truth." Scholes insists that Black's assessment of their financial results is hyperbole, but the lesson learned was an important one nonetheless.[30]

The lesson came from warrants issued by a company known as National General, which, though out-of-the-money (the stock price was below the exercise price on the warrant), appeared to be the best buy of all. In the summer of 1972, Scholes, Merton,

---

*In a kind of hands-across-the-sea gesture, Chicago granted Merton an honorary degree at the commencement exercises in June 1991.

and Black jumped in and bought a bunch of these warrants. At first, things looked great. Then, all of a sudden, there was a take-over bid for National General, and the warrants dropped rapidly in price. The takeover bid had prematurely ended the lives of the warrants but had failed to push the stock price up far enough to give the warrants value.

The lesson the MIT investors learned was that the market some-times knows things the option formula does not know. The war-rants appeared cheap because the market knew the takeover bid was a strong possibility. The three professors had never thought of that.

One of the most important early tests of the model was con-ducted in 1975 by Dan Galai, a Chicago Ph.D. candidate. Galai used daily data over the period July 1973 to April 1974 to esti-mate volatility and then used the formula to look for undervalued and overvalued options. He made some unrealistic assumptions about trading costs, but, even so, his simulated strategy was im-pressive evidence of the validity and integrity of the Black-Scholes formula.

"Opportunities like this are harder to come by these days," Black recently observed, and for a good reason: "Traders now use the formula and its variants extensively. They use it so much that market prices are usually close to formula values even in situ-ations where there should be a large difference: situations, for example, where a cash takeover is likely to end the life of the option or the warrant."[31]

The extensive use of the formula depended on the success with which it did its job, but something else was needed: an options market that would be more active than the traditional negotiated, cumbersome, primitive over-the-counter system.

By coincidence, the Chicago Board Options Exchange opened for business in April 1973, exactly one month before the Univer-sity of Chicago's *Journal of Political Economy* published "The Pricing of Options and Corporate Liabilities." That event made for a revolutionary transformation of options trading that pro-vided a perfect setting for the practical implementation of the model.

The CBOE was a success from the start, though its early days were bizarre. Trading began in the smoking lounge of the Board of Trade, a limited space that had been converted for the purpose.

Soon traders were standing on counters because there was no room on the floor.

The Chicago Board of Trade soon decided to build a new and proper floor for the CBOE. The old trading floor of the Board of Trade occupied an enormous space, about five stories high, with architecture and decoration appropriate to the importance of the commodities traded there. A new floor was suspended between the old floor and the ceiling, and in 1976 that floor of 30,000 square feet became the home of the Chicago Board Options Exchange.

From the beginning, the Exchange furnished its customers with market-makers committed to providing liquidity, standardized option contracts, strict regulation, and sophisticated electronic equipment to report all trades on computer screens the instant they occurred. Today, with an even larger trading floor, the Exchange has one and a half acres of computers in its basement, wiring for its electronic equipment that would reach twice around the Equator, and a telephone system that would service a city of 50,000 people.

On the first day of trading in 1973, with 284 members on the floor making markets, just 911 call option contracts on 16 underlying stock issues changed hands. A year later, even in the dark days of mid-1974, more than 20,000 contracts a day on 32 underlying stocks were trading, 567 members were making markets on the floor, and the cost of membership had risen from $10,000 to over $40,000. Three years later, the daily volume was up to 100,000 contracts.

At the peak of feverish market activity in 1987, daily volume averaged 700,000 call and put contracts and covered options on bonds and market indexes in addition to stocks. As each contract reflects the right to buy or sell 100 shares of stock, this was the equivalent of 70 million shares, at a time when the average daily trading on the New York Stock Exchange was 190 million shares. In 1989, a quieter year, the price of a membership on the CBOE had leapt to $250,000 and daily trading averaged about 450,000 contracts. In that same year, the competitors that had arisen since 1973—the New York Stock Exchange, the American Stock Exchange, and the Philadelphia and Pacific Stock Exchanges—together accounted for roughly another 400,000 contracts a day.

Keeping track of that volume of transactions would confound a less sophisticated system. The stocks with options trading on the CBOE have many puts and calls outstanding, with exercise prices that often range from far above to far below the current price. In September 1990, for example, Boeing had 29 puts and calls outstanding, with exercise prices ranging from 40 up to 60 at a time when the stock was trading at around 43; UAL, at the center of a takeover battle, had 60 options outstanding, with exercise prices from as low as 90 to as high as 175. Every time the price of the underlying stock changes, the prices of all those options change at the same instant.

The buyers and sellers of options have an equally elaborate task. Merton chuckles as he remembers the early days of the CBOE. In the spring of 1973, right after the CBOE opened up for business, he and Scholes designed an option pricing and hedging model for the Wall Street firm of Donaldson, Lufkin, and Jenrette, where considerable skepticism persisted about whether it would be needed. Within six months after the publication of the Black-Scholes model, Texas Instruments took a half-page advertisement in the *Wall Street Journal* to say "Now you can find the Black-Scholes value using our . . . calculator." Within a year, the transition was complete. Merton remarks:

> I got the biggest kick out of hearing those options traders routinely talk about hedge ratios and deltas, partial differential equations, and stochastic differential equations. Who would ever think that people would be talking like that. . . .
>
> People had no choice. They couldn't deal with it the way they dealt with it over-the-counter. There is no other way to deal with the complexity of the option. The models made sense intuitively and seemed to work.[32]

The important observation here is that "People had no choice." The options traders who ignored the Black-Scholes model and its variants did so at their peril: without it, they were destined to get the short end of the stick. Soon people were going about with little hand-held calculators that had been programmed to perform the necessary calculations once the inputs had been punched in. Many options traders operate with powerful computers at their beck and call.

Here, too, they have no choice. The formula is not exactly designed for quick calculations on the back of an envelope. By the time anyone figures out the answers by hand to something that looks like this:

$$C = S \, N(d_1) - E \, e^{-R_f T} N(d_2)$$

where:

$$d^1 = \frac{ln(S/E) + [R_f + (1/2) \, \sigma^2]T}{\sigma\sqrt{T}}$$

$$d_2 = d_1 - \sigma\sqrt{T}$$

$N(d_1)$, $N(d_2)$ = cumulative normal probability values of $d_1$ and $d_2$, respectively

$S$ = stock price

$E$ = exercise price

$R_f$ = the risk-free rate of interest

$\sigma$ = the instantaneous variance rate of the stock

$T$ = time to expiration of the option

the world will have moved on so far that the whole result will be obsolete even before the calculations are done.

Fischer Black was no longer in the Boston area among his MIT friends when the paper finally appeared in print. The whole experience had inducted him into the world of academe, and in 1971 he accepted a visiting professorship at the University of Chicago. Given his fascination with free-market ideas, this was the perfect place for him. As Robert Merton puts it, "Fischer out-Chicago'd Chicago."[33] In 1972, Black accepted a permanent appointment as Executive Director of the Center for Research in Security Prices (CRSP). Two years later he became Director of the Center.

In 1973, Scholes accepted Miller's offer of a temporary appointment at Chicago with the mouth-filling title Ford Foundation Visiting Research Associate Professor of Finance. In 1975, he accepted a permanent appointment as both associate professor and as Executive Director of CRSP. He became a full professor and replaced Black as Director of CRSP the following year. At CRSP, he supervised a major update of the original Fisher and Lorie study, gathering and pricing a daily data base, as well as adjusting for dividends, splits, and other capitalization changes. Meanwhile, Merton continued to hold the fort back in Cambridge, until he left MIT in 1988 for Harvard Business School.

Black's wife was not happy in Chicago and returned with their children to the Boston area, leaving Black to commute every weekend between Chicago and Boston, an expensive as well as an unpleasant arrangement. In 1975, Merton got the idea that MIT might lure Black back, not just for auld lang syne, but because he would be with his family and, incidentally, save the cost of commuting. Then Merton had another idea: Why not try to bring Scholes back at the same time?

It took Black just two days to say yes. Soon he moved into an office next door to Merton's, where they lived happily ever after until 1984, when Wall Street enticed him to New York. There he develops complex trading strategies for the customers of the investment banking firm of Goldman Sachs.

A year later, Scholes called Merton at home on a weekend to tell him that he too had succumbed. The following Monday, he called back to say he was staying at Chicago. Merton Miller, ever the power-broker, had prevailed.

Scholes continued to write as co-author with the others. Not counting the basic paper with Black on options pricing, he has published four articles with Black, two with Merton, and four with Miller.

Even before their option-pricing paper saw the light of day, Black and Scholes had shared another exciting experience. With Michael Jensen, they had conducted an important test of the Capital Asset Pricing Model and had discovered that stocks with low betas, or low volatility, tended to earn higher returns than the model predicted, while stocks with high betas did worse than expected. Their results were published in 1972.

Acting on these findings, Black and Scholes persuaded Wells Fargo to sponsor a mutual fund that would invest in low-beta stocks. In order to offer the investor a bigger bang for the buck, with more volatility than a low-beta portfolio would provide, the fund would borrow money to buy additional shares of these stocks. I remember hearing Black, in his laconic fashion, trying to make the selling pitch at a Wall Street gathering for what was to be called The Stagecoach Fund.

The horses never got attached to that stagecoach. Quite aside from the regulatory problems that would be created by a bank managing a publicly offered mutual fund, Wells Fargo planned to launch the fund just as the stock market was diving into the worst of the 1974 bear market. The environment was hardly favorable for anything as adventuresome as this, and the whole scheme died aborning. I will have more on this story in Chapter 12.

About a year later, Scholes and Merton also tried to launch a mutual fund to deal in options. This fund offered a capital-preserving strategy that they thought would be irresistible in the wake of the 1974 bear market. Here, too, events intervened. The vibrant bull market of late 1975 and early 1976 was precisely the wrong environment for a conservative strategy. A fund that the underwriters had originally pegged at $100 million turned out to raise a mere $17 million—"hardly a smashing success," as Merton admits.[34]

These disappointments aside, the three scholars at MIT had turned Thales's financial device into an instrument of great power and overwhelming importance. Options enable investors to control risk and to shape the outcomes they face: at a cost, losses can be limited while upsides can be magnified. This is the most attractive feature of options. As investors, borrowers, and lenders increased their understanding of these basic concepts, the flow of applications grew from a trickle to a flood.

Options were incorporated into the entirely new and complex debt instruments that blossomed during the 1980s. They are responsible for the mushrooming of the market for government-guaranteed home mortgages. Their hedging features made possible the development of the so-called interest rate swaps between major financial institutions, the explosion in daily trading in the foreign exchange markets, the ability of banks to shield themselves from the vagaries of the money markets, and the willingness of major investment banking firms to provide many millions of dollars of instant liquidity to their institutional customers.

Seldom has the marriage of theory and practice been so productive. Every time an institution uses these instruments, a corporation issues them, or a homeowner takes out a mortgage, they are paying their respects, not just to Black, Scholes, and Merton, but to Bachelier, Samuelson, Fama, Markowitz, Tobin, Treynor, and Sharpe as well.

# From Gown
# to Town

# Chapter
# 12

## The Constellation

*Can you really run money with this stuff?*

This chapter tells the story of a revolutionary coup, the moment when the first shots were fired, the first blood was drawn, and the first charismatic leaders stood on the ramparts. The leaders of this coup were an unlikely threesome. One was an engineer who had spent many weekend nights camped out in a sleeping bag nestled up to a main-frame computer in the basement of the Time-Life building in New York. Another had started out in Kentucky as a jazz clarinetist and saxophone player. The third was responsible for the investment management department of San Francisco's Wells Fargo Bank, who, in his own words, was "skeptical, suspicious, careful, cautious, [and] slow to change" but who ultimately became one of the revolution's most zealous and eloquent proselytizers.

Nothing about their behavior suggested a carefully coordinated team in action. Their story is typical of all revolutions, in which even a shared vision does not prevent infighting among the leaders—infighting that is often as intense as their struggle with the powers they are trying to overcome.

Difficult as their job may have been, they achieved enormous success. Before they were done, they had propelled the traditional trust department at Wells Fargo into a juggernaut that grew from about $2 billion of personal trust assets in 1970 to $14.6 billion of personal and institutional assets in 1980, and then zoomed to more than $80 billion of personal, pension fund, endowment fund, and foundation assets in 1990. That $80 billion is managed for 367 clients in 83 different strategies, every one of which stems from the theoretical ideas set forth in this book.

Wells Fargo stands today as the role model in the practical application of theoretical concepts, with a whole train of institutions around the world aiming to emulate its success.

Under most circumstances, the environment in which these three men launched their coup would have seemed singularly hostile. Although bank trust departments are never quite as bad as their customers say they are, their institutional peculiarities tend to create cadres who are set in their ways, with instinctive self-defenses that rise up at the mere whiff of innovation.

To people steeped in the conventional way of doing things, the new doctrines were heresy, beyond the pale. The transformations those doctrines required would uproot every participant in the trust investment business, either changing their roles or eliminating them altogether. No one takes a threat like that lying down.

Markowitz, for example, threatens the private preserve of portfolio managers by stressing the dominance of the portfolio over its individual components. That means that managers should not blithely stuff portfolios with their favorite picks, ignoring the overwhelming importance of diversification. In fact, the diversification Markowitz calls for often requires managers to hold stocks they do not like in order to balance out the ones they do like.

Tobin's Separation Theorem goes even further, by rejecting the conventional method of designing each portfolio specifically for each customer. Rather, Tobin prescribes identical equity portfolios for all accounts, regardless of objective or risk aversion. So who needs separate portfolio managers for each group of clients?

Security analysts are also vulnerable. Samuelson and Fama and their ilk argue that stock-picking is an activity doomed to fail and that technical analysis is a dangerous waste of time. If the stock market is efficient and stock prices are a random walk, who needs security analysts to make recommendations to portfolio managers?

The worst was yet to come. According to Sharpe, the market portfolio is the most efficient portfolio of all. If all you have to do is buy the market, or an index that replicates it, who needs anybody to carry on the traditional activities of a trust department?

It is ironic that the revolution in portfolio management got its start at Wells Fargo Bank, one of the oldest banks in the United States. The company had been founded by Henry Wells and William Fargo in 1852, to provide mail and package services as well as banking facilities for the men and women who poured into northern California after the discovery of gold at Sutter's Mill in January 1848; the banking facilities included converting gold dust into gold bars.* Before the gold rush, the population of California had been 150,000 Indian and 15,000 non-Indian; by 1852, the non-Indian population was 250,000, most of it up north in the San Francisco area.

The Wells Fargo logo is a stagecoach. The bank used its famous stagecoaches from 1852 up to the end of World War I to carry mail, packages, and treasure. These marvels of Yankee ingenuity and craftsmanship were nine-passenger vehicles built in Concord, New Hampshire, weighing 2,200 pounds and costing about $1,000. One of their longest routes ran from Cisco, California to North Platte, Nebraska, but they also reached out to major rail-heads in Montana, Idaho, and Nevada. A traveler could cover the 1,900 miles from Sacramento to Omaha in fifteen days in what Mark Twain described as a "cradle on wheels."[1] From 1852 until well into the 1860s, Wells Fargo also carried mail on its famed Pony Express.

An institution with such traditions does not normally welcome change. But Wells Fargo did not conform to the mold. Although the troops wanted to hold fast to the old ways of doing things, the chairman of the bank and the senior people in the trust and investment management departments turned out to be unexpectedly open-minded and amenable to change.

In the peaceful days before the coup, the trust department was responsible for $2 billion or so of individual trust assets, with little institutional money under management. Any resemblance to the new world to which it was about to be pulled, pushed, cajoled, and bullied was purely coincidental.

The department was functioning as it had for decades. The security analysts studied and visited the companies they were responsible for, listened to the stories and the occasionally serious pieces of analysis from Wall Street, and made appropriate recommendations to the portfolio managers. The portfolio managers, in most instances, were each responsible for over a hundred small trust accounts and worked under the supervision of an invest-

---

*Messrs. Wells and Fargo had already founded the American Express Company in 1850.

ment committee. The committee considered the recommendations of the security analysts but made its own decisions, converting the recommendations into lists of stocks OK to buy, stocks OK to hold, and stocks to be eliminated from the portfolios—tax and other individual considerations permitting.

Portfolios typically held about fifteen stocks but tended to differ a great deal from one another in their composition. Control of risk was not ignored, but interior decorating procedures took care of most of it; there was no awareness of more systematic approaches to diversification.

Clients had only the vaguest idea of how their fortunes were faring, and certainly no idea of whether their portfolios were receiving good management or bad. The only performance report was a number representing the percentage change from the inception date of the trust to the latest reporting date. No adjustments were made for money added or withdrawn. Even worse, the percentage was not converted into annual rates of return, which meant that unsophisticated customers whose portfolios had doubled over ten years might assume they were doing just as well as customers whose portfolios had doubled in five years.

The first wedge into this system was driven by a man with the fine Scottish name of John Andrew McQuown. McQuown has a boyish mop of hair that, though now grayish-white, still tumbles down over his forehead.

Like some of the other innovators in this story, McQuown had started out in engineering. While studying mechanical engineering at Northwestern, from which he received a Bachelor of Science degree in 1957, he had learned about the newly invented transistor—the chip that would replace the vacuum tube and revolutionize the world of electronics. Convinced of the future of this marvelous invention, McQuown borrowed $1,600 against the black and white Chevrolet convertible his father had given him as a graduation present and used the money to buy 400 shares of Texas Instruments, a leader in the manufacture of transistors. "My father would have killed me if he had known about it," McQuown recalls. Two years later, while serving in the Navy—he was Chief Engineering Officer on a vintage destroyer at the time of his discharge—McQuown liquidated his modest investment in Texas Instruments for more than $180,000.

The game was too tempting to give up and had the classic ending. When he left the Navy, he decided to go to Harvard Business School. He was still playing the market, using his windfall from Texas Instruments to collateralize a margin account. He had a wonderful ride, until he was wiped out in the mini-crash in the spring of 1962.

McQuown was not discouraged. He went to work at the brokerage house of Smith Barney in Wall Street and at the same time tried to help a computer programming whiz from MIT to develop a model that was supposed to distinguish cheap stocks from expensive ones. The model was cursed with a host of problems. It was extremely complicated. It produced many false signals as well as some good ones. It was such a monster that it consumed huge amounts of computer time and could operate only on the IBM 7090, then the biggest commercially available computer.

McQuown, who had been attracted to portfolio theory early on, was convinced that he could use it to make his friend's model operational. McQuown's family lived in Chicago, and he had been introduced to the theory by friends at the University, particularly Lawrence Fisher, James Lorie, and Eugene Fama (still a graduate student), whose work first attracted his attention when they began to release their findings on rates of return on equities. Through them, he became aware of the nascent development of data bases of stock market transactions, practical applications of theory, and the role of computer science in the investing world; Bankers Trust, the Bank of New York, the Boston Company, and Merrill Lynch (with the impetus coming from Jack Treynor) were all beginning to experiment along these lines. Chicago was also host to the CRSP seminars, which provided additional links to the practitioners who were exploring real-world uses for the theoretical innovations.

After an extended period of trying to beg, borrow, or steal computer time, McQuown and his friend from MIT finally made a deal and rented the 7090 in the IBM service center in the basement of the Time-Life building for $300 a weekend. The program took so long to run, and produced so many reams of uninterpretable data, that McQuown often crawled into his sleeping bag on the floor and slept while the program was running.

In the fall of 1963, these odd goings-on aroused the curiosity of the IBM people, who were always on the lookout for anything that might demonstrate to prospective customers the versatility and power of the computer. In January 1964, after hearing what

McQuown was up to, the manager of the data center invited him to San Jose, California, to describe his project at an executive forum IBM was planning to hold for customers and prospects.

One of the people attending the conference was Ransom Cook, then Chairman of Wells Fargo. Cook, who was himself an innovator in many areas of the bank, was impressed with McQuown's presentation and invited him to come up to company headquarters in San Francisco for a talk.

"Can you really run money with this stuff?" Cook asked McQuown. McQuown was confident that he could; in fact, he was convinced that there was no other way. He explained to Cook the vacuousness of the traditional methods of portfolio management, which, he pointed out, were little more than ". . . a variation of the Great Man theory. A Great Man picks stocks that go up. You keep him until his picks don't work any more and you search for another Great Man. The whole thing is a chance-driven process. It's not systematic and there is lots we still don't know about it and that needs study."

McQuown recalls that Cook "made me an incredibly attractive offer right on the spot." In March 1964, McQuown went to work in the Wells Fargo Management Sciences division to develop a project plan that came to be known as "Investment Decision Making." The goal was to make Wells Fargo a leader rather than a follower in the trust investment business.

When Cook asked McQuown about a budget, McQuown, for want of a better number, suggested "about a million a year to start." Cook responded, "That's entirely reasonable." Reasonable as this sum may have been in 1964, it was a far cry from the $12,000 annual budget that had inaugurated the Cowles Commission in 1932.

And so the great adventure began.

McQuown started off by launching an attack on the concepts to which the trust department was so attached. Together with academic consultants and the essential assistance of the computer, old practices and much investment folklore fell by the wayside.

His most important step was to demonstrate that diversification was a "trans-sovereign subject" that should dominate everything else. McQuown lights up when he recalls what went on: "There is a body of endarkenment [sic] that it's not economic to buy and hold more than a few dozen names. Owning a 13-stock portfolio is just not what you want to do. I don't care if God himself is down here making the choices—that's not the right way to play the game."

McQuown asked if anyone knew whether the bank could buy and sell large positions without so disrupting the market that the cost of the transaction would wipe out most of the gain that would accrue from just retaining the holdings. No one had an answer. So they set out to analyze the impact of transaction costs and began to recognize the importance of artful executions of trades.

This led in turn to an examination of the reporting procedures for clients. The existing reports made no sense at all. McQuown called in Lorie from Chicago to help them adjust for money added or withdrawn, for the passage of time, and for the risks incurred in generating the results.

The effort seemed so rewarding that Wells Fargo persuaded the research arm of the banking industry, the Bank Administration Institute, to support a full-fledged study of performance measurement that would be made available to the entire profession. This extraordinary document, "Measuring the Investment Performance of Pension Funds," appeared in 1968. It ran to over 200 pages and had seven academic authors, including David Durand and Lawrence Fisher as well as Lorie. The report defined the parameters and set the tone for all performance measurement guidelines established since then.

Fama contributed a 30-page appendix, "Risk and the Evaluation of Pension Fund Performance," which provides "a systematic, logically complete, non-technical discussion of the theory and measurement of risk and their relationship to the evaluation of pension fund performance."[2] This essay is one of Fama's most lucid and comprehensive reviews of theory and its applications.

The performance measurement project was by no means the only time McQuown recruited academics as consultants. He was a voracious consumer of the wisdom that the academic stars could contribute to what he refers to as "the heavy work."

Fischer Black and Myron Scholes were among his first recruits. Scholes, who had started to work with McQuown almost immediately after leaving Chicago to join MIT in the fall of 1968, began with a long report on the existing system of investment management at Wells Fargo. He reported that the input from the analysts was useless and that Wells Fargo should no longer try to outguess the market on the basis of that input. Meanwhile, Black had grown restless at Arthur D. Little and had set up his own consulting firm, Associates in Finance. At Scholes's suggestion, Wells Fargo retained Black's firm to work on analyzing the relationships between risk and return and the possibility of using option theory. Soon Wells Fargo was accounting for most of Black's consulting revenues.

According to McQuown, many other academics "were to drink from the Wells well before it was over." Those academics, not all of whom worked directly for McQuown, were to include, at one time or another, Jensen, Markowitz, Miller, Sharpe, and Treynor in addition to Lorie, Scholes, Fama, and Black. As McQuown sums up those early days, "Before we had computers, data, and good models, we didn't know which procedures were right and which were wrong. So we just started working on everything right from the start. We worked on a lot of things that weren't relevant and missed a lot that were, but we did come out with some clear ideas."

McQuown had yet to go operational by converting the ideas, discoveries, and rejections of conventional wisdom into a viable, marketable system of managing portfolios. Not at all to his surprise, he told me, the staff in the trust area were "incredibly antagonistic." At this distance, it is not altogether clear whether this early antagonism was the result of substance or of form. The new methodology was clearly threatening, but apparently McQuown was dominating and patronizing to subordinates. According to a former associate, "Education doesn't flower in an environment where the teacher starts every lecture by saying, in effect, 'Listen up, you, everything you are doing you are doing wrong and I'm here to put you straight!'"

The opposition came first from the Director of the Financial Analysis Department, James Vertin. The FAD was in effect a securities research and portfolio management organization, whose sole client was Wells Fargo's trust department. The Department hired no one without a graduate degree from a business school and, according to Vertin, was "in its own way, an innovative, highly professional organization."

Later on, seeking a more "fulsome and commanding identity," Vertin offered a $100 prize for a new name for the Division. The oil analyst came up with Wells Fargo Investment Advisors (WFIA), which won the day. This unit was subsequently spun off as a separate division of Wells Fargo's holding company. In 1990, Wells Fargo sold an interest in WFIA to Nikko Securities of Japan for $120 million in cash and changed the name to Wells Fargo–Nikko Investment Advisors.

Vertin exudes fervor. His response to McQuown's activities was natural for anyone under attack, and he felt the pressure keenly. In reminiscing about the experience, Vertin describes McQuown's Management Sciences group as ". . . guys in white smocks with computers whirring. . . . Mac the Knife was going to own this thing. I could just see the fin of the shark cutting through the water."

Vertin was a fighter, but he was too intelligent and too honest to hold out in a bunker once he recognized that it was serving no purpose except to protect obsolete methods and folklore—and their purveyors. In time, he returned to MIT for intellectual retrofitting so that he could read the academic literature and converse with its authors in a comprehensible language.

McQuown welcomed Vertin's conversion:

> Vertin, to his never-ending credit, became a professional schizophrenic. . . . I must say, from the perspective of both then and now, he was doing damn well, considering the magnitude of the required adaption. . . .
>
> Jim really did a flip. I must give him high marks. It was a battle royal at the beginning—but Jim really liked the battle. In the end, he had enough respect for our empirical work that he could change when he saw the implications. But a lot of people who worked for him never accepted it.

Vertin was responding to more than the empirical evidence produced by McQuown's group. The bear market of 1970 revealed to him the cracks in the organization he had been heading, and the wildly optimistic market of 1971–1972 confirmed the foolishness prevalent in the investment management profession. It was at this moment, in December 1972, that Myron Scholes and I had disagreed on the market outlook.

From the summer of 1970 to the beginning of 1973, the Standard & Poor's Composite had risen by more than 60 percent while the earnings of the 500 companies in the index had grown by only 25 percent. The dividends received by a typical investor in the index amounted to less than 3 percent of the amount invested. Daily trading volume on the stock exchange was 50 percent above the levels of 1969. As I have noted, the market was putting the same valuation on Eastman Kodak as on General Motors and was setting a value on International Flavors and Fragrances that was triple Union Carbide's.

I was a lonely skeptic. But when the price of oil exploded in the fall of 1973, the world of institutional investing awoke to reality. I have a vivid memory of what the environment was like around the peak. Some time during 1972 I was invited to discuss relative market values at one of the foremost bank trust companies in New York, a favorite of the biggest corporate pension funds. I pointed out that, by all rational measurements, US Steel was a lot better value than some of the Favorite Fifty growth stocks to which this bank was so attached. With about twenty people sitting around the conference table, the chief investment officer turned to me and said, "Peter, you remind me of a girl who is about to give me the crud!"

This man was hardly Vertin's type. He strode the earth like an invincible warrior. He owned a bright-red car and wore a red sports jacket in a banking environment that was far more conservative than Wells Fargo's. Like McQuown, Vertin was totally opposed to the dominance of the Great Man theory in the world of professional investing. His own metaphor is perhaps more colorful than McQuown's. He conjures up a medicine man who tries to cure a patient by jumping up and down, up and down, until finally the mere passage of time cures the patient and the medicine man takes all the credit. He also likens the process to "water-walking," in which the claims of managers that they can beat the market by some unbelievable margin year after year is the equivalent of boasting that they can walk on water.

Vertin came to recognize that the theories McQuown was trying to apply were something that no trust executive could afford to ignore. Professional performance was "just terrible," and the clients were becoming smart enough to recognize it. Just trying harder would not be enough, because everyone else was trying harder too. The "grope approach" had to give way to an approach that aimed at control of portfolio risk and that introduced rationality and discipline into the process.

Leading the revolution on the front lines would not be easy. Vertin saw that the real enemy of change was the tradition of the investment management system itself:

The guild system, in which an apprentice learns from the lore from a master craftsman [and] progresses to journeyman when he has learned to replicate the master's application of the lore . . . is not an environment in which boat-rocking is encouraged. . . . It pretends that everything worth knowing is already known and in use. The members have an overriding interest in the status quo, and this interest tends to be protected at all costs.

Vertin's conversion was neither instantaneous nor smooth, and McQuown still needed an ally. Good luck brought him William Fouse, who was just the right person for that role.

Fouse had been a skilled musician from the age of twelve and had worked his way through the University of Kentucky playing jazz clarinet and saxophone. Small, inclined to be chubby, and with a droopy moustache, he left Kentucky in 1952 with a B.S. degree in industrial administration and a graduate degree in business administration but with little idea of what he wanted to do with his life. He ended up taking a job in the trust department of the Mellon Bank in Pittsburgh, a bastion of orthodoxy in its purest form.

Fouse's description of his early days is almost a verbatim repeat of Vertin's description of the guild system: "You learn from the master to do this and do that—just doing things by rote. It was a long time before I stuck my head above the primordial ooze of traditional analysis."

Fouse was attracted by what he had read in the *Harvard Business Review* about Treynor's ideas; he was also lucky enough to meet Sharpe while he was still a "youngster." He induced Mellon to contribute financial support to CRSP, the data gathering and research group at the University of Chicago. He made congenial friends at the CRSP conferences and learned more about "these new ideas that were a-borning." He became a good friend of Treynor, who persuaded him around 1967 to represent Mellon at an informal group in New York to exchange ideas with other enthusiasts. The meetings were pure joy. "We were going to take over the world!" Fouse exclaims.

Fouse worked his way up through the Mellon hierarchy and was named Vice President and Assistant Director of Investment Research. He began to codify the stock selections of the security analysts to get a handle on what they were doing, and he also started keeping book on the performance of the portfolio managers. The results were dismal. He was finding "nothing, nothing, nothing, or worse than nothing," as he describes it, from portfolio managers who typically put a stock on their buy lists only after it had already gone up.

He was fortunate to have a sympathetic math Ph.D. on the staff and some people from IBM to help him carry out the performance measurements. They also helped with his experiments on the use of beta, industry breakdowns, company size, and other sophisticated variations on the security selection problem. Treynor was so impressed that he predicted that Mellon would be the first institution to go into the business of putting the new ideas into practice.

Fouse now felt the wind in his sails. In 1969, he recommended that Mellon launch an index fund that would replicate one of the popular market indexes, like the Standard & Poor's 500-Stock Composite. An index fund requires no one to select stocks, no security analysts, and no portfolio manager. It is a passively managed rather than an actively managed portfolio. Fouse felt that the index fund would give him an opportunity to put Sharpe's idea about the super-efficient portfolio on a real-time basis. For his efforts, Fouse recalls, he was "figuratively thrown out of the policy meeting."*

But Fouse was irrepressible. His had encountered John Burr Williams's Dividend Discount Model in business school, and he set out to apply that model to security analysis. By combining the expected returns from the dividend discount model with the beta risk measures from the Capital Asset Pricing Model, he was confident he could identify cheap stocks and expensive stocks in a systematic, disciplined manner. Fouse quite rightly considers this work one of his major accomplishments.

In the spring of 1970, he completed an elaborate study that demonstrated that his system would work. He shouted "Eureka!

---

*This was the first time a practitioner had suggested putting an index fund into operation. The only other reference to the concept that I have found was in the *Financial Analysts Journal* for January-February 1960, "The Case of an Unmanaged Investment Company," by Edward Renshaw of the University of California and Paul Feldstein, one of his graduate students. They recommended the Dow Jones Industrial Average as the index to match, but their proposal attracted no attention at the time.

Archimedes, here I come!'' and proudly took his results to his boss. Red in the face, his boss barked, ''God damn it, Fouse, you're trying to turn my business into a science.'' Fouse describes his reaction: ''I just felt the sword go right through my midsection.''

Fouse did the obvious thing under the circumstances. He got on the phone and started job-hunting. His first call was to John A. McQuown, whom he had met at CRSP conferences. McQuown in turn had found Fouse, ''a real interesting character—I always got a kick out of him.''

In a long memorandum dated May 5, 1970, Fouse presents the case for himself to McQuown. He begins by asserting that he has a reputation for being ''keenly analytical, innovative, independent of thought, dedicated to the scientific method, outspoken, and somewhat impatient with ignorance.'' He then lists his views of the investment management business, reflecting both the theoretical sophistication he had acquired and his realistic sense of what the security markets are all about.

He emphasizes the difference between earning an above-market return by taking above-average risks and winning at the expense of other players who lose more than the winners win because ''the costs of trading make the contest less than a zero-sum game.'' He expresses skepticism about winning consistently at the expense of other players in a market that is ''extremely efficient,'' because it is so difficult to tell the smart winners from those who are just lucky. He warns about the ''quicksand premise that increasing knowledge about a company guarantees greater forecasting success'' and scorns the ''trend and fetish that skillful account managers should reduce the number of names in their portfolios so as to be conversant with their individual holdings.''

Complaining that ''our business is more of a folk art than a profession . . . close to being conceptually bankrupt,'' he sets forth guidelines for moving toward a disciplined management organization:

When measurement begins, science begins . . . There is a critical need for individuals who can foster and improve communications between the management scientist and the non-quantitative traditionalist. . . . Research efforts must . . . not be mere reporting or consensus collection. . . . Portfolio managers must move away from being super security analysts to being risk managers, to the understanding that a portfolio truly is more than a sum of its parts.

Three months later, Vertin circulated a memorandum to his group announcing Fouse's arrival. He referred to Fouse's computer capabilities but emphasized that "Mr. Fouse may be viewed as this Department's 'bridge' between the theoretical new and the operating old . . . an ally in our quest for excellence."

Fouse did not find his welcome at Wells Fargo quite as warm as he had hoped. He had problems from the outset with both Vertin and McQuown.

Fouse recalls "poor Vertin trying to defend the fort. . . . The poor guy was working for a bunch of retail bankers who didn't understand anything about this stuff." When Fouse found himself assigned to Vertin's unit, "I didn't realize what a part I was playing in his [McQuown's] passion play. As it turned out, I was to be the bishop to the heathen!"

McQuown has never believed in Fouse's beloved dividend discount model and refers to it "as another old saw that just isn't right." He claims that it creates an aura of certainty where there is no certainty. At one point, which Fouse describes as "strenuous," McQuown tried to get him fired as incompetent. When Fouse found out that McQuown was trying to "have my scalp," he called up his own academic reinforcements, including Treynor, who came in for a couple of days and, according to Fouse, saved his job.

Fouse recalls that the struggle between McQuown and Vertin was by no means over when he arrived: "Mac would go into Vertin's office and close the door and pretty soon the walls would be moving. . . . Vertin's a very volatile fellow, but I understand in retrospect what he was going through. Once he came around, he became a defender of the faith."

And indeed he did. Vertin became convinced that they were in on the ground floor of a development that could mean "big things" for the members of his team and for the bank. He was so confident of the benefits the new ideas could bring to the clients of investment managers that he began a campaign to persuade potential customers of the wisdom of the Wells Fargo approach.

Vertin met with a cool reception, however. When I reminded him about how frustrating he must have found his marketing efforts in those early days, he laughed and said, "Pushin' that rock up hill."

Although other institutions were reluctant to follow its lead, Wells Fargo was making genuine progress in applying the new ideas. Portfolios were being structured around beta measurements, company size, and industry breakdowns. Analysts were developing long-run forecasts to implement the dividend discount model. Computer-based portfolios were up and running, with risk-controlled procedures and linear programming to combine the holdings into the optimal portfolio.

In 1970 further impetus came unexpectedly from outside. Keith Schwayder, a young man who had just completed his graduate study at the University of Chicago, headed for Denver to join his family's company, Samsonite, the luggage manufacturer. Upon his arrival, Schwayder discovered that the company pension fund was invested in a mixed bag of mutual funds. To someone who had sat at the feet of Lorie, Fama, and Miller, this was heresy. He began asking around to see if anyone, anywhere, was managing money in the "theoretically proper" manner in which he had been schooled. His Chicago friends immediately told him what was going on at Wells Fargo.

And so, in July 1971, the first index fund was born, with a $6 million contribution from the Samsonite pension fund. The basic design and software were developed by McQuown's Management Sciences group, but Vertin saw to the day-to-day management of the fund and asked Fouse to manage the strategy. The scheme was to hold an equal dollar amount of each of the 1,500 or so stocks listed on the New York Stock Exchange, which seemed the most appropriate replication of "the market."

The idea was fine. The Department of Finance at the University of Chicago could only approve. But the execution of the idea turned out to be a nightmare. Some stocks moved more widely than others, and a few moved in an opposite direction from the pack, so that the equal weighting would just not stand still. Heavy transaction costs were incurred for the constant re-weighting back to the original equal dollar amounts.

Although Vertin complained about the "cumbersome record-keeping and the bean-counting," he recognized that new quantitative investment services were in the making. In 1973, his group set up a commingled fund open to any and all trust accounts. The fund would track the performance of the 500 stocks of Standard

& Poor's Composite Index, which then accounted for about 65 percent of the total marketable equity market in the United States.

The first two contributions to the fund were Wells Fargo's own pension fund, with $5 million, and the pension fund of Illinois Bell, with a like amount. Those contributions fell short of the $25 million required to buy 1,000 shares of each of the 500 components of the index. So a sampling strategy had to be followed—with unfortunate errors in tracking the index—until the total reached $25 million. From that point forward, the S&P 500 index fund has held the 500 stocks in proportion to their relative market values. In 1976, Samsonite folded its equal-weighted New York Stock Exchange fund into the S&P 500 index fund.

That fund has been the model for index funds ever since, even though, as McQuown describes it, "It's a weird damn thing." The Composite includes most of the large companies in the United States, so it accounts for a major share of the market. But its composition, as determined by the Standard & Poor's Corporation that publishes it, is forever changing. When companies are merged or taken over or fail or shrink to insignificance, substitutions must be made. But those substitutions are made in an arbitrary and nontheoretical fashion. As McQuown quite rightly argues, the index is not a true sample of the stock market but, rather, a capriciously structured portfolio.

At first, people laughed at the intrepid investors who were opting for "average performance." They considered it somehow un-American not to try harder. One of my colleagues spluttered, "I wouldn't even buy the S&P 500 for my mother-in-law—it's not a prudent portfolio!" I still have in my possession a jogger's sweatband, sent to me by an active manager, inscribed "Beat that S&P 500!"

People's faith in the invincibility of active management died hard, but it did weaken over time. An article in *Pensions* magazine for October 1972 reported, "Just a few years ago, everyone was expecting to do at least 25% better than the S&P and many investment counselors . . . were promising 50%." But a 1976 survey of corporate pension officers showed that only 13 percent disagreed to any extent with this statement: "Most investment managers can't call the market successfully."[3]

No matter. Over the last twenty years or so, most managers in most years were failing to match the market averages. To perform as well as the index was to perform well above average, and at lower levels of risk.

The index funds have had the last laugh. There is nothing like solid quantitative proof to make people sit up and take notice. Once started, the indexing business grew steadily, from $6 million in 1971 to $10 billion in 1980. It is now a huge and varied business, with about 30 percent of total institutional equity assets currently indexed.

According to one authoritative count, as of mid-1990 a total of $270 billion of financial assets was in index funds, one-third of it at Wells Fargo. Not all of it was in stock funds, and not all of what was in stock funds was in the S&P 500. According to another survey, as of late 1990 112 out of the top 200 pension funds were invested in equity index funds and 56 in bond index funds. Indexes that reflect the non-S&P part of the domestic stock market have become increasingly popular. Some $67 billion is in funds that track the major indexes of the domestic bond market, while more than $20 billion is indexed to foreign stock and bond markets.

There is an irony in Wells Fargo's success in marketing and managing index funds, because the company first undertook this activity through default. Even with McQuown's whirring computers and his army of high-powered academic consultants, Wells Fargo had failed to apply theory to active management with any real success. But by the end of the 1970s, the company had completely withdrawn from the active management business and was offering only passive products.*

The Samsonite experience inspired McQuown's Management Sciences group to go into the investment management business on its own, separate from Vertin's unit. It was an ambitious move. Wells Fargo in the early 1970s was primarily a personal trust bank and a retail rather than a business-type bank at the commercial

---

*There is another irony. One of Wells Fargo's early competitors in the index fund business, Dean LeBaron of Batterymarch, made the opposite decision. He abandoned index funds and led his firm to many of the boldest and most innovative applications of the academic theories. LeBaron has also stimulated research in finance by offering three generous fellowships a year; many of the recipients are now among the leaders in financial theory.

side. If Management Sciences could move Wells Fargo into the management of corporate pension funds, it would also attract their commercial business. And if Management Sciences could make a name for Wells Fargo in the institutional investment area, the bank would increase its retail and personal trust business.

The chosen vehicle was the Stagecoach Fund, whose architects were Black and Scholes and whose theoretical basis was the tests they had carried out with Michael Jensen on the Capital Asset Pricing Model. The Fund was designed to invest in a passively managed portfolio of low-beta, or relatively stable stocks, but it would buy some of those stocks with borrowed money so as to offset the low volatility of the basic holdings. The idea brought Tobin's concepts onto center stage: If the optimal portfolio is not risky enough, borrow to finance its purchase.

Fouse thought the plan was poor. He argued that its focus on low betas would lead to a badly diversified portfolio of utilities, banks, and food stocks. The meeting at which he expressed his concern was unusually abrasive. Fischer Black, known for keeping his cool, became so angry that he stalked out.

Two years of product development and arduous marketing efforts brought a few prospects for the Stagecoach Fund, including Greyhound and Illinois Bell. But then the Investment Company Institute, the trade association of the mutual fund industry, brought suit under the Glass-Steagall Act against Citicorp because of its efforts to distribute its commingled trust funds to all customers through its branch network. The ICI claimed that Citicorp was in effect marketing mutual funds. In *ICI* v. *Camp,* the Supreme Court ruled that Glass-Steagall did apply and that banks should stay out of the mutual fund marketing business; the decision gutted Wells Fargo's plans to launch the Stagecoach Fund. The bear market of 1974 killed off whatever interest remained in this odd attempt to apply theoretical concepts.

McQuown is still enthusiastic about the Stagecoach Fund strategy. "Some day I'm going to simulate its performance," he told me. "I think it would have been sensational, even though poorly diversified and the actual undervaluedness was suspicious."

Meanwhile, Fouse was designing another product that has become increasingly important for Wells Fargo: tactical asset allocation, a method of calculating separately the expected returns for the stock market, the bond market, and the market for cash equivalents like Treasury bills. Then the assets are shifted to the market or markets that appear relatively most attractive. Although Sharpe (and Vertin, too) was skeptical about the feasibility of this idea at first, Fouse managed to successfully combine Sharpe's theoretical concepts with the ideas of Markowitz, Tobin, and John Burr Williams.

Although the notion is buy-low-sell-high, tactical asset allocation differs from so-called market timing in two ways. First, it is a scientific method of allocating assets. Second, the idea is to buy undervalued assets and to sell overvalued assets and to wait until the market corrects the perceived misvaluations; this approach differs fundamentally from flatly declaring that "this is the bottom" or "this is the top."

Fouse and Vertin soon established a fee-based consulting service within Wells Fargo to help corporate pension funds and other institutional investors to apply the ideas they were putting into practice. Soon competitors joined the clients who were flocking to Wells Fargo to attend conferences featuring Wells Fargo's academic consultants or members of its own staff. The conference at the Sloan School that Myron Scholes had organized and Robert Merton slept through was one of the conferences in this series.

The most important client of the consulting service was the College Retirement Equities Fund, or CREF, the equity portion of the pension fund of university professors and the largest single pool of equity money in the world. Harvard University was another early client. Still another was the American National Bank in Chicago, which itself was to become a leader in the application of the new ideas to trust management and a purveyor of index funds as well.

Like Moses and the Promised Land, none of the people I have mentioned here stayed on at Wells Fargo to enjoy the story's happy ending. A less than friendly sequence of events followed a change in top management in the early 1980s. Fouse's responsibilities were downgraded and he decided to return to the original fold at Mellon, where he established a competing shop that has been highly successful. Vertin was "retired" and formed a consulting firm of his own to guide others in the applications he had developed at Wells Fargo. McQuown decided to leave to plow other fields. With the structures they left in place and running, even the need for academic consultants had waned.

What was the achievement of these three men? Vertin describes their relationship to one another and to Wells Fargo as a "constellation." They enjoyed the enthusiastic support of the bank's top echelons, without whom, according to McQuown, they would have been "shut down." McQuown, who enjoyed the use of power, came upon the scene with a rich knowledge of theory and with the ability to apply theory to practical purposes. Vertin, once converted, was a heavy-duty advocate, stubborn, optimistic, and determined to make things come out right. Fouse was an intellectual firecracker. Finally, the willingness of the academics to participate at this level, and the respect in which they held the Wells Fargo people, were cardinal ingredients in the outcome.

In time, someone else would surely have put something like this together. The ideas on which it was built were too powerful to lurk forever in textbooks and journal articles. One must wonder, however, whether what others created would have had the internal consistency, coordination, and market appeal that enabled Wells Fargo to rock the world of investing to its very foundations.

The momentum that McQuown, Vertin, and Fouse created, like the momentum Moses created, was robust enough to continue in force, despite subsequent changes in leadership and even in credo. Considering how early in the game they fired their first shots, how little was known, understood, or appreciated about the theories they advanced, their achievement was indeed extraordinary. It was they who truly brought the gown to town.

# Chapter
## 13

# The Accountant for Risk

*What the hell is he talking about?*

In the summer of 1973, after more than twenty years at the task, I decided to give up managing other people's money. I had no intention of deserting the world of investing—the business was too fascinating and filled with too many attractive people for that. I was motivated by what seemed to be an unusual opportunity to capitalize on my accomplishments, and to have a lot more fun along the way.

I had always wanted to combine what I knew about economics with what I had learned in the school of hard knocks I had attended for so long as an investment advisor. Although my main activity had been in investment counseling and I had never completed my doctorate, I had published and lectured enough in the field of economics to be accepted by professional economists as one of their own. The new theories of portfolio selection, security valuation, and market behavior offered the ideal format for what I was seeking.

There was a whole world out there that my investment counseling firm had shunned. My encounter with William Sharpe at the Plaza had never lost its sting, and its meaning and importance had become more apparent to me with the passage of time. The concepts of controlling risk and concentrating on the portfolio as a whole were congenial to my characteristically conservative approach to investing, so I was confident that I could communicate those ideas with all the authority that hands-on experience could provide.

With my wife as partner on the business side of the operation, I set up as a consultant to portfolio management organizations and to their clients as well. We offered a service that focused on the linkage between the economy and the capital markets, blending that understanding with the new theoretical approaches to develop profitable investment ideas and strategies. I also recognized that the changes being forced on the profession by the theoretical innovations would require major structural and administrative decisions for money management organizations. My long experience as the chief executive of an investment counseling firm turned out to be useful in that area as well.

The venture was a success from the start. Moreover, it gave me time to advance my education in areas I had neglected while I was in the pressure-cooker of managing money. I learned to understand and, finally, to use some of the more advanced statistical techniques that had seemed like gibberish to me up to that time. I even began to read articles in the academic journals that I had formerly passed over as beyond my grasp.

During this time, I was involved with my friend Gilbert Kaplan as an investor in his successful *Institutional Investor* magazine and its associated conference business. I repeatedly told Kaplan how impatient I was with the content of the magazine, which paid little or no attention to academic innovations in portfolio management and capital market behavior.

Good-humored but persistent needling seemed to get me nowhere. When I complained that *Institutional Investor* was shamelessly turning its back on the topics being discussed in the *Financial Analysts Journal,* Kaplan laughed. He told me that his subscribers were not looking to his magazine for that kind of thing, which at that time he believed was for academics to discuss with academics. In any case, he was convinced the profession was not about to change its ways.

But events began to overtake his lighthearted rejection. The bear market of 1973–74 in bonds and stocks hit hard and deep, with a devastating effect on financial wealth that was in many ways worse than that of the 1930s. Between 1929 and 1932, at least the cost of living had fallen and bond values had risen.

The misery was not limited to the owners of wealth. Kaplan's constituency—independent investment advisors, bank trust departments, and managers of insurance company and endowment portfolios—was in total disarray. The brokerage houses that served them were in even worse shape. The day of reckoning had arrived for the hubris of the late 1960s.

One day in the late spring of 1974, Kaplan proposed that *Institutional Investor* start up a new publication to be called *The Journal of Portfolio Management,* with me as its editor. Having been assured that I would have carte blanche, I jumped at the chance. Here was an irresistible opportunity to offer a more free-form and more readable vehicle than the *Financial Analysts Journal,* where committee pressures had so painfully restrained Treynor.

In my introduction to the *Journal's* first issue in the fall of 1974, I got a lot off my chest:

> The dismal record of portfolio management over the past five years needs no elaboration. . . . With all the research input, the sophisticated economic analysis, the jolly conferences, the attention to decision making structures, and the increased understanding of risk and reward, how could so many have failed to see that all the known parameters were bursting apart? . . . None of us can avoid being haunted by the academic diagnosis. . . .
>
> The objective of this Journal is to provide a platform where practitioner, academic, regulator, and client can communicate with one another.[1]

The first two issues contained articles by Sharpe on risk and performance measurement, by Fischer Black on the random walk, by James Lorie on diversification, and by Paul Samuelson on efficient markets. I invited James Vertin to contribute the lead article in the first issue, because I knew he would come on strong. "The State of the Art in Our Profession" was an eloquent denunciation of the profession, which he described as little more than a cottage industry. He was most scathing about the refusal of most portfolio managers to learn anything new:

> [T]he full body of knowledge now available to our profession . . . can significantly improve our investment management product and our reputation. . . . Given the existing problems of the investment management community, such improvement seems well worth having. The means for obtaining it are at hand, are freely available to those who would make the effort to use them, and are usable *now.* Let's get on with it![2]

Yet change was painfully slow. In retrospect, I can see that most of the early articles in *The Journal of Portfolio Management* were elementary, in keeping with the readers' gaps in understanding. Vertin's comment that he was "Pushin' that rock up hill" was right to the point. The resistance of his own staff members was a microcosm of the opposition to change in the investment community at large.

This state of affairs was confirmed as late as April 1977, when *Institutional Investor* published a thoughtful and comprehensive article titled "Modern Portfolio Theory: How the New Investment Technology Evolved." The article contained some illuminating quotations from practitioners:

The director of portfolio management at the Crocker Bank in San Francisco, just down the street from Wells Fargo, confessed that modern portfolio theory is "something we look at, but I can't say we've been using much of it so far." Harold Arbit, vice president of American National Bank in Chicago, complained that "Most of what I see is lip service. A lot of organizations simply keep some computer guru in the back office who they drag out for dog and pony shows and then put back again." The senior vice president for investment operations at IDS, one of the country's leading mutual fund management companies, regarded the new ideas as "pretty much in the realm of classroom debate and study." The most succinct comment was that of Barton Biggs, a widely respected market strategist: "I think it's just a lot of baloney."[3]

*Institutional Investor,* to its credit, was convinced that in time the new would win out over the old. The article concluded with a forecast of the revolution's ultimate victory: "New Investment Technology demonstrates, by its example, that old investment policies . . . are inefficient, illogical, ill-conceived and frequently erroneous. . . . As the influence of NIT grows, as like hybrid seed corn it must, the investment management business seems destined for what can be considered a revolution."[4]

Victory would have been far longer in coming had the revolution not found a persuasive standard-bearer to carry the message to the Great Unwashed. If William Fouse was the bishop to the heathen in the Wells Fargo trust department, Barr Rosenberg would turn out to be the pope to investment professionals everywhere.

Rosenberg never thought of himself as an evangelist whose mission was to spread uncongenial ideas. Tall, thin, and prematurely bald, as befits a deep thinker, he is a quiet, serene, soft-spoken man who claims, "I sincerely do like virtually everyone I meet." He engages in Buddhist meditation and can read Tibetan. His wife, June, who has a master's degree in psychology and trained as an opera singer, joins him in these devotions. For most of Rosenberg's career, he has considered himself more of an econometrician than an authority in finance. He nominates John McQuown as "the prototype financial innovator, who believed intensely in the new ideas and would unswervingly push them."

Rosenberg insists, "I've made no major contributions to the literature. There is nothing intrinsically new in the system." He told me that he sees many of his ideas as "just great attention to details but very obvious . . . must seem very uninviting." He believes that, had the technology and patience been available, they could all have been developed by someone else thirty years before he developed them. He sums up his contribution as nothing more than ". . . detailed analysis of relevant real world problems, knowledge that is primarily useful because of care in details, and, at the same time, is relatively inaccessible because of the degree of detail."

Despite his modesty Rosenberg's accomplishments are formidable. He took the ideas of Markowitz, Tobin, and Sharpe and repackaged them in a new, richer, and more applicable format. His scholarly concepts brought a new dimension to the real-world relationships between managers and clients. And his success in educating the practitioners deserves primary credit for giving the new ideas credibility and acceptance by thousands of people in the field.

After coming down from his ivory tower to bring the gospel to the unbelievers, Rosenberg went on to practice what he preached. After more than ten years of extraordinarily successful consulting with money management organizations, he had the courage to go into direct competition with his former clients. In May 1985, he formed Rosenberg Institutional Equity Management, which in less than five years had $9 billion under management. Its performance record has been enviable. No less enviable is the minimum account it will accept: $75 million.

Rosenberg was born in 1942 to a family that valued intellectual achievement. His father taught dramatic arts at Berkeley and his mother wrote poetry. Rosenberg is grateful that he grew up as the son of a Shakespearean scholar, because, even as a young boy, he came to appreciate the "interplay of diverse interests enacted so eloquently by Shakespeare's characters." This fascination with diversity is evident in Rosenberg's investigations of the interaction of diverse investors and diverse securities within various groupings.

He graduated from Berkeley in the class of 1963 with a degree in economics. While still a senior, he was fortunate enough to take Gerard Debreu's graduate course sequences in statistics, economics, and mathematical economics. Debreu was already a distinguished scholar who would subsequently be awarded the Nobel Prize in economic sciences for his work with Kenneth Arrow in these areas.

Rosenberg went on to earn a master's degree in mathematical economics and econometrics at the London School of Economics. He continued to pursue those studies while working for his doctorate at Harvard. Econometrics in particular caught his fancy; this was the field of study that Alfred Cowles had helped to launch and that brings sophisticated statistical techniques to the measurement of economic variables.

Rosenberg's Ph.D. thesis was about what he calls "models with randomly dispersed parameters." When translated into plain English, this is a lot more interesting than one might expect from the scientific terminology. The members of a group share certain common characteristics that identify them as members of the group, but no group consists of members who are absolutely identical. Each individual has random features that differentiate him or her from the others. A group of human beings may all have the same illness, but each patient will respond differently to a given drug. All stocks vary with the market as a whole, but each responds to information in its own way. Even each of billions of snowflakes has unique characteristics. Shades of Shakespeare's "interplay of diverse interests"!

These variations seem random in the context of the group as a whole, but they are intrinsic, usually permanent, and very important to each individual—as with a patient's response to a new drug. The statistician starts with the broad characteristics that signify group membership and then homes in on the characteristics that distinguish one individual from all others. And the statistician must do that with a minimum number of tests but with maximum accuracy.

John Lintner was a member of Rosenberg's Ph.D. committee. Rosenberg admits that at the time he did not recognize the importance of the covariance of security returns with the market, which was then Lintner's primary focus of attention: "At first I failed to grasp the impact of this revolutionary idea."

In 1968 Rosenberg received an appointment to the faculty at Berkeley as well as a National Science Foundation grant to finance econometric research. The grant enabled him to build data bases to which he could apply the econometric techniques he had developed in the course of his graduate work.

He began by collecting two completely disparate sets of facts. One set consisted of financial information on companies with publicly traded stock. The second set consisted of data on how the responses of patients to various medications change over time. He was particularly interested in the effect of nonsystematic variations and extreme observations on the results. Rosenberg concluded that randomness is not what it seems:

> Randomness is not a mystery. Instead, it is the poorly described aspects of a process. Once you understand that, you can analyze it and think about it. This sets me off from most people in finance who say that randomness is just what their model does not capture. . . .
>
> Furthermore, changes in levels of risk can be understood better within the context of social change. Healthy societies tolerate a certain degree of randomness, but may restructure themselves in response to extreme tensions. A time of restructuring of ideas or institutions is often a time of high market variability, but for a surviving institution this is not "infinite variance."

This line of argument led Rosenberg to consider whether variability and volatility are predictable. He could readily see that they are unstable in most cases, but, if they are not chaotic in nature, we should be able to foresee how they will change. That was to remain the focus of his attention from that point forward. Although he had enjoyed working in the medical area, "my knowledge of medicine was limited—capital markets were more congenial."

By late 1969, personal finance was becoming a more urgent matter for Rosenberg than theories of finance. He and his wife, with the aid of some "counterculture architecture students and carpenters" from Berkeley, were trying to transform an ancient tugboat into a permanent residence at the Berkeley marina in San Francisco Bay. When the tugboat developed a terminal leak, they decided to build a houseboat instead. That turned out to "unpredictably need much more money than we had. . . . It was just one calamity after another."[5]

The Rosenbergs finally gave up and became landlubbers, but their financial trials and tribulations led them to search for new and larger sources of income. Walt McKibben, a Ph.D. candidate at Berkeley and an experienced Wall Street analyst, suggested that Rosenberg set up as a consultant and brought him the national brokerage firm of Dean Witter as a client. This was the point at which Rosenberg first became familiar with the meaning of the term "beta" in security analysis, "which, to my embarrassment, I had not fully appreciated before."

Another friend invited him to come to Wells Fargo to study their branch system—again a population of diverse cases in the form of individual branches with common characteristics. Rosenberg considers that experience fruitful, though he was not involved in the exciting developments taking place over in the McQuown-Vertin domain.

In the course of this work, he became interested in what he now refers to as "covariance models, the type of thing that Markowitz had done" and that fitted in with his interest in randomly dispersed parameters. He recognized at once that risk models—the use of betas and covariances to measure the riskiness of financial assets—were right up his alley. Starting with Markowitz's framework, he set out to develop a method for predicting risk by conceptualizing how the different elements of risk explain the riskiness of individual companies in a larger setting: "Economic events give rise to ripples through the economy, but individual assets respond according to their individual, or microeconomic, characteristics. If you can adequately describe the macroeconomic events, you can then model the factors that give rise to risk and the responses of the micro elements."

Along the way, Rosenberg noticed that measurements of portfolio management performance were incomplete and even misleading. The Capital Asset Pricing Model enabled the performance analyst to measure how closely a manager's returns tracked the predictions of the model, but that was as far as it went.

In the spirit of "models with randomly dispersed parameters,"

Rosenberg decided to look further into what determines a manager's residual returns—returns that vary from what CAPM predicts. Most observers had assumed that residual returns were either the result of noise and random forces or the result of an active decision by the manager to compose a portfolio that differed from the market. The distinction was no minor consideration, but no good data existed to reveal how managers actually make their decisions. Rosenberg sensed that what appeared to be random was not necessarily random.

This line of thought led to a concept he called "extra-market covariance," which means precisely what its multisyllabic nomenclature says: Many stocks move together independently of what the market as a whole is doing, for example, stocks of companies that belong to the same industry, stocks that are unusually small or large in size, or stocks that are exposed to fluctuations in the value of the dollar. At this point, Rosenberg was drawing on work by another of Chicago's productive professors, Benjamin King, whose 1966 *Journal of Business* article, "Market and Industry Factors in Stock Price Performance," had triggered a great deal of research in this area.

Rosenberg's notion of extra-market covariance added a new dimension to Sharpe's single-index model and to most versions of the Capital Asset Pricing Model; these models were all right as far as they went but they did not go far enough. Common sense suggests that the risk in owning a stock must be related to more than just the behavior of the stock's price. In the end, risk and stock price behavior will reflect such fundamental aspects of the company as its industry, its size, its financial condition, its cost structure, the diversification of its customer group, and its record of growth. These were the kinds of factors that Rosenberg identified as shaping the risk characteristics of individual stocks and, through the individual stocks, of portfolios as well.

As Rosenberg continued work on his risk modeling and return analysis, he also developed a new optimizer. This was a son-of-Markowitz computer program for identifying the efficient portfolios in a universe of securities, each with its expected return and risk. The program simplified the procedure the client had to follow, making it more "user friendly," and also accommodating the transaction costs involved in changing the portfolio around.

Rosenberg decided he was on to something really important. Nevertheless, an idea is one thing but finding the money to do research on it is something else again. A lucky turn of events during 1973 enabled him to transform what had been a one-man business operating out of the basement of his house into a full-fledged consulting operation. He called it Barr Rosenberg Associates, which soon became known as BARRA, the name it still carries even though Rosenberg himself left in 1985 to start his portfolio management company. Some of the original members of the group remain and continue to lead BARRA to new accomplishments in measuring investment risks and devising portfolio management strategies.

The lucky turn came through an invitation from the American National Bank in Chicago to design a portfolio management system for them along the lines of the Wells Fargo formulas based on the theories of Markowitz and Sharpe. Now, with assured and regular revenues coming in, Rosenberg began to build a staff that combined scholarly achievement with the ability to communicate their ideas to practitioners.

The goal at American National Bank was to develop an integrated analytical framework that could perform the whole portfolio management task right off the computer. The system would generate forecasts of security returns; it would estimate the riskiness of each individual security; it would then compose efficient portfolios that would reflect tax differences in personal accounts; finally, it would measure the performance of each portfolio, including the impact of transaction costs on the results. The bank also wanted to upgrade the sophistication of their record-keeping systems.

BARRA developed a group of monster computer programs for these purposes, involving 100,000 separate instructions to the computer and supported by over 1,000 pages of documentation to guide the user. The work took three years to complete and spawned many variations on its basic themes. It also put BARRA into business in no uncertain fashion.

Rosenberg describes BARRA's efforts for American National as "fairly innovative—always in the mode of applicability." BARRA's most significant accomplishment was an elaborate program for predicting a stock's beta, largely on the basis of company characteristics like size, earnings variability, and financial condition but including stock price behavior and trading activity as well. Soon what BARRA called the Fundamental Risk Management Service was in great demand, and the predicted betas came to be known fondly throughout the profession as "Barr's bionic betas." The bionic betas, and the risk model in which they were embedded, have been Rosenberg's pride and joy.

To Rosenberg's surprise, new clients started to come along and growth accelerated. By the end of 1976, sixteen firms had joined American National Bank as clients for his risk models and portfolio management systems, including Prudential Insurance Company, Wells Fargo, the College Retirement Equities Fund, and the Travelers. June Rosenberg suggested that BARRA conduct a series of seminars on its methodology and selected the beautiful amenities at Pebble Beach on the Monterey Peninsula. Those Pebble Beach seminars became famous. As the new theories gained currency, no one in the investing world—either manager or client—who had not been to Pebble Beach could claim a place among the cognoscenti. Rosenberg recalls, "It was a wonderful opportunity for me to share ideas with congenial people."

For at least the first five years, all the participants in these seminars were from the United States. Europe and Asia have been slow to adopt the modern theories of portfolio selection, security valuation, and market behavior and have been even slower to apply them. For reasons that must reach deep into history and tradition, economics in general and financial economics in particular have been dominated by English and American scholars, with only a few notable exceptions such as Karl Marx and Friedrich von Hayek.

The new gospel was being spread early on in England, especially at the London Business School, and in France, at the major French business school, CESA (Centre d'Enseignement Supérieur des Affaires), in Joüy-en-Josas outside Paris. But until well into the 1980s applications were few and far between. Today, applications are common and the funds involved are substantial. Moreover, BARRA and other high-powered consulting organizations have an impressive roster of foreign clients. And yet the number of foreign managers and corporations applying the theoretical innovations is still low relative to the United States.

The Rosenberg magic was compelling. In its May 1978 issue *Institutional Investor* portrayed him on the cover sitting in a pink robe on a mountain top with his hands lifted in prayer, flowers in his hair and on his shoulders, and little people around him performing a variety of obeisances. The cover story, titled "Who is

Barr Rosenberg? And what the hell is he talking about?'' referred to the "sheer megavoltage of his mind" and described his charismatic presence:

> As Rosenberg speaks, a hush typically falls over the audience. In the manner of sinners, heads are slightly bowed. Eyes are moist and a bit glassy. One can almost hear murmurs of "Amen, Brother" and "Praise the Lord. . . ."
>   Being plugged into Barr is now considered by many managers a sine qua non of a winning marketing pitch. (Nobody these days would ever ask, "Barr who?" Like Cher, he is a one-name celebrity.)[6]

The article goes on to quote the pension officer of a major company who protested that "practically everyone we see brings his name up. I just don't see how Barr could possibly be in that many places and eat that many dinners." Arbit, who could well claim to have put Rosenberg on the map, questioned the seriousness of those who came to genuflect: "A lot of people who are signing up with Barr are just glomming onto him as a security blanket without understanding him. It's just like they glommed onto beta a few years ago. . . . I wish more people were *really* listening."[7]

One attentive listener was Douglas Love at the Prudential, who has described Rosenberg as "an accountant for risk." Love went around to see him and asked, "Barr, here we have these different managers. How do we combine them?" Rosenberg answered the question with a program called MULMAN, an acronym for multiple manager risk analysis. Its reverberations echoed to the furthest reaches of the world of investing.

Traditionally, pension funds and other institutional investors, like individual investors, hired a single portfolio management organization, usually a bank. This overall manager had total responsibility for bonds as well as stocks, for determining the mix between the two, and for selecting the securities in each sector. After a time it became common to have one manager for equities and another for fixed-income securities, but in the early 1970s the idea of having a bevy of equity managers was still a novelty.

Rosenberg could see no reason why Markowitz's ideas about individual stocks would not apply equally well to a stable of individual portfolio managers. A properly diversified portfolio of risky stocks would have a high expected return but would be far less risky than any of the single holdings considered alone. Why not hire a group of high-risk, aggressive managers with distinctly different management styles to achieve the same result?

Rosenberg's sermons began to include parables for the pension funds among his clients and students at Pebble Beach. He berated them for favoring managers who were excessively cautious about making big bets against the market and who as a result were "closet-indexers." There was no point, he insisted, in paying full management fees for results that closely tracked an index fund that would itself be far less costly to maintain. To justify the fees they charged, managers should be willing to take on more risk, to have the courage of their convictions—just as long as the client employed a diversified group of managers.

The idea took hold. Today, it is a rare fund that has only one equity manager, and many have multiple managers for fixed-income investments and international securities as well. Clients ride herd on their active managers to stick to their appointed style and show a willingness to take on higher risks to bring in improved rates of return.

When I reminded Rosenberg that MULMAN had changed the world, he replied, with typical understatement, "That's interesting. Well, I don't know. It did improve the dialogue between the more thoughtful clients and their managers."

Looking back over his career, Rosenberg recognizes that he has traveled a long road in less than fifty years. That road has taken him all the way from total theoretician to the most real-time of practitioners. His academic work at Berkeley and the London School of Economics was all theoretical. Computers were nowhere in sight. His first introduction to the power of computing was at Harvard, when econometrics caught his fancy. But though he worked with hard data, his early work on predicting volatility and in building risk models had theoretical objectives. Perhaps if the tugboat had been more seaworthy or the houseboat more affordable, he might never have made the decision to earn his living as a consultant. Once he had made that decision, however, his mission has been practical rather than academic.

Rosenberg is convinced that BARRA succeeded because it was committed to the idea that investment systems should be useful, not just "interesting." BARRA provided valid risk models, data bases that were extensive, accurate, and timely, decision systems to make the models useful in realistic situations—all delivered at a price that clients could afford and in language they could understand.

Rosenberg offers interesting insights into the reason for the early resistance of practitioners to the new theoretical concepts. He refers to certain "unattractive motivations": defense of entrenched power, fear of the unknown, intellectual laziness, and naive pride of place. These motivations were most apparent in the stubborn refusal to understand that one investor's gain against the rest of the market had to be another investor's loss, and that active investment management is a zero-sum game, and less than zero after transaction costs are figured in. This disagreeable but logically irrefutable feature of investing was a challenge to the fraternity's conviction that they could all be winners. It was what had bruised my ego that day in New York when Sharpe subjected me to his persistent interrogation.

Rosenberg was still encountering stubborn resistance as late as 1977. Charles Ellis recalls the occasion when Rosenberg addressed the Tenth Annual Institutional Investor conference at the New York Hilton, at a time when his popularity and following were firmly established. In his talk on the applications of portfolio theory, he made such observations as this: "Inescapably, a properly constructed index fund should outperform the average performance you provide."[8] When he sat down, not a single person in the packed ballroom applauded.

Rosenberg tried to understand why practitioners resisted rigorous analytical techniques so stubbornly. One reason, he suspects, is that most of the people in the profession in the early 1970s had gone to college and graduate school before computers were available on campuses and so were unable to appreciate the computer's capacity to integrate and organize information. He admits he would have felt the same way if he had been in their shoes. These were precisely the kinds of concerns that the BARRA systems tried to accommodate and overcome.

He still recognizes that a difficulty arises when an organization attempts "the blending of rigorous formal methods with associative freewheeling styles of search and decision." Ideally, an organization that combines the formal with the creative should be more than the sum of its parts. And yet, he finds, "organizations seem to gravitate toward one pole of the other, as if the formal structure is antithetical to the creative process."

In describing how his career path has differed from that of academics, he says he "built factories" while they built individual asset models:

> Markowitz, Sharpe, Cootner, and Fama and the others had fine, really nifty ideas, stated clearly from the beginning, and they were ideas everyone had to have in their heads— although it took a long time to evaluate them.
>
> I wish I'd thought of all those ideas of Fischer [Black]'s. . . . Fischer says his articles are built on very obvious foundations, but no one else had those ideas, which are profoundly original to me.

He sees the computer as the key piece of equipment in his "factories," because it can make a big problem seem much smaller. He is also a compulsive manager of data bases, constantly searching for errors and making certain that every entry is accurate and precise. His patience seems unlimited.

Rosenberg was an early user of data bases from IDC—Interactive Data Corporation, a pioneer marketer of economic and financial data. He had his clients use them as well. So IDC gave him free access to their data in an era when computer time was brutally expensive. As his clientele grew, he put his programs onto the IDC system and his clients, no matter where they were, could log into IDC and apply his programs in any manner they wished. Without the computer, the arrangement would have been impossible.

The most impressive combination of computer and data is at Rosenberg Institutional Equity Management. When Rosenberg and his associates set up this organization in 1985, they decided they would have to reinvent everything from portfolio management itself right down to the record-keeping system.

Their data base covers 3,500 companies based in the United States and 1,800 based in Japan, each broken down into 150 different categories; work is currently under way for a global data base that will include another 3,000 securities from markets around the world. The balance sheet, operating earnings, and sales for each company are compared with the data for similar companies and are adjusted for taxes and variations in capital structure. An optimizer program continuously reviews each of the securities and selects efficient portfolios based on the prices continuously fed into the computer from the ticker tape. Rosenberg claims that RIEM is the only investment organization that has a real-time optimizer like that, but would not have anything less.

The computer makes all the investment decisions, and those decisions cannot be overridden by people. The only way people can influence the outcome is by changing the programs or the data. A typical portfolio may contain as many as 350 holdings, but with the computer ceaselessly evaluating the universe of companies and their market prices, about 75 percent of the portfolio turns over in the course of a year—a turnover rate typical of institutional activity at the present time.

The process is pure Rosenbergiana—the nitty-gritty is essential to its success. Every transaction is booked into the records at the instant it occurs. Trading systems are state-of-the-art. The data bases are scrutinized for errors and inconsistencies as they arrive. Changes in tax rules or accounting rules receive immediate attention. Officers carry beepers to warn them of computer breakdowns. Vertin's nightmare of "guys in white smocks with computers whirring" has become a vivid reality at RIEM.

A man who reads Tibetan, who sincerely likes almost everyone he meets, and who wishes he could have lived on a houseboat seems an odd figure to be advancing the frontiers of portfolio management. But there he is!

# Chapter
# 14

---

# The Ultimate Invention

*Lifestyles were in danger, and it was time for invention.*

Investment advisors and brokers love to regale one another with stories about clients who want to make money in the market without taking the risk of losing any. The characters change, the locale shifts, and the details vary, but the stories are much the same.

Those clients are not as foolish as they seem. Even though risk and return are inseparable, there are certain schemes that can limit losses while providing virtually unlimited gains. And they are respectable schemes, not crazy gimmicks designed to fleece little old ladies and other innocents.

These risk-controlling schemes come under the heading of insurance. Albert Einstein is reputed to have said that insurance is one of humanity's most brilliant inventions. Insurance makes disaster tolerable. Insurance will restore the value of a house burned to ashes, replace part of the earning power of breadwinners who lose their jobs, pay the medical and hospital bills of a catastrophic illness, protect depositors from bank failures, and even reimburse customers for errors and omissions made by their stock brokers. Piano virtuosos can insure their hands against accidents, women can insure their diamonds against robbery, and automobile drivers can insure themselves against accusations of negligence. Why should investors be denied the opportunity to insure their security portfolios against a decline in the market?

No one had ever thought of such a stratagem until Hayne Leland, a 35-year-old finance professor, hit on the idea during a sleepless night in September 1976. What emerged from his bout with insomnia has had a lasting and profound influence on the world of investing. Had Leland fallen asleep in the process of his cogitations, he might have had a nightmare about what lay ahead—the crash of October 19, 1987.

But Leland was more concerned at the moment with personal finance than with market crashes. He and his French-born wife had recently returned from France to Berkeley, where he was teaching finance. Leland was in a less than happy mood. The rapidly weakening dollar had spoiled their trip to Europe, and Governor Ronald Reagan's persistent attack on the purchasing power of academics in California posed a more serious threat. As he considered the situation, Leland concluded, "Lifestyles were in danger, and it was time for invention."[1]

The idea that occurred to him that night brought him into theoretical territory that was largely foreign to him. He would have to learn his way around before he could transform the untested notion into a reality.

Actually, the seed had been planted by his older brother, John, who was a top executive at Rosenberg Capital Management (no relation to Barr Rosenberg), a San Francisco investment counseling firm. Shortly after the stock market crash of 1974, John had deplored the decision of many pension funds to yank most of their money out of the market when it hit bottom, apparently with no intention of coming back. The funds have lived up to that intention: Equities fell from a peak of 71 percent of total corporate pension fund assets in 1972 to 54 percent in 1974 and have remained below 60 percent, except for brief moments, ever since.

Ruminating about this experience, John had remarked to his brother, "It's too bad there is no way you could buy insurance on your portfolio. Then people wouldn't have to sell out at the very worst time and have no way to participate in the subsequent market rally."[2] John's observation is an example of what Robert K. Merton describes as "specified ignorance."* By stating precisely what was not known about how to protect a portfolio from market declines, John's specified ignorance was to set his brother off in search of a solution to the problem.

Leland had found his brother's observation interesting at the time and had filed it away for consideration "at a later date." On his return from Europe in 1976, he decided that that date had

---

*Robert K. is a sociologist and the father of Robert C. of MIT, who played such an important role in the development of the theory of option pricing.

arrived. He sat down at his desk and started to think. "It took me quite a while," he recalls, "something like two hours."[3]

He began by stating the problem in the simplest possible terms. What was needed, he saw, was an instrument that would work like an insurance policy. It would pay off if the market went down but would entail a relatively small cost if the market went up. Home insurance pays off if the house burns down but costs no more than the premium if it does not.

But there the resemblance ends. Conventional insurance works because people pool their risks and the risks are diversified. Diamonds are stolen, houses burn down, and drivers have accidents, but disaster does not strike all insured women, homeowners, and drivers at the same moment. Some never suffer any loss at all. The premiums paid by the lucky ones cover the losses incurred by the less fortunate.

When the stock market goes down, all portfolios, whether insured or not, go down with it. There is no way to diversify the risks. All insured portfolios would turn unlucky at the same moment. It would be as if all drivers were to have an accident on the same day and end up suing one another like crazy.

Leland considered once again what he was trying to get at—something that paid off when there was a loss but that also entailed a relatively small premium. "That's a put option!" he exclaimed to himself.[4] It all boiled down to a problem in options.

As we have seen, an investor who buys a put option has the right to sell the stock at a specified price within a specified time period, although the owner of a put option has no obligation to sell the stock—the premium paid merely carries the *option* to sell it. On the other hand, the investors to whom the premium is paid are in the opposite position: they *must* buy the stock if the owner opts to put it to them. Under the rules of the exchanges, the seller of a put option must provide collateral to assure the owner of the option that the money will be there if the option is exercised.

The two parties to the deal are seeking opposite outcomes. The investor who buys the put is looking for protection against the possibility that the price of the stock will fall. If the price does fall, the investor can exercise the option and sell the stock at a price that will then be above the market price. If the price of the stock rises, the investor can let the option lapse and will be out only the cost of the premium paid to buy it. The seller of the put then pockets the premium. That is the end of the deal.

Leland decided that the put option was just the instrument he was looking for. The trick was to make it serve as protection for a whole portfolio of stocks, not just one stock. But in 1976 there were no organized markets for put options on individual stocks, much less for options on a whole portfolio. Leland then recalled that Black and Scholes had created the equivalent of a risk-free asset by combining shares of stock with an option. If you could combine stock and an option to create something that performed like cash, why not combine cash and stock to create something that would perform like an option?

After all, if $3 = 2 + 1$, then $2 = 3 - 1$, and $1 = 3 - 2$ as well. If you can perform the first two steps, you can perform the third: combine cash and stock to perform like an option. If synthetic cash and synthetic stocks can be created, it should also be possible to create a synthetic option.

The mathematics involved would be relatively simple. By studying the changing values of put options as the prices of the associated stocks move up and down with the passage of time, the procedure should reveal how to adjust the ratios of cash and stock so that the package would exactly mimic the performance of the put option. Then Leland recalled that a student in a seminar he had taught at Stanford had suggested a technique for working out the Black-Scholes stock/option combination along precisely these lines.

Portfolio insurance and a conventional put option would be identical twins. The owner of the portfolio would set some minimum value, or "floor," below which the portfolio would not be allowed to go—the equivalent of the selling price specified in the put option contract. The idea would be for the owner to sell stocks and invest in cash as the market fell and to switch from cash to stocks as the market rose.

The program would be set so that the portfolio would consist of virtually 100 percent cash and zero stocks at the precise moment when the portfolio reached the specified floor value. As with a put option, further market declines could then do no harm. The portfolio would be fully insured. As the market rose, the investor would gradually use the cash to buy stocks until the portfolio was fully invested. From that point onward, the portfolio would share fully in the rising market.

The difference between the value of the portfolio at the outset and the floor value would be the "deductible" for the insurance policy. The investor would lose some money as the market pulled the portfolio down toward the floor, just as a deductible requires the owner of a conventional insurance policy to share in the first part of a loss. Thereafter, the policy covers 100 percent of the losses. Similarly, after the portfolio had reached its floor, the 100 percent cash position would protect it from any further loss.

The "premium" would be what the investor would sacrifice if the portfolio was less than 100 percent in stocks when the market started to go up. The allocation between stocks and cash in a rising market would depend on the same factors that determine the premium on a conventional option or an insurance policy. The two most obvious factors are the time involved until the expiration date and the interest the investor can earn on the cash holdings that represent the insured portion of the portfolio.

Moreover, just as a conventional premium depends on the difference between the exercise price of the option and the actual price of the underlying stock (the deductible), so the cost of portfolio insurance would depend on the difference between the floor value selected and the value of the portfolio at the outset of the program. The closer the floor is to the original value of the portfolio, the larger the allocation to cash must be at the beginning, and the smaller the portfolio's participation if the market goes up instead of down.

The cash allocation at the outset will depend on what the investor expects the volatility of the portfolio to be—an estimate that almost always reflects recent experience. If it looks as though the market is going to make big moves rather than modest fluctuations, more cash will be needed at all times to protect the portfolio from steep declines. That extra cash, however, will also limit the portfolio's gain if the market shoots upward instead of downward.

Recalling his classical education, Leland shouted, "Eureka! Now I know how to do it."[5]

But when he got up the next morning after his sleepless night, he realized that he did not know enough about options to develop the idea in detail. There was a host of unanswered questions. What was the appropriate ratio between cash and stock? Would the insured investors ever have to sell stock short—that is, sell stock they did not own and borrow the shares to deliver to the buyer? How could all the relevant data be fed into a computer? Might everything go wrong—the equivalent of all the insured houses burning down on the same day?

That same morning, Leland took his problems to a younger Berkeley colleague, Mark Rubinstein. Rubinstein shared his fascination with mathematics, was knowledgeable in economics and finance, and had recently published a paper that made a significant contribution to option-pricing theory. Most important, Leland was confident that Rubinstein would not run off and put the idea into practice himself or spill the beans to someone with less integrity. "Mark is the most honest person I've ever known," Leland told me. Rubinstein was "a computer nut" as well. He fit the bill to perfection.[6]

Leland and Rubinstein had both gone to Lakeside School in Seattle, but four years' difference in their ages meant that they barely knew each other, and Leland had transferred to Exeter before going on to Harvard in 1960.

Leland entered Harvard with the intention of studying math and physics, but he soon decided that economics would bring him closer to the real world. As it turned out, he found that economics was fun but not irresistible. He graduated uncertain about whether to continue with it.

But he still wanted to stay in an area where he could use mathematics. Math had captivated him even as a boy. In his early teens, shortly after his family had moved to Seattle from Boston, he had developed a model to explain people's perception of time based on how long they had lived. He concluded that he had experienced one-half of his total perceptive life by the time he was 11 years old!

Rubinstein is just as rhapsodic in recalling his early exposure to mathematics. Recently he had to work out a problem that involved the formula for the sum of the squares of all the numbers in a long series. When he started to figure out what the formula would be, he remembered that he had worked through the whole thing back at Lakeside. That was one of the easiest problems he had solved back in those days.

Lakeside, incidentally, was not just a haven for math freaks, though it also produced Bill Gates, the Wunderkind founder of Microsoft who became a self-made billionaire before the age of 31. The University of Washington used the Lakeside football team for scrimmage practice, and Lakeside had the best ski and tennis teams in the state. Rubinstein also has fond memories of the Shakespeare course, which inspired an enthusiasm that has never waned.

After graduating from Harvard, Leland enrolled in the London School of Economics; but not because of intellectual compulsions: he was following a girlfriend who had taken a job in Europe. He found the work at LSE solid in content and much more quantitative than anything he had been exposed to as a Harvard undergraduate. The people he met struck him as unusually brilliant and stimulating. Among them was a fellow American from the West Coast, Barr Rosenberg, who became a lifelong friend.

When Leland returned to Harvard to study for his doctorate, he began to take notice of the stock market. His family were all investors, and the market appealed to his interest in how people handle uncertainty. Stocks also lent themselves to mathematical analysis, enriched by the vast data base of market transactions.

The stock market was hardly mainstream material for an academic economist in the mid-1960s, however: "I kept looking for how it fitted into then-current economic theory. It didn't. . . . The stock market . . . was off to the side, a seeming casino that didn't really fit in. In economics, firms maximized profits and that was that."[7]

The hot topic in economics at the time was what was known as optimal growth theory, which sought to show how the economy can best adjust the mix of saving, investment, and consumption to fiscal and monetary policy to attain the highest sustainable rate of real growth. The leading economists in this area included Robert Solow and Kenneth Arrow, both of whom became Nobel laureates.

Leland was convinced that the stock market played a role in determining optimal outcomes for the real economy. To prove his point, his doctoral dissertation combined the dynamics of the real economy with the uncertainty of portfolio theory. "This was fun to work on," he told me.[8]

Leland began his teaching career at Stanford, where Harry Markowitz's skirmish with Milton Friedman in 1952 still haunted scholars in the field of finance. Stanford was never satisfied that the research Leland was doing was really "economics." So tenure with a full professorship grew increasingly elusive and doubtful.

In 1973 he joined the faculty of the business school at Berkeley and has remained there ever since. By coincidence, Rubinstein had tried unsuccessfully to land a teaching job at Stanford while Leland was there, and he had been happily ensconced at Berkeley for a year when Leland appeared on the scene.

Rubinstein had done his graduate work at the University of California in Los Angeles, where he studied under many of the same people William Sharpe had worked with just a few years earlier. Like Sharpe, Rubinstein found the UCLA faculty interesting and inspiring. And like Sharpe, he was especially attracted by Jack Hirshleifer ("He really opened my mind to the beauty of economic reasoning").[9] But, also like Sharpe, he was disappointed in what the UCLA faculty could offer him in the field of finance. Sharpe had had to look elsewhere and left UCLA to study with Harry Markowitz at RAND. And Rubinstein decided to go elsewhere to strengthen his command of the field.

He read everything that had been written on the subject—some 2,500 articles, 500 of which he read with care. He compiled a bibliography of his readings and then wrote a summary that runs to over a hundred pages, a document that was an invaluable asset to me in writing this book.

After earning his degree at UCLA in 1971, Rubinstein went to Berkeley to teach corporate finance, but he found the subject less appealing than he had expected. He wanted theoretical work and looked around for something more to his taste. He offered to teach a course in options, even though his knowledge of options was behind the times—the recent publication of the Black-Scholes and Merton papers had unleashed a flood of articles that Rubinstein had not yet studied with care. To teach options, he had to learn about them. So he set to work.

A disturbing thought occurred to him along the way. He wanted to be a theorist, but could he be a good theorist without a better sense of the real world? "I felt like a kid trying to play with my model trains in the basement," he told me. "Anyway, the students were not really interested in options. They wanted to know how things worked."[10]

This was in early 1976, and the Pacific Stock Exchange, following in the footsteps of the Chicago Board Options Exchange, had just launched an options trading operation. Rubinstein and two fellow academics decided to see whether the models they were putting on the blackboard could actually earn them some money: "We must know more than the guy who is just trading there," they reasoned.[11] His associates were John Cox of Stanford and Stephen Ross of the University of Pennsylvania, both of whom were becoming distinguished options theorists in their own right. Ross was about to publish his first paper on Arbitrage Pricing Theory.

The three put together $24,000 out of their own pockets. They spent $9,000 to buy a seat on the exchange and another $4,000 to program their computer. That left $11,000 for them to trade with. They decided that Rubinstein would go on the floor and do the trading, Cox would work on the models, and Ross would measure the variance of the stocks on which they would trade the options.

The $4,000 for programming went to two Italian students. "They were the smartest students I ever had," says Rubinstein. "They programmed like crazy at my house. Later I found out that one of them lived in a home in Italy that many people would regard as a palace."[12]

Rubinstein had become fascinated with a computer language known as APL: "I am a very orderly person. When I see something as orderly as a computer language, I just get sucked in— it's just awful. . . . I won a programming prize at Stanford as an undergraduate without knowing programming. When I saw APL, all I could say was, 'Boy, that's incredible!'"[13] He proceeded to buy himself one of the first desktop computers, the IBM 5100. It cost $20,000, looked like a typewriter, had a video screen "the size of a postcard," and sported 64K memory—about a tenth of today's most modest desktop computers. But the little computer had one irresistible feature: It came with APL built in, as well as the more conventional programming language known as BASIC.[14]

When it came to the practicalities of trading, the computer program was limited to identifying trades based on the previous day's closing prices, which Rubinstein and his partners found unsatisfactory for their purposes. The beloved computer "was very good at picking out trades you couldn't do," Rubinstein laments. On the other hand, he is grateful for "a good lesson in empiricism."[15] Later on, after they had closed out their venture, advances in programming techniques made intraday trading a simple matter.

Despite the programming obstacle, the trading operation was running with an accumulated profit of $3,000 when Rubinstein made a careless but nearly fatal mistake. Meaning to sell one in-the-money option and buy four out-of-the-money options on a stock, he inadvertently offered to sell four in-the-money-options and buy one out-of-the-money option. As he saw the crowd on the floor rushing to take the other side of his transactions, he gloated, "Boy, do I have them!"[16] Then reality dawned: The crowd on the floor had been nice to him as the new boy in town, but he sensed that they were acting a little *too* nice on this occasion. It took only a minute and a half for Rubinstein to realize that even a move of as little as half a point in the underlying stock would wipe him and his partners out. He hastened to reverse the transaction at a cost that just about used up their $3,000 profit.

He feels the experience was worth it: "When I walked into the classroom, at least I knew what was going on. I could stop teaching corporate finance and begin to teach investments."[17] The association with Cox and Ross also bore rich fruit later on. In 1979, the "Cox-Ross-Rubinstein" option pricing model appeared in print and has rivaled the popularity of the Black-Scholes model among practitioners ever since.

Rubinstein listened eagerly when Leland, groggy after his sleepless night but also a little manic, dropped by his office to outline his scheme for portfolio insurance. Rubinstein immediately recognized the implications of what Leland had dreamed up. His first reaction was to chuckle: "I'm surprised I never thought of that myself!"[18]

At that very first meeting, the two arrived at a verbal agreement to form Leland-Rubinstein Associates. They also had what Leland describes as "a most delightful argument," with each insisting that the other should have a larger share of the partnership.[19]

They were optimistic about the outlook for their product. Even if conventional puts and calls became available on the leading market indexes, like the Standard and Poor's 500 Stock Composite, those options would have too short a life to suit the needs of most institutional investors. Nor would they insure portfolios that included bonds and short-term paper as well as stocks in proportions unique to each investor.

But progress was slow. Both men had other projects to pursue and teaching responsibilities to honor. That was the least of it, for major questions remained unsolved. The mechanics of the dynamic strategy had to be formulated, the impact of trading costs had to be incorporated into the procedures, and the role that Leland-Rubinstein Associates would play in the process had to be specified. At first, they thought they had no choice but literally to sell insurance to investors, in which case all the risks would be theirs if the strategy failed to work as promised. Further analysis proved that this frightening obligation would not be necessary. They figured out how to function simply as investment advisors to their clients in return for a regular percentage fee.

The most stubborn problem was how to handle volatility in calculating the cost of the insurance. The volatility of the underlying asset is the only uncertain variable in determining the value of an option. The expiration date, exercise price, interest rate, and current stock price are all known facts, but volatility is extraordinarily difficult to forecast. That is why most investors base their estimates of volatility on what it has been in the recent past.

The penalty for making a bad estimate of future volatility can be ruin. If the program assumes a level of volatility that turns out to be too low, the insurance will fail to deliver on its promise to protect the investor against losses; the portfolio will be holding too little cash and too much stock as the market tumbles. The portfolio will also be carrying too much cash and too little stock when the market rises. These unhappy outcomes would be the equivalent of a life insurance company selling a man fire insurance on the assumption that his house is fireproof, when in fact it is nothing but tinder in an arson-prone neighborhood, with a high probability of burning down before more than three or four premiums have been paid in.

In the summer of 1978—two years after the first meeting with Rubinstein, and now back in France—Leland finally figured out how to handle unexpected changes in volatility. Once again, he derived his insight from the Black-Scholes procedure. The Black-Scholes option pricing formula includes, among its inputs, the time to the expiration of the contract as well the expected volatility of the underlying stock. Indeed, it multiplies time by the volatility estimate.

This simple piece of arithmetic supplied the missing piece to the puzzle. Instead of insuring a portfolio for a fixed time period with a fixed estimate of volatility, why not insure it for a total amount of market fluctuation? The greater the rate of actual fluctuation, the sooner the insurance coverage will expire. This arrangement would be identical to an insurance company offering a policy to a family with three cars that protects them against a total of five accidents, regardless of which car or cars sustain the damage. The policy will automatically expire when (and if) five accidents have occurred.

The idea sounded great. Rubinstein, who had been doing some theoretical work along similar lines, went to the computer to simulate the results over a variety of historical situations. An unpleasant surprise greeted him. As the computer printed out sheet after sheet of paper, the results were not at all what he had expected.

Rubinstein could not believe his eyes. After going over and over his material, he discovered that he, of all people, had made a mistake in the programming instructions. When he fixed up the program, the results conformed closely to his expectations. Errors shrank from 5 percent to less than 0.1 percent, and the necessary number of transactions held to acceptable levels. The first sales material for Leland-Rubinstein's portfolio insurance product contained an example of protection against five market moves of 5 percent, with the protection in force until the maximum number of moves had taken place.

Rubinstein set out to prove to the world that this splendid product really worked: he tried it out with his own money, shifting between a money market fund and a mutual fund that tracked the S&P 500 Index over a period of six months. Everything worked out exactly as expected. The experiment was so successful that *Fortune* magazine published an article about it.

Marketing began in earnest in 1979. Armed with a letter from Barr Rosenberg endorsing the validity of the principles behind the product, Leland visited a number of bank trust departments in the East and Midwest, including Morgan Guaranty in New York and American National Bank in Chicago. Interest seemed high. Meetings ran several hours over schedule.

Back at Berkeley and full of enthusiasm, Leland waited for the phone to ring. "By God," he exclaimed to me, "no one ever called!"[20] To anyone in the investment business who has gone on one of these marketing sprees, Leland's experience was by no means unique. But it was hard for Leland and Rubinstein to realize that investors seldom find any product irresistible—and complicated ones least of all. A complicated product involves an unavoidable learning process first and then the tiresome, often impossible, job of trying to explain the product to superiors. No matter how fascinating intellectually, few products appear to be worth all that trouble to people who have more pleasant ways to spend their time.

Leland and Rubinstein decided that they had to have a professional marketing person with the analytical skills to understand and explain their novel product. They chose John O'Brien, whom they had met at a seminar on finance at Berkeley in which they both participated. With degrees from MIT and UCLA, O'Brien was already an old hand at consulting with institutional investors and in explaining the applications of financial theory. As far back as 1970, he had written a superb article for the *Financial Analysts Journal* whose lengthy title, "How Market Theory Can Help Investors Set Goals, Select Investment Managers, and Appraise Investment Performance," summarizes its lucid and concise introduction to most of the ideas I have set forth in this book.

In the fall of 1980, Leland-Rubinstein Associates became Leland O'Brien Rubinstein Associates, Inc.—now known as LOR. The founders have described the firm at that point as having "three principals, two part-time secretaries, one computer, and no clients."[21]

The first client came along almost immediately. John Mabie of MidContinent Capital Management, an old friend of O'Brien's, gave them $500,000 to insure against six moves of 4 percent over six months. The program worked perfectly: six moves of 4 percent took place over exactly six months. Mabie was delighted and LOR was delighted. They launched a second program. This time the term of the insurance coincided with the bumpy markets of late 1981 and early 1982; six insured moves occurred within four months instead of being spread out over six months. Now Mabie was more puzzled than delighted. Although he had been insured against the market's volatility, he felt he had not got his money's worth.

This time Leland and Rubinstein came up with a revised version of their product in which they could still promise the client that— as long as trading was possible and other investors would readily buy the stocks the portfolio had to sell—the portfolio would not fall below some level specified in advance, no matter how volatile the market. The price of this protection would be some sacrifice in how fully the portfolio would participate in rising markets, which meant that the size of the insurance premium would be more difficult to estimate in advance.

Investors seemed to find this new arrangement acceptable. O'Brien, concentrating on investors who owned the assets rather than following Leland's practice of trying to sell to investors who *managed* the assets, brought $135 million into the fold the first year. Before long their roster of business was in the billions. Later, they licensed other managers to use their system, including Wells Fargo and Aetna Insurance. Aetna used its own assets to back its guarantee of minimum rates of return on equity investments. At its zenith in mid-1987, LOR's portfolio insurance system covered more than $50 billion in assets of institutional investors; Rubinstein estimates the total as high as $70 billion.

Despite the momentum O'Brien had built up for LOR's product, some snags remained. A mechanical glitch developed as the insured portfolio moved from stocks to cash or vice versa. If the client had even one portfolio manager picking stocks or varying the composition of the portfolio—and most clients, heeding the prescriptions of Barr Rosenberg, had more than one manager by that time—the orders from some outside authority mandating them to buy or sell was neither welcome nor easily coordinated among the managers. Furthermore, each manager's portfolio had a different degree of sensitivity to movements in the market as a whole. The whole process entailed significant transactions costs that further hobbled the bottom-line performance numbers.

The opening up of the market for futures in the major stock indexes in 1983 was a godsend. A futures contract is a commitment by the owner to deliver a designated item at a specific date in the future at a specified price. The buyer hopes that the price at the date the contract expires will be higher than the price at which the deal was made; the seller hopes the price will fall. In the case of futures contracts on stock indexes, nobody actually delivers all the stocks in the index at the expiration of the contract. Buyer and seller settle up in cash, paying or receiving the difference between the contract price and the price of the S&P 500 prevailing when the contract comes due and expires.

The market for stock index futures was a success from the beginning. The futures contract bypasses the messy business of buying and selling 500 different stocks while trying to trade each of them as close to the same moment as possible. The investor can bet on the market as a whole with a single transaction at a cost far below the cost of buying and selling each of the 500 stocks individually. The volume of trading in the futures tied to the Standard & Poor's index has been active at all times, so that the contracts are highly liquid. On many days, the volume of trading on the futures market represents more shares of stock than actually trade on the New York Stock Exchange.

Now the purveyors of portfolio insurance could change the mix of the overall portfolio without ever disturbing the client's managers. As the market declined, portfolio insurance called for the investor to sell futures; as the market rose, the investor would repurchase the futures. The system was convenient, inexpensive, and efficient. By 1986, the use of futures on the S&P 500 index had replaced buying and selling individual stocks in nearly all LOR accounts.

Leland and Rubinstein were also concerned about what would happen if stock prices fell far enough to trigger selling from $50 billion to $60 billion of insured portfolios that would hit the market all at once. An act of faith in the efficiency of the capital markets eased LOR's worries about this dire possibility. Although some skeptics continued to raise the question, the purveyors of insurance, and the big brokerage firms that enjoyed their busy trading activities, asserted confidently and repeatedly that other investors would be delighted to absorb these liquidations at only a minimal discount from current prices. After all, the insured sellers would be offering stock for sale, not because they had some kind of negative information, but simply because they wanted to protect their portfolios from further loss. Experience up to that point demonstrated that the market stood ready to accommodate such so-called "informationless" sellers at much better prices than sellers who were suspected of "knowing something." The rationalizations about the ability of the market to absorb concentrated and heavy selling persisted right up to the day of reckoning that arrived on October 19, 1987.

Leland's sleepless night in September 1976 had led to the creation of an immensely attractive investment strategy for clients and an equally attractive outlook for LOR's profitability. Competition from well-known organizations soon made an appearance, but no one ever threatened LOR's lead, especially when coupled with the performance of its licensees.

Leland had one disturbing experience with a competitor. During 1981, he conducted a series of all-day seminars on portfolio insurance, including one in Chicago. Six months later, he saw an announcement of "Protected Investment Programs" offered by the prominent brokerage firm of Kidder Peabody, where interest in quantitative products had been high for some time. When Leland went to listen in on their presentation to a meeting of prospective clients, he was dumbfounded to see that they were using slides almost identical to his and examples that were identical to his. At the moment when the speaker was about to explain what the premium would be on the example he was displaying, Leland astonished the person next to him by leaning over and predicting, accurate to the fourth decimal place, that the number would be 5.875 percent. The irony of the story is that Kidder Peabody later decided that portfolio insurance was not an appropriate product for a brokerage house and became a major source of referrals to LOR and a major trader in futures for the accounts of LOR's clients.

It is interesting to speculate on why portfolio insurance was such a hot product during the bull market of the 1980s. Assets under portfolio insurance more than quadrupled during 1987 alone.

Protection against losses is always appealing, but nothing comes without a cost. The more fully a portfolio is insured, the more limited will be the client's participation in a rising market. Nevertheless, spectacular as it was, the bull market of the 1980s climbed up a wall of worry: the budget deficit, the trade deficit, lurking inflationary pressures, the persistently low savings rate, the fluctuating dollar, lagging productivity, disappointing profits, and high real interest rates. All these distressing realities haunted investors. Portfolio insurance provided the comfort of knowing that the huge and often unexpected gains would not vanish on the day the bear market arrived.

Yet something more than protection had to be involved. There was almost no talk of bear markets as stock prices rose 60 percent from 1982 to 1984 and then doubled between the end of 1984 and the summer of 1987. The explanation, in my opinion, is that portfolio insurance became a justification for carrying heavier positions in equities than would have seemed acceptable without it.

Without portfolio insurance, risk-averse investors who had piled up enormous profits in the bull market of the 1980s would have had to sell off their shares in order to lock in their profits. This strategy would have sharply reduced their returns if they sold too soon and the market continued to climb. With portfolio insurance in place, they acquired downside protection with greater upside participation than they would have had by adhering to traditional investment practice.

The assumptions underlying portfolio insurance (and the option-pricing theory on which it was based) underwent a crucial test in October 1987. For the strategy to be fully effective, the investors without portfolio insurance must accommodate the investors with portfolio insurance, at all times and under all conditions. Changes in stock prices must be continuous—a stock must not close at $25 and open the next day at $22. And the market must be willing to absorb whatever selling is necessary at prices very close to the price prevailing when the sell decision is made. In short, the market must be liquid.

At this point, the difference between portfolio insurance—a synthetic put option—and the real thing turned out to be fateful. A conventional put option *commits* the seller of the put to buy the underlying shares at a specified price; the contract to do so is secured by cash collateral. The arrangements as to price and purchase are set in advance and are secured by an agreement enforceable in a court of law.

The events of October 1987 shattered the underlying assumptions of how markets, and therefore portfolio insurance, would work in practice: The investors without portfolio insurance flatly refused to play the part of the seller of the put. They had made no advance commitment whatsoever to oblige the investors with portfolio insurance by taking stock off their hands at the current price, and they had no intention of putting up the cash to do so. On the contrary, everyone seemed to be joining the insurance bandwagon by trying to sell. With so few hardy investors willing to stand up and buy stock, market liquidity evaporated.

To make matters worse, portfolio insurance became a focal issue in the market's wild gyrations and was pilloried for being both the villain and the victim of the chaos. The dust had hardly settled when insurance came in for a large part of the culpability for the crash itself.

The stock market had peaked in mid-August 1987, drifted downward during the rest of the month, wobbled through September, and then started to weaken perceptibly as October progressed. The whole five-year bull market appeared to crumble in the course of the trading week that ended on Friday, October 16. The Dow Jones Industrials fell by 250 points, or just about 10 percent, over those five days, with nearly half of that drop occurring on Friday alone. Similar patterns were emerging in stock markets all around the world.

Panic set in even before trading began on Monday morning, October 19. A huge overhang of sell orders had built up over the weekend. Sell orders placed with brokers so outnumbered buy orders that 187 stocks—nearly 10 percent of all the listed stocks—were not able to trade at the opening at all, an unprecedented event. Two hours later, more than 40 stocks had still failed to trade.

The Dow Jones Industrial Average was down more than 100 points by noon, but the worst was yet to come. The drop amounted to 190 points between 11:40 and 2:00 alone, and the free-fall came to nearly 300 points during the final hour and a quarter of trading. When, at long last, the gong sounded at 4:00 PM to end the day's trading, the market had plunged 508 points, or 23 percent, a record decline for a single day. Prices closed only a shade above the worst prices of the day. At 1749, the Average was almost a thousand points below the zenith it had reached only two months earlier.

A mind-boggling 604 million shares worth almost $21 billion changed hands—mostly into the hands of market-makers rather than permanent holders. This was four times the average daily volume of the preceding nine months of 1987, and nearly eight times the average daily volume as recently as 1985.

The drama was by no means limited to the floor of the New York Stock Exchange and other stock exchanges around the world. Much of the stress and high excitement of the day was generated by the market for futures on the major stock market indexes, such as the Standard & Poor's Composite of 500 stocks. The tight interrelationship between the futures market and the underlying indexes of stock prices added to the tempest of selling that was already overwhelming the ability of the market structure to deal with the pressures bearing down on it. On October 19, values on the futures market sank by 29 percent—even worse than the losses on the exchange—on trading volume of about $20 billion.

Since the price of a futures contract on the S&P 500 index is based on the prices of the 500 individual stocks in the index at the moment the contract is struck, the price of the contract and the total market value of the shares of the 500 component companies should bear a close resemblance to each other. Most of the time, they do. This is no accident or coincidence. If the price of the futures contract falls too far below the prices of the stocks, traders engaging in arbitrage will buy the futures and ask their brokers to sell the 500 stocks in the index. The arbitragers know that they can reverse the procedure with an assured gain on the day the futures contract expires, at which point the two must be precisely equal to each other.

During the week preceding the crash, the prices of the futures had, as usual, faithfully tracked the movement of the index itself. They continued to do so all week, even though the market came close to disorder on occasion and even though insured portfolios were steady sellers all through the week. On Friday the 16th, selling from insured portfolios accounted for about 15 percent of all futures trades; from 12:00 to 12:30, the figure rose as high as 40 percent.

This neat relationship between the futures contracts and the underlying stocks in the index burst apart during the very first minutes of trading on October 19. At the opening, the quoted prices on the 500 stocks in the index indicated an index value of 282; the futures contract opened at 262, at a record discount of about 7 percent. Except for a brief period around 11:00, the futures and the prices of the stocks in the index never came close to converging. When the trading day finally came to a close, the discount stood at 10 percent.

What had caused this enormous disparity between two markets that should theoretically be almost identical? The gap opened up because investors who wanted to raise cash found the stock market too chaotic to satisfy their needs. It was easier to sell futures and be done with it. As a result, the price of the futures contracts appeared to be falling much faster than the prices of the stocks, but no one knew with any certainty the prices at which stock transactions would actually take place. The actual gap between the futures market and the stock market may have been smaller than indicated by the yawning differential that appeared to be developing, because the "last sale," which determines the value of the index, was stale news most of the day. Stock prices would have been a good deal lower if the tremendous numbers of shares offered for sale had found buyers and trades had been executed.

But this was only one step in an even more terrifying sequence of events. The arbitragers who would normally have supported the futures market by buying the futures when they were at such a large discount from the stock market failed to make their usual appearance. Some of them had run out of money during the decline of the preceding week. Those who stayed in the game on Monday found that they could buy the futures all right, but they were unable to execute the offsetting sales on the stock market at prices anywhere near what they expected to receive. Like everyone else, they were just plain scared. So the prices kept dropping on the futures market, pulling stock prices down with them, and adding to the fright suffered by everyone.

The most authoritative and comprehensive chronicle of these terrible hours appears in the report prepared by a presidential task force under the direction of Nicholas Brady, then chief executive of the investment banking firm of Dillon Read and later Secretary of the Treasury under George Bush. As my wife and I wrote in a critique of the task force's work in *Institutional Investor,* the Brady report's "painstaking analysis [was] a powerful effort indeed . . . consistently objective and professional."[22]

Nevertheless, Brady and his associates were convinced that the leading cause of the chaos on October 19 was the cumulative impact of "mechanical, price-insensitive selling by a number of institutions employing portfolio insurance strategies and a small number of mutual fund groups reacting to redemptions [by their stockholders]." The whole disaster and the "consequent threat to the financial system," they argued, resulted from the unprecedented volume of selling that was "concentrated in the hands of surprisingly few institutions."[23]

The Brady report provides a great deal of evidence that appears to support this case. The top four sellers in the stock market accounted for 14 percent of total sales on October 19; the top fifteen sellers accounted for 20 percent of the total. Concentrated liquidation was even greater in the futures market, where the top ten sellers contributed 50 percent of the volume aside from traders whose business was to make the markets in the futures.

Portfolio insurance was itself a major factor. According to the Brady report, three portfolio insurers accounted for just under 10 percent of the total selling on the stock market on October 19; insurance programs were responsible for 40 percent of the volume on the futures market, of which 70 percent came from just three insurers:

An example may help illustrate the extent of the portfolio insurance overhang by Friday's close. One portfolio insurance client had followed exactly the instructions of its advisor during the Wednesday to Friday period. Over the weekend, the advisor informed the client that, based on Friday's market close, it should sell on Monday 70% of its remaining equities in order to conform to the parameters of the insurance model. This is, of course, an extreme example. But the typical portfolio insurance model calls for stock sales in excess of 20% of a portfolio in response to a 10% decline in the market. . . .

[The insured portfolios] approached Monday with a huge amount of selling dictated by their models. With the market already down 10%, their models dictated that, at a minimum, $12 billion (20% of $60 billion) of equities should already have been sold. Less than $4 billion had in fact been sold.[24]

The shortfall in planned sales was a direct result of frenzied conditions that violated the underlying assumptions of portfolio insurance: that ready buyers are always willing to accommodate the sellers in the insurance camp. In other words, the market would be liquid. But the opposite set of forces came into play. The traders on the floor of the Exchange and many other large investors knew that heavy selling from the insured portfolios was in the wings. Nothing can discourage even the most venturesome buyers faster than information like that. The job of the traders executing the portfolio insurance game plans became next to impossible.

In all the confusion of October 19, LOR made the decision to accept the prices on the stock exchange as the "correct" prices and to reduce their selling into the futures market. They reasoned that the extremely depressed prices of the futures were unrealistically low relative to the prices in the stock market, because the arbitragers who would normally keep the futures in line with the underlying stocks were either unable or unwilling to act; in any case, their absence was obvious. Selling futures into these conditions seemed unacceptable. But selling the underlying stocks was also impossible, because LOR's arrangements with its clients limited its trading to the futures markets.

LOR's decision to cut back on the liquidation of the futures mandated by their programs was a costly decision at the moment, for stocks continued to fall throughout the day of October 19. By the end of the week, after stocks had rebounded considerably, this may have turned out to be the wiser move.

The Wells Fargo traders took the opposite tack. They decided that prices in the futures market were "correct" rather than unrealistically low and kept selling into that market, even though, unlike LOR, they had the choice of selling the underlying stocks instead. For October 19, at least, this looked like the better decision to have made, although Rubinstein argues that "Wells Fargo was lucky, not right."[25]

The Wells Fargo customers happened to have another advantage over the customers of LOR: they had floors for their portfolios that were closer to the peak levels of mid-summer. When Monday morning, October 19, rolled around, most of the Wells Fargo customers had already liquidated a significant portion of their stocks. They took their beating on the transactions executed on Monday, but, considering the heavy equity positions they had carried a few weeks earlier when the market started to sink, they came out a lot better than they would have without the insurance program. The LOR clients were less fortunate, although they probably came out better than they would have with no insurance.

Even the most enthusiastic proponent of portfolio insurance cannot deny its disappointing performance during this critical test of its capabilities. The problem was not in a failure to keep portfolios above the promised minimum value—the minimum values were seldom penetrated by more than 1 percent or 2 percent. The problem was the unexpected failure of market liquidity, which made the effective premium much more expensive than had been anticipated: under more normal conditions, the necessary selling would have been executed at significantly higher prices.

And yet the Brady report may have overstated the case against portfolio insurance. Despite the hard facts cited in the report concerning the contribution of portfolio insurance to the cascade of stock prices on October 19, it is fair to take issue with the conclusion that "surprisingly few institutions" in general, and portfolio insurance in particular, "outstripped the capacity of market infrastructures" and, as a result, deserve the blame for the magnitude of the crash.[26]

Institutions do most of their buying and selling in block trades of 10,000 shares or more. The Brady report shows that there were 12,000 block trades on October 19; the average block ran to about 25,000 shares for a dollar value of approximately $1 million—no higher than normal, by the way.

Therefore, block trading accounted for a total of 300 million shares and $12 billion, or about half the share volume and 60 percent of the dollar volume of transactions on that day. This was only two percentage points above the average for the preceding fifty days and almost identical to the average for the last fifty trading days of 1986, suggesting that the admittedly savage selling pressure from the institutions was only a part, and not an unusually large part, of the appalling story of October 19.

The Brady report includes another statistic that has received too little attention. Compared with the 190,000 nonblock transactions that were actually executed, the 12,000 block transactions occupied only a tiny amount of the time of the market makers and a minimal amount of space on the computer screens. The ballooning volume of nonblock transactions was nearly triple the average daily number in 1986 and well above the previous high of 145,000. This avalanche in the sheer number of orders coming into the system overwhelmed the whole communications network and explains the unanswered telephones in the brokerage offices and the darkened computer screens that intensified the chaos and fed investor panic. If you do not know what the last price was, you are incapable of making an informed decision; if you cannot reach your broker at all, you are in never-never land.

A survey of investors conducted immediately after the crash by Robert Shiller of the Cowles Foundation at Yale reported that 20 percent of the respondents admitted to "difficulty concentrating, sweaty palms, tightness in the chest or rapid pulse." More than half who had sold on October 19 said that they were "experiencing a contagion of fear." Close to 40 percent who sold had stop-loss orders in place, orders to sell whenever a stock breaks below a specified price and a strategy that is just as "mechanical" as portfolio insurance.[27]

Shiller hypothesizes that all investors worry that somebody else knows something that other investors do not know. In an article that appeared in the *American Economic Review* in December

1990, Leland and his Berkeley colleague Gerard Gennotte developed a full-scale model of crashes that reflects the same set of investor responses. It catches the sweat and pressure of real-time investing: All of us read and talk and listen and calculate and compute for hours on end and still never feel secure that we have as much—forget more—information than others. Even Ivan Boesky and Michael Milken were never certain they had the informational upper hand.

The only hard information we have is the movement of stock prices themselves. "How's the market?" is no idle question for most investors. The answer to that question on October 19, even when available, was devastating. The inundation of selling during the week preceding the crash and the tumultuous events of the early morning created a pervasive sense that "they" knew something awful. It was an ideal prescription for panic, and all too many investors, large as well as small, behaved accordingly.

The Brady report touches on another problem, but takes an odd road to its solution. The infrastructure and trading rules of the financial markets, in particular the specialist system at the New York Stock Exchange, have been in place for decades while the technology of investing has moved into the space age: computers at every stage of the process, trading in entire portfolios instead of individual stocks, global time differences, single transactions in the millions of dollars, and strategies never dreamed of even twenty years ago. The situation is comparable to trying to run a bullet train on the railbed between New York and the eastern tip of Long Island. The Brady report proposed slowing down the train. The effort to slow down the train is likely to get in the way of the more natural and rapidly evolving innovations to improve the quality of the roadbed.

Whatever the role of portfolio insurance may have been, the crash played a major role in the decline of portfolio insurance as an accepted investment strategy. Only a few clients remained after October 1987—mostly Japanese—and even fewer signed up to start new insurance plans. Why did the Japanese clients remain so loyal while the Americans fled the scene? Leland speculates that the Japanese " . . . hung in, in part, because they took the time to more fully understand the product. They realized that the problems of portfolio insurance in the crash were related to problems of market liquidity, not to some 'fundamental flaw' of the underlying technique."[28]

Two years of famine were to pass before LOR took on its first new domestic client. The general impression was that insurance had failed just at the moment when it was most needed. Furthermore, expectations of a further sharp decline in stock prices gradually diminished as nothing serious happened after the crash, and, in time, stocks resumed their long upward climb.

Did portfolio insurance "fail"? Rubinstein denies that it did. After all, he points out, "the market was nice enough to provide proper conditions for more than fifty years."[29] As a result, it was the market that failed to provide conditions where portfolio insurance could work.

The experience has kept Leland and Rubinstein busy at their drawing boards. They have designed new techniques and new financial instruments to avoid the disappointments of October 1987. They are convinced that the underlying concepts of portfolio insurance are valid and that the inversion of the Black/Scholes argument from $3 = 2 + 1$ into $1 = 3 - 2$ lends itself to a many different permutations. Hedging is always in demand; products that hedge while they expose the portfolio to high returns when available should continue to find a ready market.

The experience of October 1987 has increased the market for products that offer precision in the control of investment risk. Many other purveyors have entered this market, some with offerings more unfamiliar and complex than anything on the menu at LOR. And the strategy has been applied with considerable success in the market for fixed-income securities.

The most interesting applications derive from the essential promise of portfolio insurance: Over time and on the average, portfolio insurance allows the investor to enjoy the return on the better-performing of two assets, stocks and cash, while reducing the exposure to the asset with the lower rate of return. Why limit the arrangement to just stocks and cash? Why not stocks and bonds, or stocks in New York and stocks in Tokyo? One vendor is offering a strategy that provides the return of the best of three markets, or even more. Another has a strategy that promises the investor the right to sell at the highest price hit during a contract period, with the current price as a minimum guarantee. Synthetic equity created from a combination of options and cash permits investors to structure the uncertain trade-off between risk and return precisely to the taste of each.

None of these arrangements comes free; in some instances, the costs may appear prohibitive compared with more orthodox approaches to investing. Many of these deals are put together informally, tailor-made by investment bankers and others to match the requirements of both sides but often lacking the cash collateral that the organized exchanges require to assure the buyer of the option that the other side will live up to the terms of the contract. Despite the hazards of these credit risks, the concept seems to know no limits. In a volatile world, control of risk has become a paramount investment objective.

These exotic offshoots of Hayne Leland's sleepless night in 1976 spring from the same deep theoretical roots that shaped the original structure at LOR. Harry Markowitz taught the wisdom of optimizing the trade-off between risk and return. William Sharpe showed how to do it. Black, Scholes, and Merton converted these concepts into the creation of synthetic securities offering many varieties of risk control. Franco Modigliani and Merton Miller emphasized the critical role played by arbitrage in determining the value of securities. And Paul Samuelson and Eugene Fama were there to remind investors that, in an unpredictable market, they had better not venture forth unprepared. Preparation for unpredictable situations is what LOR is all about.

# PART
# VI

# The Future

# Chapter
## 15

# The View from the Top
# of the Tower

*. . . The triumph of economic law after competition has
done its best.*

"NEVER HAVE SO FEW TAKEN SO MUCH FROM SO MANY."
This heading, in letters an inch high, appeared over a full-
page advertisement in the financial section of *The New York
Times* on June 25, 1990. In only slightly smaller type, the ad continued: "The speculators and their political friends ruined the
S&L industry. Now they have the power to ruin the stock
market."

This ad was not paid for by Ralph Nader or by one of the groups
usually associated with attacking the rich and powerful. It was
placed by a respected brokerage firm that is a full-fledged member
of the Wall Street establishment.

Just a few months later, Michael Milken, who had earned
$25,000 in 1970 and $500 million in 1989, wrote to Judge Kimba
Wood that "I never dreamed I could do anything that would result in being a felon." The government's measure of the damage
he had done to others came to $685,614. Judge Wood sentenced
him to ten years in jail.

The stock market crash of October 19, 1987 wiped out $600
billion of wealth in six and a half hours. The Brady report explained this tragedy by denouncing "mechanical, price-insensitive selling . . . concentrated in the hands of surprisingly few institutions" and proposed a series of constraints to bring the
market's penchant for wildness under control.

The popular literature about the world of investment in the 1980s carries titles that reflect those events: *Bonfire of the Vanities, Barbarians at the Gates, The Predators' Ball,* and *Liars' Poker.* The main characters are arrogant, greedy, cynical, and shady. At one point or another in their careers, they grow rich beyond the dreams of most of us—largely because they have profited from the new technologies, novel financial instruments, and mysterious investment strategies that emerged from the revolution in finance and investing.

These angry words and charges of evil-doing emanating from respectable, capitalist sources, could have been written by socialist reformers. They suggest that the world might be better off if the authorities shut down the financial markets altogether. If the bathwater is contaminated, maybe we should throw the baby out along with it. If the stock market is a casino, who needs it?

We all need it, even those of us who do not invest in it. Our economy would grind to a halt without it, leaving us with no alternative but the socialist model. And as we went through that door, we would collide with the former socialist economies struggling to come the other way. On April 16, 1991, on the occasion of the opening of the Warsaw Stock Exchange for the first time since World War II, one of the senior participants noted that this was "a significant moment in the nation's progress from a centralized economy to a free market system. . . . We now have the central institution of a capital market."[1]

The stock market is more than a place where traders buy and sell bits and pieces of corporate ownership. It is more than an outlet for our savings or a source of finance for corporations seeking more capital. It is more than an instrument for valuing giant corporations. It is more than a means for transforming fixed capital assets into a liquid form that can be converted into cash.

The stock market is all these things. It could not be one without being the others as well. If the market failed to bring buyers together with sellers, shares would not be liquid and deals to buy or sell them could no longer easily be reversed. If shares were not liquid, companies would find it a lot more expensive to raise cash and would grow more slowly as a result. If the market were not a place where people could trade fractions of corporate ownership, it would be far more difficult to place a credible value on the corporations that trade there. If the market did not provide liquidity and did not set a value on corporations, it would not attract people to trade outstanding shares or to buy newly issued shares.

Without the stock market, the market for corporate ownership would be like the market for houses. The seller of a house offers the entire house, not just a piece of it. Only rarely do brokers use their own capital to buy a house for resale. They have to advertise or resort to more cumbersome methods for finding the other side of the deal; no wonder realtors earn a commission of 6 percent (the commission on a typical stock transaction is less than 1 percent), and no wonder transactions involve such extended negotiations. After the house has been sold, only the principals and their close friends know what the price was. Transactions are few and far between. With trading so difficult, so expensive, so infrequent, and so secret, the buyer and seller seldom know whether the price they settled on was the right price or whether they might not have struck a better deal with someone else.

If nobody knows whether or not the price was right, then nobody has a way of searching out the best value in the market. The inability to discover "the best at the price" may not matter when a house is a home. But when a profit-making business that sells goods and services to the public is involved, the most efficient allocation of the nation's productive resources is at stake. The misallocation of those resources would have catastrophic effects on living standards, employment, and economic growth. In socialist economies it is the absence of free and active markets for corporate ownership that deprives citizens of the goods they want, with the quality they demand, and at prices they can afford to pay.

Some people argue that valuing corporations is unnecessary when most big companies no longer need to raise new capital from the stock market and when so many of them have been buying their shares back in from the market. That is a simplistic view. We learned during the 1980s that the price of a company's stock exerts a powerful influence on the behavior of its managers. Managers who are asleep at the switch or who prefer their own perks to the stockholders' interest soon find their companies on the bargain counter and a corporate raider shoving them out the door. The stock market is a huge voting booth in which the ballots are counted every minute of the business day. No officeholder in a publicly held corporation can afford to ignore it.

But there is a more subtle force at work. Takeovers make big headlines, but most investors, even the biggest, are in the stock market to buy fragments of companies, not whole companies. They come there precisely because they do not want the whole thing, to meet sellers who want to sell parts of the whole.

That is what makes diversification feasible: It creates many baskets in which investors can carry their eggs. People do not buy twenty, forty, or a hundred houses at a time, but they can go to the stock market and buy bits and pieces of as many corporations as they wish.

As Markowitz reminds us, big risks are scary if you cannot diversify them, especially if they are expensive to unload; even the wealthiest families hesitate before they decide which house to buy. But big risks that can be diversified are not scary; investors find them interesting. No single loss will make anyone go broke. Even if investors lose on some of their purchases, their overall expected return will be high. *Because the stock market makes diversification easy and inexpensive, the average level of risk-taking in society is enhanced.* *

The distinguishing feature of our economic system is the anticipation of high reward for those who are willing to take risk, who have the courage to make decisions that may go wrong. This creates a force that planned economies cannot emulate. Outside the military-scientific complex, technological innovation has been nil in the postwar socialist economies of Eastern Europe, the USSR, and China. Until private ownership of productive property became the norm during the seventeenth and eighteenth centuries, economic development was slow everywhere.

It is no coincidence that stock markets are both a feature of all free-market economies and a goal of all countries moving toward free enterprise. Institutions that encourage risk-taking are essential if a society is to grow and raise its living standards. Granted, risk-taking involves social costs. But the capitalist nations have no monopoly on pollution, maldistribution of income, inadequate education, poverty, speculation, crime, or corruption.

There is nothing new in the observation that private ownership of productive property and a healthy appetite for risk have much to do with the pace of economic progress. That the stock market plays a central role in the dynamics of our economic system is a

*I am grateful to Jack Treynor for this important insight.

more novel idea. Our understanding of the interplay between the stock market and risk, and of the role of risk in motivating the economy, derives directly from the contributions of the innovators we have met in the course of this history. Those contributions have had a profound impact on our understanding despite the controversies they triggered on their first appearance. Ninety years ago, Louis Bachelier's work was brushed aside because his topic was "somewhat remote." In 1952, Milton Friedman refused to accept Harry Markowitz's thesis as "economics." Only twenty-five years ago, Hayne Leland was complaining that to economic theorists "the stock market was off to the side."

If their only contribution had been to advance our comprehension of how the system works and the nature of the forces that drive it, Dayenu! But that was by no means all. Our heroes may not be household names among the investing public, but the spirit that ignited their revolution now touches virtually every decision that investors make.

Individual investors, armed with the power of their personal computers, are using quantitative techniques for appraising risk and expected returns and for analyzing stock price movements at a level of complexity Harry Roberts could never have imagined in 1959. Diversification is now a goal of the investment process, not just a byproduct. The burgeoning mutual fund industry supports index funds that track the S&P 500, an even wider market index, the bond market, and European and Pacific stock markets. The industry also offers many vehicles to satisfy the increasing demand for home-made diversification: the number and types of funds has proliferated to the point where their price quotations now fill nearly a full page in the daily newspapers. In addition to hundreds of specialized stock funds, there are funds that invest in every segment of the bond market from Treasury bonds to junk bonds. And there are funds for market timing strategies, options and futures, variable and fixed-rate home mortgages, and bond and stock markets all around the world.

Among institutional investors, diversification is no longer a casual, unstructured procedure, even for those who are unconverted by the academic theories. Institutional investors have moved rapidly into the global diversification of investment assets. They have come to recognize, belatedly, that the investor is concerned with a portfolio, not just a list of stocks. Trading entire portfolios, or major pieces of portfolios, has became standard practice through the futures markets and program trading, which is the name applied to the purchase or sale of baskets of stocks in one transaction. The markets for futures and options allow dealers to hedge the risks they incur when they accommodate institutional clients who want to buy or sell large blocks of stocks; such transactions would be prohibitively expensive if the hedging facilities were not available. Risk-hedging is not limited to market-makers: it has become an integral part of corporate finance as well.

In response to the demand for risk-hedging facilities and other applications of the new instruments, the markets for futures, for options, and for complex synthetic securities have experienced spectacular growth. The futures market alone has expanded by 12 percent a year since 1985. At this writing, new exchanges to handle these kinds of instruments are under development in London, Paris, Hong Kong, Sydney, Toronto, Singapore, Brazil, Osaka, Zurich, Frankfurt, and Tokyo.

The junk bond market, the most controversial of the markets of the 1980s, flourished because it satisfied the needs of both the investors who bought junk bonds and the relatively small companies that issued them. The issuers did not want to dilute their ownership by selling more stock, but they needed capital that their banks either could not or would not supply. The buyers would have been reluctant to buy shares in small, unknown companies, but they were willing to provide capital that offered a higher yield and less risk than common stock.

Milken recognized that the parties could do business. No one was fooled that these were triple-A obligations, but the high interest rates seemed to compensate for the risks involved. Many small companies got financing and created new jobs that would have been impossible without the junk bond market. Most of the junk bonds that subsequently defaulted were issued to finance takeovers rather than to finance the expansion of smaller corporations.

Although the revolution inspired by the new theories of finance has been profound, it has been less than total. Nor has the investment world split into faithful users of the new methodology and inflexible believers in the orthodox approach. The lines are blurred.

*302*

About half of all shares of stock outstanding are still owned by individual investors. Many of them continue to manage their affairs as they always have—and as their fathers did. Their portfolios are badly diversified, they seize on the latest market gossip, and they have no idea of how to measure whether they are doing well or poorly at the game; they are the noisiest of the noise traders. Others, perhaps out of inertia, fear, or stubborn unwillingness to pay capital gains taxes on old holdings, sit tight and do nothing.

Even in the institutional world, old ways die hard. Two-thirds of institutional money remains outside the index funds and is handled by active managers seeking to outwit the market—or trying to outperform one another. The salespeople at major institutional brokerage houses like Morgan Stanley and Goldman Sachs continue to meet each morning as they have for twenty years or more; they listen to the latest views of their security analysts and hurry to phone their favorite clients in the hope of stimulating a trade. Robert Kirby, who speaks with authority as a former lecturer at the Stanford Business School and as President of Capital Guardian Trust, which manages with more than $20 billion of pension fund and other institutional accounts the oldfashioned way, once declared: "Modern portfolio theory has become another very complicated piece of sleight of hand . . . designed to make the client believe that the Tooth Fairy is alive and well."[2]

Traditional money managers like Capital Guardian, who remain stock pickers at heart, and many of the brokerage firms who execute their orders, regard the new markets and the new trading strategies as enemies that distort values and cause abrupt shifts in stock prices. Many of them support attempts to hobble the markets with regulatory constraints on the new instruments and the new trading strategies.

The facts about market volatility dispute the charges that enjoy so much currency. Countless academic studies reveal no increase in monthly stock price volatility since the introduction of the S&P 500 futures contract in April 1982, and only minor changes in daily volatility. In a recent analysis, G. William Schwert of the University of Rochester reviewed the data all the way back to 1802 and concluded that "volatility estimates show remarkable homogeneity through time" with the exception of the high volatility from 1928 to 1937, when investment and trading practices were entirely different from what they are today.[3] Nor is there any evidence that stocks in the S&P 500 index are any more volatile than the stocks of similar companies that are not in the index, even though the S&P stocks are more likely to be involved in program trading and arbitrage transactions.

These studies are unanimous in agreeing that the events of October 1987 were an anomaly, as volatility returned to pre-crash levels within just a few weeks after the market break. Even during the worst moments of the sharp drop on October 13, 1989, the futures market was having no effect at all on the market for stocks, because the regulators had shut it down. Brief episodes of high volatility have appeared in other markets around the world, where modern financial theory has received far less notice than here and where many of the instruments derived from it are still relatively uncommon.

Another line of analysis indicates that the market is becoming more, rather than less, efficient. Fama's theoretical work on the efficient market hypothesis, and Alexander's empirical study of market behavior, both argued that in an efficient market changes in stock prices would be random rather than occurring in sequential patterns like trends. A study in 1990 by Kenneth Froot of MIT and André Perold of Harvard Business School shows that the occurrence of price trends has been diminishing rather than increasing. In a range of zero to one, the correlation between a stock's change in price at one moment and its change over the next fifteen minutes was 0.4 in 1983; today it is essentially zero. Similar measures of daily and weekly correlations over the past twenty years have also fallen. If the walk is more random than ever, information must be moving faster, prices must be holding closer to intrinsic values, and outguessing the market must be growing increasingly difficult.

There is one problem with the market that warrants attention, however. The brokers and dealers who make markets in stocks have seen their incomes shrink as a result of the 1975 deregulation of brokerage commissions and rising competition from new market-makers and from markets outside the United States. Consequently, the market for many stocks tends to be less liquid and individual price changes are wider than they would be otherwise. This deterioration in liquidity helps to explain the rapid growth in the markets for options and futures, where transaction costs are lower and spreads between bids and offers are smaller than on the stock market itself. If carried far enough, this trend could destroy the traditional markets, which is why so much attention is now being directed toward the structure of the established stock exchanges and the variety of instruments and securities that may be traded there.

The frantic, raucous capital markets that we see today, with their many new instruments and novel approaches to portfolio management, form a sharp contrast with the quiet atmosphere in which the scholars plotted their revolution. The world of the towers of ivory is far more antiseptic and innocent than the world of Wall Street. There are tears and sweat, but fortunes are neither won nor lost in the process.

There is Louis Bachelier in 1900, holed up in the Sorbonne scratching out eternal verities about the behavior of speculative markets. Harry Markowitz stumbles upon a great truth while perusing John Burr Williams's book during a quiet afternoon in the library at the University of Chicago. James Tobin freely admits to being an "ivory tower economist." Paul Samuelson, for whom finance serves as Sunday painting, is ambivalent over whether he has found something trivially obvious or dramatically sweeping. William Sharpe survives an abrasive confrontation with John Lintner and launches the beta revolution, but his phone does not ring. Harry Roberts publishes charts designed for security analysts in a journal read only by academics. The astronomer Osborne chooses an obscure Navy Department publication for his thoughts on "the epitome of unrelieved bedlam." Eugene Fama deserts the football field for the academic groves of Chicago, where he confirms Alfred Cowles's gloomy view that portfolio managers who try to beat the market are impotent. Franco Modigliani and Merton Miller, cheek-by-jowl at Carnegie Tech, say much the same about corporate financial officers, though the *Wall Street Journal* takes no notice. Fischer Black, Myron Scholes, and Robert Merton change the whole world of finance by staring at differential equations. Through it all, the only sound we hear is the clanking of primitive computers.

They surveyed the scene from the top of the ivory tower. Let us now share their perspective, which reaches beyond the dickering business of eighths and quarters on a block trade and the flashing numbers on a computer screen. As the derring-do of Michael Milken and his cohorts fades from view, as financial innovation advances, and as the global economy fosters increasingly competitive financial markets, the vitality and flexibility of the capital markets come into sharp focus.

These markets are the marvel of the capitalist system that the world yearns to emulate. The clatter of the computer and the roar of the trading floor are the sounds of a great battle in which investors compete with one another to determine who can buy at the lowest and sell at the highest. In no other market, regardless of product, structure, or institutional arrangement, is competition as free, as vigorous, as effective as here. In no other market do prices convey so much information about what people are buying and selling. Harry Markowitz himself, in a recent address to his students, reminded them that: "Granted that the invisible hand is clumsy, heartless, and unfair, it is ever so much more deft and impartial than a central planning committee."[4]

This is what fascinated the instigators of the revolution in finance. It was not the fun and games of investing that caught their fancy. It was the purity of the free market dynamics, the best that the study of economics can offer. Remember Paul Samuelson's reaction when he heard about Kendall's Demon of Chance: "Work the other side of the street! The nonpredictability of future prices from past and present prices is the sign, not of failure of economic law, but the triumph of economic law after competition has done its best."

If the final product of the efforts of the financial theorists was only an assemblage of abstractions, those abstractions are the essential insights into how people do act and how people should act as they engage in the competitive battle. Mere abstractions cannot tell investors whether to buy or to sell—in the end, that secret remains hidden from us—but they can tell us how to manage our affairs so that the uncertainties of human existence do not defeat us.

But there is more. If we join the theorists in their fascination with free markets, we will find that they not only help us to appreciate what we have. They can also help us to make our system even better.

# Notes

"PC&I" refers to personal correspondence and interviews.

### Chapter 1
### INTRODUCTION: THE REVOLUTION IN THE WEALTH OF NATIONS

1. Hansell (1989).
2. I am grateful to McCloskey (1992) for the quotation from Dante.
3. Wien (1990).
4. *Institutional Investor* staff (1977).
5. The editor of this book read the term in a journal article of the 1970s.
6. Vosti (1990).
7. Treynor, PC&I.
8. Judson (1979).
9. Gould (1991).
10. Vertin (1974).

### Chapter 1
### ARE STOCK PRICES PREDICTABLE?

1. Cootner (1964).
2. Bachelier (1900).
3. Bachelier (1900).
4. Bachelier (1900).
5. All the quotes in this paragraph are from Mandelbrot (1987).
6. Bachelier (1900).
7. Bachelier (1900).
8. Bachelier (1900).
9. Bachelier (1900).
10. Bachelier (1900).
11. Bachelier (1900).
12. Bachelier (1900).

13. Fama, PC&I.
14. Bachelier (1900).
15. Wallis (1981).
16. Wallis (1981).
17. Wallis (1981).
18. Samuelson, PC&I.
19. Samuelson (1973).
20. Wendt (1982).
21. Wendt (1982).
22. Wendt (1982).
23. Wendt (1982).
24. Wendt (1982).
25. Kopcke (1989).
26. Bloom (1974).
17. Bloom (1974).
28. Bloom (1974).
29. Rhea (1935).
30. Clapesattle (1984).
31. All quotes in this paragraph from Galbraith (1972).
32. Bloom (1974).
33. Cowles (1933).
34. Cowles (1933).
35. Rhea (1933).
36. Rhea (1933).
37. Rhea (1933).
38. Rhea (1933).
39. Cowles (1933).
40. Bloom (1974).
41. Cowles (1944).
42. Bloom (1974).
43. Quoted in Jones and Wilson (1989).
44. Cowles (1938).
45. Bloom (1974).

## Chapter 2
### FOURTEEN PAGES TO FAME

1. *Financial Analysts Journal* (1967).
2. Markowitz, PC&I.
3. Markowitz, PC&I.
4. Markowitz, PC&I.
5. Markowitz, PC&I.
6. Dimson (1982).
7. Keynes (1939).

8. Keynes (1983).
9. Loeb (1935).
10. Markowitz, PC&I.
11. Markowitz (1952).
12. Markowitz (1952).
13. Biel (1972).
14. Markowitz (1952).
15. Markowitz (1959).
16. Markowitz, PC&I.
17. Roy (1952).
18. Roy (1952).
19. Roy (1952).
20. Markowitz, PC&I.
21. Markowitz, PC&I.
22. Markowitz, PC&I.

## Chapter 3
### THE INTERIOR DECORATOR FALLACY

1. Roy (1961).
2. Tobin, PC&I.
3. Tobin, PC&I.
4. Tobin, PC&I.
5. Tobin, PC&I.
6. Tobin (1986).
7. Keynes (1936).
8. Tobin (1958).
9. Tobin (1958).
10. Tobin (1986).
11. Tobin (1958).
12. Tobin, PC&I.

## Chapter 4
### THE MOST IMPORTANT SINGLE INFLUENCE

1. Markowitz (1959).
2. Markowitz (1959).
3. Markowitz (1959).
4. Sharpe, PC&I.
5. Sharpe, PC&I.
6. Sharpe, PC&I.
7. Sharpe, PC&I.
8. Weston and Beranek (1955).
9. Weston and Beranek (1955).
10. Sharpe (1963).
11. Sharpe (1963).

12. Sharpe (1962).
13. Sharpe (1963).
14. Sharpe (1963).
15. Sharpe (1963).
16. Sharpe (1963).
17. Markowitz, PC&I.
18. Sharpe, PC&I.
19. Sharpe (1963).
20. Leibowitz (1990).
21. Sharpe (1963).
22. *Institutional Investor* (1968).
23. Goodman (1969).

## Chapter 5
### ILLUSIONS, MOLECULES, AND TRENDS

1. Galbraith (1972).
2. All quotes in this paragraph from Galbraith (1972).
3. Samuelson, PC&I.
4. Samuelson, PC&I.
5. Working (1934).
6. Working (1934).
7. Kendall (1953).
8. Kendall (1953).
9. Kendall (1953).
10. Kendall (1953).
11. Kendall (1953).
12. Samuelson, (1973).
13. Brealey, PC&I.
14. Miller, PC&I.
15. Roberts (1959).
16. Roberts (1959).
17. Scheinman (1991).
18. Roberts (1959).
19. Roberts (1959).
20. Osborne, PC&I.
21. Osborne, PC&I.
22. Osborne, PC&I.
23. Osborne (1959).
24. Osborne (1959).
25. Osborne (1959).
26. Osborne (1959).
27. Osborne (1959).
28. Osborne (1959).
29. Osborne (1959).

30. Sharpe, PC&I.
31. Osborne (1962).
32. Osborne (1962).
33. Kendall (1953).
34. Fama, PC&I.
35. Alexander (1961).
36. Alexander (1961).
37. Alexander (1964).
38. Roberts (1959).
39. Sametz (1990).

## Chapter 6
### ANTICIPATING PRICES PROPERLY

1. Samuelson, (1986c).
2. Samuelson, PC&I.
3. Samuelson (1974).
4. Samuelson, PC&I.
5. Samuelson (1983).
6. Samuelson (1983).
7. Samuelson (1983).
8. Samuelson, PC&I.
9. Samuelson (1983).
10. All quotes in this paragraph from Samuelson (1983).
11. Samuelson, PC&I.
12. Samuelson, PC&I.
13. Samuelson, PC&I.
14. Samuelson, PC&I.
15. I am grateful to Tvsersky (1990) for this metaphor.
16. Keynes (1936).
17. All quotes in this paragraph from Samuelson (1965).
18. Samuelson (1965).
19. Samuelson, PC&I.
20. Samuelson, PC&I.
21. Samuelson (1986b).
22. Samuelson, PC&I.
23. All quotes in this paragraph from Samuelson, PC&I.
24. Merton (1983).
25. All quotes in this paragraph from Samuelson, PC&I.
26. All quotes in this paragraph from Black (1986).
27. Black (1986).
28. Black (1986).
29. Black (1986).

## Chapter 7
### THE SEARCH FOR HIGH P.Q.

1. Samuelson, PC&I.
2. Fama, PC&I.
3. Fama, PC&I.
4. Fama, PC&I.
5. Fama, PC&I.
6. Fisher and Lorie (1964).
7. Smith (1924).
8. Schweiger (1967).
9. Samuelson, PC&I.
10. Fisher and Lorie (1964).
11. *Institutional Investor* (1968).
12. Hartwell (1968).
13. Rinfret (1968).
14. Fama (1965b).
15. Fama (1965b).
16. Fama (1965b).
17. Sharpe (1970b).
18. Black (1973).
19. Fama (1970).
20. Fama (1970).
21. Jensen (1965).
22. Buffett (1984).
23. Samuelson (1974).
24. Samuelson, PC&I.
25. Samuelson, 1974.

## Chapter 8
### THE BEST AT THE PRICE

1. Williams (1959).
2. Williams (1959).
3. Williams (1959).
4. Williams (1938).
5. Williams (1938).
6. Williams (1938).
7. Markowitz (1952).
8. Williams (1938).
9. Williams (1938).
10. Kaplan (1968).
11. Tsai (1968).
12. Durand (1957).
13. All quotes in this paragraph from Durand (1957).

14. Durand (1957).
15. Fridson (1990).
16. All quotes in this paragraph from Graham and Dodd.
17. All quotes in this paragraph from Graham and Dodd.
18. Kahn and Milne (1977).
19. Kahn and Milne (1977).
20. Kahn and Milne (1977).
21. Graham and Dodd (1962).

## Chapter 9
### THE BOMBSHELL ASSERTIONS

1. Miller, PC&I.
2. All quotes up to this point from Miller, PC&I.
3. Modigliani, PC&I.
4. Modigliani, PC&I.
5. Samuelson (1983).
6. Modigliani, PC&I.
7. Miller, PC&I.
8. Miller, PC&I.
9. Modigliani and Miller (1958).
10. Williams (1938).
11. Miller, PC&I.
12. Modigliani, PC&I.
13. Modigliani and Miller (1958).
14. Miller, PC&I.
15. Modigliani and Miller (1958).
16. Miller, PC&I.
17. Miller, PC&I.
18. Miller (1988).
19. Miller (1988).
20. Miller (1988).
21. Miller (1989).
22. Miller (1989).
23. Miller (1987).
24. Vertin (1990).

## Chapter 10
### RISKY BUSINESS

1. Miller and Modigliani (1961).
2. Treynor (1972).
3. Treynor, PC&I.
4. All quotes in this paragraph from Treynor, PC&I.

5. All quotes in this paragraph from Treynor, PC&I.
6. Treynor, PC&I.
7. Treynor, PC&I.
8. Treynor, PC&I.
9. Modigliani, PC&I.
10. Treynor, PC&I.
11. Merton (1990).
12. Treynor (1961).
13. Treynor, PC&I.
14. All quotes in this paragraph from Treynor (1961).
15. Treynor (1961).
16. Treynor (1961).
17. Treynor, PC&I.
18. Sharpe (1964).
19. Sharpe (1961).
20. Sharpe (1961).
21. Sharpe (1964).
22. Welles (1971).
23. All quotes in this paragraph from Welles (1971).
24. Welles (1971).
25. Welles (1971).
26. Sharpe (1964).
27. Welles (1971).
28. Sharpe, PC&I.
29. Sharpe, PC&I.
30. Sharpe, PC&I.
31. Sharpe (1964).
32. Treynor, PC&I.
33. Sharpe, PC&I.
34. Treynor, PC&I.
35. Treynor, PC&I.
36. Treynor, PC&I.
37. Treynor, PC&I.
38. Milne, in Molodovsky (1974).
39. Treynor, PC&I.
40. Vertin, PC&I.
41. Treynor, PC&I.
42. Sharpe, PC&I.
43. Sharpe, PC&I.
44. Miller, PC&I.
45. Sharpe, PC&I.
46. Sharpe, PC&I.
47. Sharpe, PC&I.
48. Sharpe, PC&I.

49. All quotes in this paragraph from Grauer (1989).
50. All quotes in this paragraph from Treynor, PC&I.
51. Grauer (1989).
52. Welles (1971).
53. Welles (1971).
54. Welles (1971).

## Chapter 11
### THE UNIVERSAL FINANCIAL DEVICE

1. Samuelson, PC&I.
2. Black (1989).
3. Black (1988b).
4. Black, PC&I.
5. Treynor, PC&I.
6. Black (1989).
7. Black (1988b).
8. Black and Scholes (1973).
9. Merton, PC&I.
10. Scholes, PC&I.
11. Scholes, PC&I.
12. Scholes (1972).
13. Scholes, PC&I.
14. All quotes in this paragraph from Merton, PC&I.
15. Samuelson, in Merton (1990).
16. Merton, PC&I.
17. Merton, PC&I.
18. Markowitz, PC&I.
19. Merton (1990).
20. Merton (1990).
21. Scholes, PC&I.
22. Scholes, PC&I.
23. Scholes, PC&I.
24. All quotes in this paragraph from Merton, PC&I.
25. Merton, PC&I.
26. Merton, PC&I.
27. Scholes, PC&I.
28. Black (1988a).
29. Merton, PC&I.
30. Black (1988b).
31. Black, PC&I.
32. Merton, PC&I.
33. Merton, PC&I.
34. Merton, PC&I.

## Chapter 12
### The Constellation

All quotes in this chapter are from interviews or personal correspondence with Fouse, McQuown, and Vertin, with the following exceptions:
1. Wells Fargo & Company publicity brochure.
2. Fama in Bank Administration Institute (1968).
3. Ellis (1979).

## Chapter 13
### The Accountant for Risk

All quotes in this chapter are from the interview or personal correspondence with Rosenberg, with the following exceptions:
1. Bernstein (1974).
2. Vertin (1974).
3. All quotes in this paragraph from *Institutional Investor* (1977).
4. *Institutional Investor* (1977).
5. All quotes in this paragraph from Welles (1978).
6. Welles (1978).
7. Welles (1978).
8. Ellis (1979).

## Chapter 14
### The Ultimate Invention

1. Leland, PC&I.
2. Leland, PC&I.
3. Leland, PC&I.
4. Leland, PC&I.
5. Leland, PC&I.
6. Leland, PC&I.
7. Leland, PC&I.
8. Leland, PC&I.
9. Rubinstein, PC&I.
10. Rubinstein, PC&I.
11. Rubinstein, PC&I.
12. Rubinstein, PC&I.
13. Rubinstein, PC&I.
14. Rubinstein, PC&I.
15. Rubinstein, PC&I.
16. Rubinstein, PC&I.
17. Rubinstein, PC&I.

18. Leland, PC&I.
19. Leland, PC&I.
20. Leland, PC&I.
21. Leland and Rubinstein (1988).
22. Bernstein and Bernstein (1988).
23. All quotes in this paragraph from Presidential Task Force (1988).
24. Presidential Task Force (1988).
25. Rubinstein, PC&I.
26. Presidential Task Force (1988).
27. All quotes in this paragraph from Shiller (1989).
28. Leland, PC&I.
29. Rubinstein, PC&I.

## Chapter 15
### THE VIEW FROM THE TOP OF THE TOWER

1. Engleberg (1991).
2. Kirby (1979).
3. Schwert (1990a).
4. Markowitz (1991).

# Bibliography
# and Other Sources

ALEXANDER, SIDNEY S. 1961. "Price Movements in Speculative Markets: Trends or Random Walks." *Industrial Management Review,* Vol. 2, No. 2 (May), pp. 7–26. Also in Cootner (1964).

ALEXANDER, SIDNEY S. 1964. "Price Movements in Speculative Markets: Trends or Random Walks, No. 2." *Industrial Management Review,* Vol. 5, No. 2 (Spring). Also in Cootner (1964).

ARISTOTLE. *Politics.* Book I, Chapter 11.

BACHELIER, LOUIS. 1900. *Theory of Speculation.* Paris: Gauthier-Villars. Translated by A. James Boness and reprinted in Cootner, *loc. cit.*

BANK ADMINISTRATION INSTITUTE. 1968. *Measuring the Investment Performance of Pension Funds.* Park Ridge, IL.

BARTLETT, SARAH. 1990. "A California Pension Fund Cuts the New York Umbilical Cord." *The New York Times,* August 26, p. 12.

BAUMOL, WILLIAM J. 1966. "Mathematical Analysis of Portfolio Selection." *Financial Analysts Journal* (September–October), pp. 95–99.

BERNOUILLI, D. 1930. "Exposition of a New Theory on the Measurement of Risk." *Papers of the Imperial Academy of Science,* Vol. II, pp. 175–192. Translated by Louise Sommer, *Econometrica* (January 1954), pp. 23–36.

BERNSTEIN, PETER L. 1974. "What This Journal Is About." *Journal of Portfolio Management* (Fall), pp. 5–6.

BERNSTEIN, PETER L. 1977. "Hate: The New Force in the Stock Market." *Institutional Investor,* November.

BERNSTEIN, PETER L. 1987. "Liquidity, Stock Markets, and Market Makers." *Financial Management* (Summer), pp. 54–62.

BERNSTEIN, PETER L. and BARBARA S. BERNSTEIN. 1988. "Where the Postcrash Studies Went Wrong." *Institutional Investor,* April.

BIEL, HEINZ. *Forbes,* November 15, 1972.

BISHOP, GEORGE W., JR. 1961. "Evolution of the Dow Theory." *Financial Analysts Journal* (September–October), pp. 23–26.

BLACK, BERNARD S. and JOSEPH A. GRUNDFEST. 1987. "Shareholder Gains From Takeovers and Restructurings Between 1981 and 1986: $162 Billion Is a Lot of Money." *Midland Corporate Finance Journal* (now *Journal of Applied Corporate Finance*), Vol. 1, No. 1, pp. 6–15.

BLACK, FISCHER. 1973. "Yes, Virginia, There Is Hope: Tests of Value Line Ranking System." *Financial Analysts Journal,* Vol. 29 (September–October), pp. 10–14.

BLACK, FISCHER. 1986. "Noise." *Journal of Finance,* Vol. 41 (July), pp. 529–543.

BLACK, FISCHER. 1988a. "On Robert C. Merton." *MIT Management* (Fall), p. 28.

BLACK, FISCHER. 1988b. "Option Formulas and Nikkei Options." Unpublished manuscript.

BLACK, FISCHER. 1989. "How We Came Up With the Option Formula." *Journal of Portfolio Management* (Winter), pp. 4–8.

BLACK, FISCHER, MICHAEL C. JENSEN, and MYRON S. SCHOLES. 1972. "The Capital Asset Pricing Model: Some Empirical Tests." *Studies in the Theory of Capital Markets,* Michael C. Jensen, ed. (New York: Praeger), pp. 79–121.

BLACK, FISCHER and MYRON S. SCHOLES. 1972. "The Valuation of Option Contracts and a Test of Market Efficiency." *Journal of Finance,* Vol. 27 (May), pp. 399–418.

BLACK, FISCHER and MYRON S. SCHOLES. 1973. "The Pricing of Options and Corporate Liabilities." *Journal of Political Economy,* Vol. 81 (May/June), pp. 637–654. Also unpublished manuscript, dated January 29, 1971.

BLOOM, MURRAY TEIGH. 1974. *Rogues to Riches.* New York: Warner Books.

BREALEY, RICHARD A. 1983. *An Introduction to Risk and Return.* Cambridge, MA: MIT Press, 2nd Edition.

BUFFETT, WARREN E. 1984. "The Superinvestors of Graham-and-Doddsville." Address on the occasion of the 50th anniversary of the publication of *Security Analysis.*

CHRIST, CARL F. 1952. "History of the Cowles Commission, 1932–1952." *Economic Theory and Measurement: A Twenty Year Research Report.* Chicago: Cowles Commission, pp. 3–66.

CLAPESATTLE, HELEN. 1984. *Dr. Webb of Colorado Springs.* Colorado Springs: Colorado Associated University Press.

COWLES, ALFRED 3rd. 1933. "Can Stock Market Forecasters Forecast?" *Econometrica,* Vol. 1 (July), pp. 309–324.

COWLES, ALFRED 3rd and ASSOCIATES. 1938. *Common Stock Indexes.* Indianapolis, IN: Principia Press.

COWLES, ALFRED 3rd. 1944. "Stock Market Forecasting." *Econometrica,* Vol. 12, Nos. 3 & 4 (July–October), pp. 206–214.

DEBREU, GERALD. 1991. "The Mathematization of Economic Theory." *American Economic Review,* Vol. 81, No. 1 (March), pp. 1–7.

DE BONDT, WERNER F. M. and RICHARD H. THALER. 1990. "Do Security Analysts Overreact?" *American Economic Review,* Vol. 80, No. 2 (May), pp. 52–57.

DIMSON, ELROY and PAUL MARSH. 1982. "Calculating the Cost of Capital." *Long Range Planning,* Vol. 15, No. 2, pp. 112–120.

DURAND, DAVID. 1957. "Growth Stocks and the Petersburg Paradox." *Journal of Finance,* Vol. XII, No. 3 (September), pp. 348–363.

DURAND, DAVID. 1959. "The Cost of Capital, Corporation Finance, and the Theory of Investment: Comment." *American Economic Review,* Vol. 49, No. 4 (September), pp. 639–655.

DURAND, DAVID. 1960. "Portfolio Selection: Efficient Diversification of Investments, Review." *American Economic Review,* Vol. 50, No. 1 (March), pp. 234–236.

ELLIS, CHARLES D. 1979. *Investment Policies of Large Corporate Pension Funds.* Ann Arbor, MI: University Microfilms International.

ENGLEBERG, STEPHEN. "Warsaw Turns on the Stock Tickers." *The New York Times,* April 17, 1991, Business Section.

FAMA, EUGENE F. 1963. "Mandelbrot and the Stable Paretian Thesis." *Journal of Business,* Vol. 36, No. 4 (October), pp. 420–429. Also in Lorie and Brealey (1972) and in Cootner (1964).

FAMA, EUGENE F. 1965a. "The Behavior of Stock Prices." *Journal of Business,* Vol. 37, No. 1 (January), pp. 34–105.

FAMA, EUGENE F. 1965b. "Random Walks in Stock Prices." *Financial Analysts Journal* (September–October), pp. 55–59.

FAMA, EUGENE F. 1968a. "What 'Random Walk' Really Means." *Institutional Investor,* April, pp. 38–40.

FAMA, EUGENE F. 1968b. "Risk and the Evaluation of Pension Fund Performance." *Measuring the Investment Performance of Pension Funds.* Park Ridge, IL: Bank Administration Institute, pp. 191–223.

FAMA, EUGENE F. 1970. "Efficient Capital Markets: A Review of Theory and Empirical Work." *Journal of Finance,* Vol. 25, No. 2 (May), pp. 383–417. Also in Lorie and Brealey (1972).

FINANCIAL ANALYSTS JOURNAL. 1967. *Index, 1945 through 1966.* New York: Financial Analysts Federation.

FISHER, LAWRENCE and JAMES H. LORIE. 1964. "Rates of Return on Investments in Common Stocks." *Journal of Business,* Vol. 37, No. 1 (January), pp. 1–24.

FRIEDMAN, BENJAMIN M. and DAVID I. LAIBSON. 1989. "Economic Implications of Extraordinary Movements in Stock Prices." *Brookings Papers on Economic Activity,* 2, pp. 137–189.

FRIEDMAN, MILTON and ANNA SCHWARTZ. 1991. "Alternative Approaches to Analyzing Economic Data, Appendix." *American Economic Review,* Vol. 81, No. 1 (March), pp. 48–49.

# Bibliography and Other Sources

FRIDSON, MARTIN S. 1990. "Applying Contemporary Analytical Techniques to the High-Yield Bond Market." *Conference on High-Yield Bonds: Analysis and Risk Assessment,* Frank Reilly, ed. Charlottesville, VA: Institute for Chartered Financial Analysts, July 15.

FORTUNE, PETER. 1989. "An Assessment of Financial Market Volatility: Bills, Bonds, and Stocks." *New England Economic Review,* November/December, pp. 14–28.

FROOT, KENNETH A. and ANDRE F. PEROLD. 1990. "New Trading Practices and Short-Run Market Efficiency." Cambridge, MA: National Bureau of Economic Research, Working Paper #3498.

GALBRAITH, JOHN KENNETH. 1972. *The Great Crash.* New York, Houghton Mifflin, 3rd edition.

GOLDSTEIN, MICHAEL L. 1990. "Back to the Future: The Changing Focus of Money Management in America." Sanford C. Bernstein, Inc. Strategic Decisions Conference, New York, June 13.

GOODMAN, GEORGE W. ("ADAM SMITH"). 1969. Introduction to *The Money Managers,* edited by Gilbert Kaplan and Chris Welles. New York: Random House.

GORDON, MYRON J. 1989. "Corporate Finance Under the MM Theorems." *Financial Management,* Summer, pp. 19–28.

GOULD, STEPHEN JAY. 1990. *Natural History,* October, p. 17.

GOULD, STEPHEN JAY. 1991. "More Light on Leaves." *Natural History,* February, pp. 16–23.

GRAHAM, BENJAMIN and DAVID L. DODD. *Security Analysis: Principles and Techniques.* New York: McGraw-Hill, various editions.

GRAUER, FREDERICK L. A. 1989. "On the Occasion of the 25th Anniversary of the Capital Asset Pricing Model." *Currents,* Wells Fargo Investment Advisors, July.

HALL, BRONWYN H. 1990. "The Impact of Corporate Restructuring on Industrial Research and Development." *Brookings Papers on Economic Activity: Microeconomics,* pp. 85–124.

HANSELL, SAUL. 1989. "The Wild, Wired World of Electronic Exchanges." *Institutional Investor,* September, pp. 91–119.

HARRIS, LAWRENCE. 1989. "S&P 500 Cash Stock Price Volatilities." *Journal of Finance,* Vol. 44. No. 5 (December), pp. 1155–1175.

HARTWELL, JOHN M. 1968. "Where Does Performance Go From Here?" *Official Proceedings of the First Annual Institutional Investor Conference.* New York: Kennington Publishing Corporation, pp. 81–87.

HENDRICKS, DARRYLL, JAYENDU PATEL, and RICHARD ZECKHAUSER. 1990. "Hot Hands in Mutual Funds: The Persistence of Performance, 1974–1987." Cambridge, MA: National Bureau of Economic Research, Working Paper #3389.

INSTITUTIONAL INVESTOR STAFF. 1977. "Modern Portfolio Theory: How the New Investment Technology Evolved." *Institutional Investor,* April.

JENSEN, MICHAEL C. 1965. "The Performance of Mutual Funds in the Period 1945–64." *Journal of Finance,* Vol. 23 (December), pp. 587–616.

JONES, CHARLES P. and JACK W. WILSON. 1989. "Is Stock Price Volatility Increasing?" *Financial Analysts Journal* (November–December), pp. 20–26.

JUDSON, HORACE F. 1979. *The Eighth Day of Creation.* New York: Simon & Schuster.

KAHN, IRVING and ROBERT D. MILNE. 1977. *Benjamin Graham: The Father of Financial Analysis.* Charlottesville: Financial Analysts Research Foundation.

KAPLAN, GILBERT E. 1968 "Opening Remarks." *Official Proceedings of the First Annual Institutional Investor Conference.* New York: Kennington Publishing Corporation, pp. 1–4.

KAPLAN, GILBERT E. and CHRIS WELLES, eds. 1969. *The Money Managers.* New York: Random House.

KENDALL, MAURICE G. 1953. "The Analysis of Time Series, Part I: Prices." *Journal of the Royal Statistical Society,* Vol. 96, pp. 11–25. Also in Cootner (1964).

KEYNES, JOHN MAYNARD. 1925. "An American Study of Shares Versus Bonds as Permanent Investments." *Nation and Athenaeum,* May 2, pp. 247–252.

KEYNES, JOHN MAYNARD. 1936. *The General Theory of Employment, Interest, and Money.* New York: Harcourt Brace.

KEYNES, JOHN MAYNARD. 1939. Memorandum for the Estates Committee, Kings College, Cambridge, May 8. *The Collected Writings of John Maynard Keynes,* Donald Moggridge, ed., Vol XII. New York: Cambridge University Press, 1983, pp. 66–68. Also in Ellis and Vertin (1989).

KEYNES, JOHN MAYNARD. 1983. "Letter to F. C. Scott, February 6, 1942." *The Collected Writings of John Maynard Keynes,* Donald Moggridge, ed., Vol XII. New York: Cambridge University Press, pp. 81–83. Also in Ellis and Vertin (1989).

KIRBY, ROBERT G. 1979. "Ethics, Gimmicks and Modern Portfolio Theory." *Financial Analysts Journal* (September–October), p. 22.

KOPCKE, RICHARD. 1989. "The Roles of Debt and Equity in Financing Corporate Investments." *New England Economic Review* (July/August), pp. 25–48.

LEAVENS, D. H. 1945. "Diversification of Planning." *Trusts and Estates,* Vol. 80 (May), pp. 469–473.

LEIBOWITZ, MARTIN. 1990. *Speech in Honor of William F. Sharpe.* October 17.

LELAND, HAYNE E. and MARK RUBINSTEIN. 1988. "The Evolution of Portfolio Insurance." *Portfolio Insurance: A Guide to Dynamic Hedging,* Donald Luskin, ed. New York: John Wiley & Sons, pp. 3–10.

LEROY, STEPHEN F. 1989. "Efficient Capital Markets and Martingales." *Journal of Economic Literature,* Vol. XXVII (December), pp. 1583–1621. This article contains an extensive bibliography.

LICHTENBERG, FRANK. 1990. "Industrial Diversification and Its Consequences for Productivity." Cambridge, MA: National Bureau of Economic Research, Working Paper #3231.

LICHTENBERG, FRANK and DONALD SIEGEL. 1989. "The Effects of Leveraged Buyouts on Productivity and Related Aspects of Firm Behavior." Cambridge, MA: National Bureau of Economic Research, Working Paper #3022.

LINTNER, JOHN. 1965. "The Valuation of Risk Assets and the Selection of Risky Investments in Stock Portfolios and Capital Budgets." *Review of Economic Statistics* (February), pp. 13–37.

LOEB, GERALD M. 1935. *The Battle for Investment Survival.* New York: Simon & Schuster. Extract also in Ellis and Vertin (1989).

MANDELBROT, BENOIT. 1987. "Louis Bachelier." *The New Palgrave: A Dictionary of Economics.* New York: Macmillan Publishing, Vol. 1, pp. 168–169.

MARKOWITZ, HARRY M. 1952. "Portfolio Selection." *Journal of Finance,* Vol. VII, No. 1 (March), pp. 77–91. Also in Lorie and Brealey (1972).

MARKOWITZ, HARRY M. 1959. *Portfolio Selection: Efficient Diversification of Investments.* New York: John Wiley & Sons.

MARKOWITZ, HARRY M. 1991. "Markets and Morality: Or Arbitrageurs Get No Respect." Robert Weintraub Memorial Lecture. Reprinted in *Journal of Portfolio Management,* forthcoming.

McCLOSKEY, DONALD N. 1992. "The Art of Forecasting, From Ancient to Modern Times." *Cato Journal* (January).

MERTON, ROBERT C. 1973. "Theory of Rational Option Pricing." *Bell Journal of Economics and Management Science,* Vol. 4 (Spring), pp. 141–183.

MERTON, ROBERT C. 1974. "On the Pricing of Corporate Debt: the Risk Structure of Interest Rates." *Journal of Finance,* Vol. XXIX, No. 2 (May), pp. 449–470.

MERTON, ROBERT C. 1983. "Paul Samuelson's Financial Economics." In *Paul Samuelson and Modern Economic Theory,* Cary E. Brown and Robert M. Solow, eds. New York: McGraw-Hill Book Company.

MERTON, ROBERT C. 1988. Personal statement (unpublished manuscript).

MERTON, ROBERT C. 1989. "On the Application of the Continuous-Time Theory of Finance to Financial Intermediation and Insurance." *The Geneva Papers on Risk and Insurance,* Vol. 14 (July), pp. 225–262.

MERTON, ROBERT C. 1990. *Continuous-Time Finance.* Cambridge, MA: Basil Blackwell.

MILLER, MERTON H. 1986. "The Academic Field of Finance: Some Observations on Its History and Prospects." Address at Katholieke Universiteit te Leuven, Leuven, Belgium, May 15.

MILLER, MERTON H. 1987. "Behavioral Rationality in Finance: The Case of Dividends." *Midland Corporate Finance Journal* (now *Journal of Applied Corporate Finance*), Vol. 4, No. 4 (Winter), pp. 6–15.

MILLER, MERTON H. 1988. "The Modigliani-Miller Propositions After Thirty Years." *Journal of Economic Perspectives,* Vol. 2, No. 4 (Fall), pp. 99–120.

MILLER, MERTON H. 1990. "Leverage." Nobel Prize Lecture, Stockholm.

MILLER, MERTON H. and FRANCO MODIGLIANI. 1961. "Dividend Policy, Growth, and the Valuation of Shares." *Journal of Business,* Volume 34, No. 4, pp. 411–433. Also in Lorie and Brealey (1972).

MODIGLIANI, FRANCO and MERTON H. MILLER. 1958. "The Cost of Capital, Corporation Finance, and the Theory of Investment." *American Economic Review,* Vol. 48, No. 3 (June), pp. 655–669.

MODIGLIANI, FRANCO and GERALD A. POGUE. 1974. "An Introduction to Risk and Return: Concepts and Evidence." *Financial Analysts Journal* (March–April), pp. 18–30.

MOLODOVSKY, NICHOLAS. 1974. *Investment Values in a Dynamic World: The Collected Papers of Nicholas Molodovsky,* Robert D. Milne, ed. Charlottesville, VA: Financial Analysts Research Foundation.

MOSSIN, JAN. 1966. "Equilibrium in a Capital Asset Market." *Econometrica,* Vol. 34 (October), pp. 768–783.

MYERS, STEWART. 1985. "The Capital Structure Puzzle." *Midland Corporate Finance Journal* (now *Journal of Applied Corporate Finance*), Vol. 3, No. 3 (Fall), pp. 6–19.

NEW YORK STOCK EXCHANGE. *Year Book,* various.

O'BRIEN, JOHN W. 1970. "How Market Theory Can Help Investors Set Goals, Select Investment Managers, and Appraise Investment Performance." *Financial Analysts Journal* (July–August), pp. 91–103.

OSBORNE, M. F. M. 1959. "Brownian Motion in the Stock Market." *Operations Research,* Vol. 7 (March–April), pp. 145–173. Also in Cootner (1964).

OSBORNE, M. F. M. 1962. "Periodic Structure in the Brownian Movement of Stock Prices." *Operations Research,* Vol. 10 (May–June), pp. 245–279. Also in Cootner (1964).

PRATT, SHANNON P. 1968. "Bibliography on Risks and Rates of Return for Common Stocks." *Financial Analysts Journal* (May–June), pp. 151–166.

RENSHAW, EDWARD F. and PAUL J. FELDSTEIN. 1960. "The Case for an Unmanaged Investment Company." *Financial Analysts Journal* (January–February), pp. 43–46.

RHEA, ROBERT. 1933. "Random Comment." *Dow Theory Comment,* Supplement to Mailing #9, January 18.

RHEA, ROBERT. 1935. *Comment, July 6.* Quoted in Richard Russell's *Dow Theory Letters,* Letter #1040, La Jolla, CA, April 4, 1990.

RINFRET, PIERRE A. 1968. "Do Investment Managers Earn Their Keep?" *Official Proceedings of the First Annual Institutional Investor Conference.* New York: Kennington Publishing Corporation, pp. 417–424.

ROBERTS, HARRY V. 1959. "Stock Market 'Patterns' and Financial Analysis: Methodological Suggestions." *Journal of Finance,* Vol. XIV, No. 1 (March), pp. 1–10. Also in Lorie and Brealey (1972) and in Cootner (1964).

ROHRER, JULIE. 1989. "Inside the Alpha Factory." *Institutional Investor,* September.

ROY, A. D. 1952. "Safety First and the Holding of Assets." *Econometrica,* Vol. 20 (July), pp. 431–439.

ROY, ARTHUR. D. 1961. "Review of Portfolio Selection: Efficient Diversification of Investments." *Econometrica,* Vol. 29, No. 1 (January), pp. 99–100.

SAMETZ, ARNOLD. 1990. "Arnold Sametz and the Salomon Brothers Center Over the Last Twenty Years." *Stern School Festschrift,* prepared by Robert A. Kavesh and Lawrence S. Ritter.

SAMUELSON, PAUL A. 1965. "Proof That Properly Anticipated Prices Fluctuate Randomly." *Industrial Management Review,* Vol. 6 (Spring), pp. 41–50.

SAMUELSON, PAUL A. 1972. *Collected Scientific Papers of Paul A. Samuelson,* Vol. III, Chapter 198. Cambridge, MA: MIT Press.

SAMUELSON, PAUL A. 1973. "Mathematics of Speculative Price." *SIAM Review* (Society for Industrial and Applied Mathematics), Vol. 15, pp. 1–42.

SAMUELSON, PAUL A. 1974. "Challenge to Judgment." *Journal of Portfolio Management,* Vol. I (Fall), pp. 17–19.

SAMUELSON, PAUL A. 1983. *Paul Samuelson and Modern Economic Theory,* Cary E. Brown and Robert M. Solow, eds. New York: McGraw-Hill Book Company.

SAMUELSON, PAUL A. 1986a. "Economics in My Time." *Collected Scientific Papers of Paul A. Samuelson,* Vol. V. Cambridge, MA.: MIT Press.

SAMUELSON, PAUL A. 1986b. "My Life Philosophy." *Collected Scientific Papers of Paul A. Samuelson,* Vol. V. Cambridge, MA.: MIT Press.

SAMUELSON, PAUL A. 1987. "Paradise Lost and Refound: The Harvard ABC Barometers." *Journal of Portfolio Management* (Spring), pp. 4–9.

SAVAGE, LEONARD JIMMIE. 1981. *The Writings of Leonard Jimmie Savage—A Memorial Selection,* W. Allen Wallis, ed. American Statistical Association and The Institute of Mathematical Statistics.

SCHEINMAN, WILLIAM X. 1991. "All Win." *Timings,* January 28.

SCHOLES, MYRON S. 1972. "The Market for Securities: Substitution versus Price Pressure and the Effects of Information on Share Prices." *Jour-*

*nal of Business,* Vol. 44, No. 2 (April). Also in Lorie and Brealey (1972).

SCHOLES, MYRON S. 1990. "In Honor of Merton H. Miller's Contributions to Finance and Economics." *Journal of Business,* Vol. 63, No. 1, Part 2 (January), pp. 81–85.

SCHWEIGER, IRVING. 1967. "The Journal of Business." *The Newsletter,* University of Chicago Graduate School of Business, Vol. XIV, No. 1 (Spring), pp. 14–16.

SCHWERT, G. WILLIAM. 1990a. "Indexes of Stock Prices from 1802 to 1987." *Journal of Business,* Vol. 63, No. 3.

SCHWERT, G. WILLIAM. 1990b. "Stock Market Volatility." *Financial Analysts Journal* (May–June), pp. 23–34.

SHARPE, WILLIAM F. 1962. "Quadratic Programming as a Technique for Portfolio Selection: Progress and Prospects." Paper represented to joint meeting of Econometric Society and Institute of Management Sciences, Ann Arbor, MI, September.

SHARPE, WILLIAM F. 1963. "A Simplified Model for Portfolio Analysis." *Management Science,* Vol. 9 (January), pp. 277–293. Also in Lorie and Brealey (1972).

SHARPE, WILLIAM F. 1964. "Capital Asset Prices: A Theory of Market Equilibrium Under Conditions of Risk." *Journal of Finance,* Vol. XIX, No. 3 (September), pp. 425–442. Also in Ellis and Vertin (1989) and in Lorie and Brealey (1972).

SHARPE, WILLIAM F. 1970a. *Portfolio Theory and Capital Markets.* New York: McGraw-Hill.

SHARPE, WILLIAM F. 1970b. "Comment on 'Efficient Markets: A Review of Theory and Empirical Work.'" *Journal of Finance,* Vol. 25, No. 2 (May), pp. 383–417. Also in Lorie and Brealey (1972).

SHARPE, WILLIAM F. 1990a. "Investor Wealth Measures and Expected Return." *Quantifying the Market Risk Premium Phenomenon for Investment Decision Making.* Charlottesville, VA: Institute of Chartered Financial Analysts.

SHARPE, WILLIAM F. 1990b. "Capital Asset Prices With and Without Negative Holdings." Nobel Prize Lecture, Stockholm.

SHILLER, ROBERT. 1989. *Market Volatility.* Cambridge, MA: MIT Press, Chapter 23.

SMITH, EDGAR LAWRENCE. 1924. *Common Stocks as Long-Term Investments.* New York: Macmillan Publishing. Also in Ellis and Vertin (1989).

TOBIN, JAMES. 1958. "Liquidity Preference as Behavior Toward Risk." *Review of Economic Studies,* Vol. 67 (February), pp. 65–86.

TOBIN, JAMES. 1982. "Le Laureat: Notice Biographique." Published in *Nobel Foundation, Les Prix Nobel 1981.* Stockholm: Almquist & Wiksell International, pp. 307–311.

TOBIN, JAMES. 1986. "James Tobin." *Lives of the Laureates: Seven Nobel Economists,* William Breit and Roger W. Spencer, eds. Cambridge, MA: MIT Press.

TOBIN, JAMES. 1988. "Keynesian Economics and Harvard: A Revolution Remembered." *Challenge,* July–August, pp. 35–41.

TREYNOR, JACK L. 1961. "Toward a Theory of Market Value of Risky Assets." Unpublished manuscript.

TREYNOR, JACK L. 1965. "How to Rate Management of Investment Funds." *Harvard Business Review,* Vol. 43, No. 1 (January–February), pp. 63–75.

TREYNOR, JACK L. 1971. "The Only Game in Town." *Financial Analysts Journal* (March–April), pp. 12–14, 22.

TREYNOR, JACK L. 1972. "The Trouble with Earnings." *Financial Analysts Journal,* Vol. 28 (September–October), pp. 41–46. Also in Lorie and Brealey (1972).

TREYNOR, JACK L. and FISCHER BLACK. 1973. "How to Use Security Analysis to Improve Portfolio Selection." *Journal of Business,* Vol. 46, No. 1 (January), pp. 66–86.

TSAI, GERALD JR. 1968. "An Investment Strategy for Today's Market." *Official Proceedings of the First Annual Institutional Investor Conference.* New York: Kennington Publishing Corp., pp. 441–450.

TVERSKY, AMOS. 1990. "Commentary." *Journal of Economic Perspectives* (Spring), pp. 209–210.

VERTIN, JAMES R. 1974. "The State of the Art in Our Profession." *Journal of Portfolio Management* (Fall), pp. 10–12.

VERTIN, JAMES R. 1991. "Comment." Appended to abstract of J. Fred Weston, "What MM Have Wrought," *CFA Digest,* March, p. 57.

VOSTI, CURTIS. 1990. "Nobel Prize Recognizes Financial Economists." *Pensions & Investments,* October 29, p. 3.

WAGNER, WAYNE H. and SHEILA LAU. 1971. "The Effect of Diversification on Risk." *Financial Analysts Journal* (November–December), pp. 48–53.

WALLIS, ALLEN W. 1981. "The Writings of Leonard Jimmie Savage—A Memorial Selection." American Statistical Association and The Institute of Mathematical Statistics.

WELLES, CHRIS. 1971. "The Beta Revolution: Learning to Live with Risk." *Institutional Investor,* September.

WELLES, CHRIS. 1978. "Who is Barr Rosenberg? And What the Hell Is He Talking About?" *Institutional Investor,* May.

WELLS FARGO & COMPANY. "Wells Fargo Since 1852." Publicity brochure.

WENDT, LLOYD. 1982. *The Wall Street Journal: The Story of Dow Jones & the Nation's Business Newspaper.* New York: Rand McNally & Co.

WESTON, J. FRED and WILLIAM BERANEK. 1955. "Programming Investment Portfolio Construction." *The Analysts Journal* (May), pp. 51–55.

WIEN, BYRON. 1990. "The Coming Squeeze in Investment Management." *Investment Research,* Morgan Stanley, March 13.

WILLIAMS, JOHN BURR. 1938. *The Theory of Investment Value.* Cambridge, MA: Harvard University Press. Subsequently Amsterdam: North Holland Publishing, 1956.

WILLIAMS, JOHN BURR. 1959. *Fifty Years of Investment Analysis: A Retrospective.* Charlottesville, VA: Financial Analysts Research Foundation.

WILSON, JACK W. and CHARLES P. JONES. 1987. "A Comparison of Annual Common Stock Returns: 1871–1925 with 1926–85." *Journal of Business,* Vol. 60, No. 2, pp. 239–258.

WORKING, HOLBROOK. 1934. "A Random Difference Series for Use in the Analysis of Time Series." *Journal of the American Statistical Association,* Vol. 29 (March), pp. 11–24.

### THREE EXCELLENT COLLECTIONS OF READINGS

COOTNER, PAUL H., ed. 1964. *The Random Character of Stock Prices.* Cambridge, MA: MIT Press.

ELLIS, CHARLES D. and JAMES R. VERTIN. 1989. *Classics: An Investor's Anthology.* Homewood, IL: Dow Jones-Irwin.

LORIE, JAMES and RICHARD BREALEY. 1972. *Modern Developments in Investment Management.* New York: Praeger Publishers.

# Name Index

# Name Index

# Name Index

# Subject Index

*333*

## Subject Index

Insurance companies, investments of, 110, 168

*Intelligent Investor, The* (Graham), 157

Interactive Data Corporation (IDC), 267

Interest/interest rates, 68, 69–71, 72, 159, 203
  corporate debt, 222–23
  junk bonds and, 178
  payments, 179
  risk-free, 200
  stock indexes and, 84
  stock prices and, 159, 201, 207
  stock valuations, 207
  swaps, 230

International Flavors and Fragrances, 52, 242

Intertemporal capital asset pricing model, 215, 224

Institute for Quantitative Analysis in Finance, 85–86

Investment Company Institute (ICI), 250

Investors
  active vs. passive, 135
  corporate/institutional, 8, 166–68, 301
  equity, 168
  individual, 8–9, 264, 301, 303
  response of to risk, 185

Invisible hand market theory, 122, 306

"Is American Business Worth More Dead Than Alive?" (Graham), 158

*Journal of the American Statistical Association,* 94

*Journal of Business,* 129, 131, 132, 140, 175, 195, 196, 261

*Journal of Finance,* 41, 42, 46, 55, 80, 91, 98, 137, 155, 194, 195, 198

*Journal of the History of Ideas,* 214

*Journal of Political Economy (JPE),* 220, 221, 222, 225

*Journal of Portfolio Management, The,* 14, 113, 180, 225–56

*Journal of the Royal Statistical Society,* 96

Kidder Peabody, 283–84

Law of the Conservation of Investment Value, 169, 170

Law of One Price: *see* Arbitrage

Leland O'Brien Rubinstein Associates, Inc. (LOR), 281–82, 283, 284, 289–90, 293, 294

Leland-Rubinstein Associates, 278–79, 281

Leverage, 172–73, 176, 178, 179

Leveraged buyouts, 178–79

Liquidity
  management, 68–69
  market, 190, 289, 293, 304
  money, 69
  Preference theory, 69, 70, 71
  stock, 7, 8

"Liquidity Preference as Behavior Toward Risk" (Tobin), 64

Linear programming, 45–46, 49, 50, 78–79, 165, 247

Loading charges: *see* Brokerage commissions

London School of Economics (LSE), 275

London Stock Exchange, 5

Macroeconomics, 65, 168–69

*Management Science,* 78, 82, 85

Marginal utility concept, 59

"Market and Industry Factors in Stock Price Performance" (King), 261

Market theories (general discussion), 17–18, 30–31, 42, 43, 112, 200–201. *See also specific theories and types of securities*
  competitive, 134–35, 171, 173, 192
  disaster avoidance, 55–57
  invisible hand, 122, 306
  linear regression/econometric, 31–38
  seasonal fluctuations, 144, 290
  stochastic process, 18–23, 186

Mathematical economics, 129n

*Mathematical Theory of Non-Uniform Gases, The,* 103–4

Maximum expected return concept, 53, 63, 73

McCormick Harvester, 28

Mean-Variance Analysis, 54–55, 84

*Mean-Variance Analysis in Portfolio Choice and Capital Markets* (Markowitz), 55

"Measuring the Investment Performance of Pension Funds," report, 239

Mellon Bank, 243, 244

Merck, 51

Merrill Lynch, 129, 237

Minnesota Mining, 149

MIT, 46, 114, 128, 130, 131, 208

MM Theory, 174–78, 179, 181–82, 209, 222

"Modern Portfolio Theory: How the New